MEASURING THE CORRELATES OF WAR

Measuring the Correlates of War

Edited by
J. David Singer and Paul F. Diehl

Ann Arbor
THE UNIVERSITY OF MICHIGAN PRESS

Copyright © by The University of Michigan 1990
All rights reserved
Published in the United States of America by
The University of Michigan Press
Manufactured in the United States of America

1993   1992   1991   1990   4   3   2   1

Library of Congress Cataloging-in-Publication Data

Measuring the correlates of war / edited by J. David Singer and Paul
   F. Diehl.
        p.   cm.
   Includes bibliographical references and index.
   ISBN 0-472-10166-8 (alk.)
   1. War.   2. World politics—19th century.   3. World politics—20th
century.   4. Military history, Modern—19th century.   5. Military
history, Modern—20th century.   I. Singer, J. David (Joel David),
1925–   .   II. Diehl, Paul F. (Paul Francis)
U21.2.M43   1990
355.02'072—dc20   90-47151

TP

Foreword

Richard L. Merritt and Dina A. Zinnes

The growth of systematic, quantitative research on international conflict has accelerated sharply in the century's latest three quarters. This scientific thrust can be seen in the articles published in major journals, papers presented at scholarly conferences, and a host of books and edited volumes. An impetus for this new, systematic approach came partially through a growing recognition by statesmen that they needed complete, accurate, and replicable data on politically relevant events. The major stimulus, however, came from the academic community itself, from scholars, such as J. David Singer, who were deeply dissatisfied with the anecdotal fashion in which arguments were developed and documented. International conflict, crises, and war, they said, were far too serious to be left to armchair speculation. The Correlates of War (COW) Project, as shown by the chapters in this volume, has been at the forefront of the drive to make the study of international conflict systematic, precise, and replicable.

Origins of Data on International Conflict

At the heart of any science is the compilation of data. One of the most important contributions of the COW Project is the multiple data sets it has generated and made available to the research community. Though its war-related data sets are currently far and away the most complete and accurate, COW's data sets owe their origins to several earlier efforts. The first study of note was begun around 1909 by an eminent biologist, Frederick Adams Woods, who reports having been "greatly struck by the failure of the modern centuries to give much diminution in the proportion of time devoted to the horrible art of war." Six years of collaboration with a young political scientist, Alexander Baltzly, produced *Is War Diminishing?* (Woods and Baltzly 1915). This volume provides, for the period 1450–1900 (and back to 1100 in the cases of England and France), a list of wars in which most of the major European states participated. Chapters on each of the eleven countries indicate the years when a national war was initiated and terminated and, hence, the duration of the war. Statistical graphs show the percentage of each decade during which the countries engaged in interstate, imperial, and civil wars.

Although a useful beginning, by modern standards their study is remarkably incomplete. Woods and Baltzly do not differentiate among the three types of wars they include. They provide no criteria for inclusion and exclusion other than their own judgment. The unit of analysis is the war rather than the year, but the wars are listed separately for each state rather than for the system as a whole. The national focus leads the authors to disaggregate national war behavior into bilateral wars, making it difficult to use the data for system-level analysis. Furthermore, the absence of casualty data, as a measure of a war's seriousness, limits the data set's usefulness for numerous, important theoretic questions. Woods and Baltzly's research was nevertheless an important beginning.

Three major breakthroughs came during the late 1930s, at a time when Europe seemed once again to be careening toward sanguinary conflict. The first of these is found in the four-volume study of *Social and Cultural Dynamics,* in which Pitirim A. Sorokin (1937) of Harvard University identified "almost all the known wars" from antiquity to 1925 for the major states in Europe. The countries included are ancient Greece, ancient Rome, and nine European nation-states. The periods covered vary for each state, though most of the modern states are begun somewhere between A.D. 900 and 1500. Sorokin includes internal disturbances as well as interstate, civil, and imperial wars. He provides the dates of initiation and termination (by year), duration of the war for each major state, and estimates of the average army size, percentage of casualties, and total number of casualties for each state.

Sorokin's data, though more complete than those of Woods and Baltzly, also provide no explicit operational criteria for interstate, imperial, or civil wars. This raises questions of both validity and reliability. The accuracy of the casualty data is also open to question. Moreover, like Woods and Baltzly's data, Sorokin's organization of the data by state makes it difficult to use them for system-level analysis.

The second scientific development in the 1930s took place at the University of Chicago. Quincy Wright (1942), in his massive book, *A Study of War,* lists wars involving either major or minor states during the period 1480–1964. He includes "all hostilities involving members of the family of nations . . . which are recognized as states of war in the legal sense or which involved over 50,000 troops," and additional hostilities of lesser magnitude or nonlegal standing that led to "important legal results." The wars—classified roughly as balance of power, civil, imperial, and defensive (of "modern civilization against an alien culture")—are listed chronologically for the international system rather than for each state. The data set includes, for each war, the dates of initiation and termination, identity of the participants, their individual date of entry (if different from the war's initiation), and the number of important battles. Wright also provides data on the frequency and types of battles, casualties, and internal disturbances in the system per decade or quarter-century, aggregated over all the major European powers. He also lists, for each half-century period since 1100, the number of years each of the major powers was at war.

Wright's data set is limited by the questionable validity of his legalistic criteria for including or excluding wars. Significant differences exist between the wars Wright identifies on the one hand and, on the other, Woods and Baltzly (1915), Sorokin (1937), and, more recently, Levy (1983). Another major limitation is the absence of severity data for individual wars.

A third product of the 1930s, generated in England, was not complete before the scientist died. With the posthumous efforts of his intellectual supporters, Lewis Fry Richardson (1960) compiled the *Statistics of Deadly Quarrels,* that is, conflicts that caused death to humans, for the period 1820–1949. Imperial wars, civil wars, and other forms of domestic conflicts are included along with interstate wars.[1] Deadly quarrels as the unit of analysis are organized by magnitude and then chronologically within magnitudes. The data on each war include the magnitude, dates of initiation and termination (in years), participants, and identity of the initiators, together with the ostensible cause or issue at stake and numerous conditions that might have contributed to amity, ambivalence, and dislike.[2]

Richardson's criteria for inclusion and exclusion are more explicit than those of Woods and Baltzly or Sorokin. Nevertheless, there are serious questions about the reliability of the data and validity of the categorical codings. This data set, widely used in earlier studies, has been superseded by the Correlates of War Project.

The Correlates of War

In the 1960s, J. David Singer at the University of Michigan initiated a line of thinking and data generation that has come to dominate the quantitative study of international war. Concerned for many years about the "war-peace question," Singer (1976, 21–22) reports experiencing a growing distaste for existing answers to the question, "Why war?" They were overly simplistic, he said, and based on very selective choices of evidence. Singer felt that the problem of conflict and war needed more systematic and rigorous analysis,

---

1. Although Richardson discusses murder and "ganging," data on quarrels involving fewer than 315 deaths (corresponding to a magnitude of $m = 2.5$, where $m = \log_{10}[\text{deaths}]$) are not included.

2. Contributory causes include, for example, trade rivalry, desire for territory, and similarities or differences in languages and marriage customs.

covering the entire international system for long historical periods, and with carefully defined variables and systematically collected data.

The Correlates of War Project began formally in 1963 with a modest grant from the Carnegie Corporation. Following in the footsteps of Sorokin, Wright, and Richardson, Singer and his associate, Melvin Small, systematically culled historical texts to obtain, for all wars since 1815, as complete a listing as possible, together with major identifying characteristics such as the number of participants, battle deaths, and durations (Singer and Small 1972; Small and Singer 1982).

Singer's focus was on the *correlates* of war, those factors that seemed to covary and thus be associated with the occurrence, duration, and magnitude of wars. Accordingly, the data set on the attributes of war comprised only one part of the project, the dependent variable. Understanding the occurrence of war meant obtaining information on other attributes of the international system that theorists had argued were the "causes" of war. Principal among these were configurations of power, as indicated by national capabilities, as well as alliances and other variables, as shown in some of the essays in this volume.

In subsequent years the research question shifted from the identification of national and systematic attributes associated (correlated) with the outbreak of war to the question of the difference between international disputes that evolve into war and those that do not. This changed focus led to the expansion of the original war data set to include data on militarized interstate disputes (Gochman and Maoz 1984, reprinted in this volume)[3] and "behavioral COW," the systematic collection of the events that characterized international crises (Leng and Singer 1988, reprinted in this volume).

More recently, Jack Levy (1983) extended COW's war data set back to 1495 for some fifteen major powers. These interstate wars, including civil and imperial wars, each entail more than 1,000 battle deaths. Levy's *War in the Modern Great Power System* uses as sources Woods and Baltzly (1915), Sorokin (1937), Wright (1942), and, for validity checks, additional studies.[4] With individual wars as the unit of analysis, wars are listed chronologically for the system, although a separate list of wars for each great power is also

---

3. Unaware of Singer's new data collection efforts on militarized interstate disputes, Randolph Siverson and Michael Tennefoss (1982 and 1984), at the University of California, Davis, independently developed a data set on major international crises since 1815. The data set overlaps with but is not equivalent to Michigan's militarized interstate dispute data set.

4. Additional overlapping but not identical data sets have been developed by Robert Butterworth (1976), Michael Brecher and Jonathan Wilkenfeld (1982), and Hayward R. Alker, Jr., and Frank L. Sherman (1982; cf. Sherman, in progress). These data sets report significant attributes of international crises since World War II. With a slightly different view, Frederic S. Pearson (e.g., 1974) collected data on international interventions in the post–World War II period.

available. The operational definitions are comparable to those developed for the COW Project.

The Correlates of War Project has had multiple effects. It generated a series of significant data sets and it heightened the professional commitment to the systematic, quantitative study of international conflict. Researchers within the COW Project have raised a range of significant theoretic issues, from the systematic analysis of age-old questions, such as the balance of power, to more recently minted arguments about status inconsistency and war. It has refined and extended earlier data sets on war and gone on to compile other data sets on different facets of international conflict and their possible correlates.

And, not the least of its contributions, the COW Project has been a major stimulus to the research community at large on the causes and consequences of international conflict. Research reported in fifteen key journals that focus on quantitative international politics found that, from 1974 to 1986, COW was the most frequently cited data project (McGowan et al. 1988, 106). It accounted for 31 percent of the 279 citations of the eight leading projects. A survey conducted in 1984 among 161 specialists in international and comparative political research, 63 (39 percent) of whom responded, found COW and the *World Handbook* project at the top of the list of currently archived data sets that "should be designated national data resources for maintenance, improvement, and expansion" (McGowan et al. 1988, 107). The uses and reputation of the COW Project have clearly marked it as one worthy of updating and expansion.

Data Development for International Research

The need for enhanced scientific attention to COW, of course, supported a general effort begun in the mid-1980s to expand other data sets as well. Important development needs for the systematic analysis of international behavior included, beyond conflict studies, data sets on the attributes of nation-states, as presented in the *World Handbook* series, and such event data sets as World Event/Interaction Survey (WEIS), Conflict and Peace Data Bank (COPDAB), and Comparative Research on the Events of Nations (CREON). The sense that scientists in the field needed to take concrete action led to the creation in 1986 of an organizational framework, Data Development for International Research (DDIR), located at the Merriam Laboratory for Analytic Political Research, University of Illinois at Urbana-Champaign. Its genesis sprang from four premises:

- The last four decades have seen an explosion in the scientific study of national development and international interaction processes;

- Data sets are integral for the continuing feedback relationship between theory and research;
- Advanced attention and improved techniques are expanding the means to conduct quantitative data analysis; but, finally,
- Sporadic funding of data development has significantly hindered such research.

Funding from the National Science Foundation permitted DDIR to support eleven projects developing data on international conflict and national development. Of these, five are linked directly to COW research.

As DDIR moves toward the end of its first three-year phase, most of the research projects have now been or soon will be completed, and the DDIR staff at the University of Illinois at Urbana-Champaign is engaged in completing uniform formats and working toward integrated data sets. It is also developing procedures for its second phase, which will emphasize international events and international political economy. The goal is to broaden the relevant, data-based research indicated inter alia by the chapters included in this volume. COW continues to make its solid contribution to systematic, quantitative research on international politics.

Preface

Until the "behavioral" movement arrived, research in international politics differed from the study of diplomatic and military history only in that the former was more polysyllabic and conceptually rich and more contemporary in its empirical focus. Although we spent more time interviewing decision makers than in perusing archives, and were perhaps more willing to speculate about the past and offer predictions and prescriptions about the future, we pursued knowledge in essentially the same fashion as our colleagues in history departments. That is, we held and articulated rather vague "theories," rested them on an uncounted number of inarticulate and imprecise assumptions, and let those assumptions shape the stories that we told and the inferences that we drew. It is only in the last thirty years that scholars have begun to conduct systematic, empirical research on international political phenomena.

Despite the widespread view to the contrary, the behavioral movement never became dominant in scholarly circles, and its impact on the policy-making and media communities remains negligible. Even among those scholars who have adopted the scientific approach, success has been slow and somewhat limited. After the euphoria associated with the rigorous methods of the physical sciences died down and the fascination with statistical techniques was muted, a cold reality set in. The scientific approach to international politics would have to clear at least two hurdles before it could begin to make significant progress toward its goals of description, explanation, and prediction. First, scholars would have to define operationally the key concepts and variables that would form the centerpieces of their analyses. This proved to be more difficult than many had initially believed; the amorphous notions of power, polarity, and war, for example, were quite elusive as scholars argued over the best indicators for these key concepts.

Second, the difficult search for indicators was mirrored in the attempt to produce complete data sets on a variety of phenomena. Rather than encouraging scholars to pick and choose cases according to their own recollections and biases, an accurate record of *all* cases of a given phenomenon was necessary to test hypothesized relationships with broad generalizability across time and space. Yet, the construction of a data set is an arduous task that requires great expenditure of time as well as considerable support from often skeptical foundations.

While the scientific study of international politics has faced a number of obstacles, that should not imply that the tasks of indicator construction and data generation have been completely unsuccessful. The Correlates of War (COW) Project has devoted a good portion of the over quarter century of its existence to these tasks. Not surprisingly, the loose network of COW researchers has wrestled with serious measurement and data problems over the years and allocated a fair fraction of its resources to that process. As indicated in the concluding chapter, the results to date have generally been judged a success, but much remains to be done.

In one sense, the contents of this book provide a road map to COW strategies and procedures to indicator construction and data collection in international politics and, we believe, research in the other social sciences as well, and it might be useful to discuss some of the assumptions and strategies that have guided the enterprise.

First, one will find almost no attention to such domestic factors as level of development or elite ideology, even though such attributes not only figure heavily in the literature, but pose relatively manageable problems of observation and measurement. Our sense—and the empirical work of others to date—suggests that those account for little of the variance in state behavior; such cross-national comparisons seem to serve better for mobilizing public opinion than for explaining the conflict behavior of the state. On the other hand, and as implied in the realpolitik model, we find that such attributes as national capabilities—military, demographic, and industrial—carry us some distance down the postdictive road. As the relevant pages make clear, this is true despite the need for more attention to the validity of the indicators used.

Second, and perhaps more surprising in light of Singer's early and frequent attention to the matter, one also finds absolutely no attention to the decision process of states in conflict. Justifying this omission is more complicated, and we emphasize at the outset that it is temporary. That is, we have no doubt that any complete explanation must include the national decision process as one of the links in the allegedly causal chain that culminates in war—or any other outcome of a rivalry or conflict. There are, however, two grounds for not pursuing that route at this juncture, the first of which is theoretical-empirical. Although it has yet to be put to any conclusive historical test, there is some basis for believing that all nations of a given class follow highly similar decision rules. As indicated above, these classes are likely to be based on size, strength, prestige, and influence, whereas regime type, economic system, elite ideology, and so forth are rather unlikely to generate classes of nations that follow divergent decision rules or differentiate among decision-rule configurations. Thus, if this postulated uniformity is empirically correct, and if, in addition, we are concentrating on major powers, then we can afford to defer inclusion of the decision process in our analyses.

A second, and more compelling, justification rests not on evidence but on logic and epistemology. Here, the argument is that the more we discover about which policy decisions are taken under which given sets of circumstances, the more confidently we can reject some of the contending models of the decision process. Ranging from the rational choice, goal-maximizing and highly purposive approaches at one extreme, to the largely stochastic, random walk at the other, one finds many rival models in the literature. Although we tend toward a psycho-political orientation and conventional wisdom view of the national security decision process in the major powers of the past two centuries, we will be on much firmer ground in deciding which versions of which models should be empirically examined first if we know which ones could not—given the observed inputs and outputs—possibly be correct.

Before opening the black box of decision making, we must therefore sort out which behaviors of states occur under particular conditions. In effect, we are concerned with how the context that decision makers face influences their policy choices. Beyond a possible similarity of decision rules, decision makers may also face the same menu of policy choices conditioned by the context of the decision. A state that faces a militarily inferior opponent who has no allies is less constrained than if the opponent is militarily superior, has numerous allies, and is geographically proximate to the site of any confrontation. To use the menu analogy, the items on the menu may not always change, but the prices of some items (and thereby their probability of selection) will vary. When we have identified the constraints and opportunities from the context of decision making, the investigation may profitably proceed to assess different models of decision making and ascertain what differences in outcomes can be explained by the contents of the black box.

Also worth nothing is the strong realpolitik flavor. All of our studies to date are state-centered, and the central variables arise out of the three basic concerns in that literature: capabilities, commitments, and contiguities. This is not because we believe that the territorial state is a particularly effective or humane form of social organization; while it may have been appropriate to the industrial revolution, it is essentially anachronistic in a global village that has been made so interdependent by that very revolution. Nor can a strong case be made for it in the context of the not-yet (and perhaps never) developed nations of the world. On the other hand, it has been the dominant mode of human aggregation in the West since the Napoleonic War and remains so today, while trends toward both larger and smaller entities of significance are clearly evident in recent decades, the territorial state demonstrates a considerable staying power in the industrial and postindustrial regions, not to mention those in the preindustrial phase of development. Although this state of affairs may not be realistic in terms of bettering the human condition, there is little doubt that the "realists" remain very much in the political saddle.

Let us turn next to a brief overview of the contexts in this effort to observe and measure some of the putative correlates of international war in the same period since the Congress of Vienna. The opening essay, written well after quite a few of the basic ones had been completed, was therefore less a guide in our early efforts than a set of later reflections on the role of measurement and an exploration of the connections among theoretical constructs, verbally defined variables, the empirical domain, and the operational indicators that emerge. Had all of these ideas been more thoroughly appreciated in the discipline at an earlier point in the Project, we would surely have experienced fewer false starts, dead ends, and unproductive investments of time, energy, and money.

In the body of the anthology there are four basic sections, reflecting the general taxonomy that has shaped the enterprise from its inception: attributes of the nations themselves; attributes of the international system and its subsystems; the links and bonds between the nations; and, finally, the behavior and interaction of these political entities and those who act on their behalf. While each of the substantive papers begins with a discussion of the key concept and its role in theory building before addressing the specifics of index construction and data generation, a short overview of each might be useful here.

The section on national attributes focuses on indicators of characteristics of nations that are thought to have some explanatory link to the onset and escalation of conflict. One theme is that of status inconsistency, borrowed from the social psychological literature, reflecting the notion that when nations acquire certain capabilities (achieved status), their elites will expect commensurate benefits in the form of international prestige (ascribed status). When this ascribed status lags behind actual achievements, as might be the case with an emerging major power, the dissatisfied state might be more aggressive in pursuit of the spoils and respect that were not forthcoming. Small and Singer attempt to capture the notion of *ascribed* status by constructing an indicator of the attributed diplomatic importance of a state, using the number and rank of the diplomatic missions accredited and dispatched to its capital. This is one instance in which relationships at one level of analysis (dyadic bonds) may be used to develop indicators at another level of analysis (national status).

The other part of the status inconsistency equation is *achieved* status. We now move to the central, but often elusive, concept of power. The difficulty of accurately measuring the intangible degree of influence that nations exercise over each other had led some scholars to focus on "potential power" or national capabilities for assessing a nation's achieved status. In the second essay, Singer does precisely that, and the resulting multidimensional indicator—demographic, industrial, and military—of capabilities is widely used in the field. Some controversy has arisen over the validity of such an indicator in a world of nuclear weapons and high technology, but the development of an indicator that can be used across a broad spatial-temporal domain is a valuable contribution (see Stoll and Ward 1989).

Finally Goertz and Diehl focus on the various indicators used to signify a nation's allocations to its military, often misleadingly referred to as its "defense burden"; such measures are critical in the study of arms races, alliance military spending, and economic development. Whereas the previous essay outlines procedures to enhance the validity of the indicator through precise conceptualization and careful data collection, this essay outlines a strategy for validating indicators vis-à-vis empirical criteria. The results suggest that we have a long way to go, and that we especially need to attend to the specific nations under study inasmuch as the validity of various indicators may well differ from one group to another.

The next section of the book is devoted to systemic attributes. A common theme in other related COW research is the importance of international system characteristics in conditioning national behavior. Traditionally, system structure—one dimension of which is often defined by the distribution of capabilities among the major actors in the system—has been viewed as a key explanatory variable (a dissenting view is found in Bueno de Mesquita and Lalman 1988). Ray's essay opening this section provides a valuable conceptual overview of the problems and considerations in measuring system structure.

The next essay is an actual illustration of how systemic attributes might be measured. Ray and Singer attempt to measure the extent to which capabilities are concentrated in the hands of one or more members of the international system. Although it has been over a decade since this essay was first published, it might still be used to assess propositions suggested by the "long cycle" approach or those that stem from the study of major power decline.

There is a tendency in international relations research for indicators of a certain phenomenon to be as numerous as the number of studies on the subject. This makes the cumulation of knowledge difficult in that one is never sure that the strength of the relationship reported in a study (and its convergence or lack thereof with other studies) is a function of the actual correlation of factors or the product of the particular indicator chosen. Sometimes, the most valuable work involves a comparison and discussion of different measures of key concepts. In a previously unpublished essay, Wayman and Morgan review various measures of systemic polarity and find much less convergence than might be hoped. The theoretical and practical implications of their analysis are worth noting for scholars interested in international systems research, but also reveal the problems and limitations inherent for all scholars in their quest for valid indicators.

The fourth section of the book looks at the connections, links, bonds, and associations between nations. Small and Singer operationally define and classify the most formal of those relationships, alliances, and demonstrate along the way that the adoption of operational criteria does not negate the need for an understanding and use of history. As alliances are considered a critical component of models of conflict initiation and expansion, their typology and list of alliances has become a standard in analyses on the subject. Among other data sets designed to measure bondedness between nations are geographical proximity, shared membership in international organizations, and the diplomatic bonds mentioned earlier in connection with the diplomatic importance index; all of these have been generated, but space limits preclude inclusion of their descriptions here. Others that await further investigation are trade, investment, military and economic aid, as well as communication and transport links.

The fifth section of the book offer a description of two data sets on hostile behaviors between nations. Gochman and Maoz identify all "militarized interstate disputes"—and the actions that comprise them—since 1816, noting their general characteristics as well as their variations across space and time. This data set is well-suited to developing generalizations about the processes that often culminate in warfare across a wide variety of nations and historical epochs. Along with those developed by Siverson and Tennefoss (1982) and Brecher, Wilkenfeld, and Moser (1988), this data set is one of the few of its kind available, and forms the centerpiece of much recent COW work (for a general discussion of data sets in this area, see Alker and Midlarsky 1985 and Cioffi-Revilla 1989). Then, in order to describe in finer detail the behavior of the protagonists within those disputes, including the specific diplomatic, economic, and military actions taken, Leng and Singer describe an additional data set containing this information for a limited number (now forty) of the disputes.

The final essay is a concluding chapter by Wayman and Singer providing a reflection of past COW accomplishments and consideration of a future research agenda. The extent to which the COW research agenda has proved effective (see also Vasquez 1987), and which indicators have proved useful and why, as well as what revisions and extensions are underway or are in the planning stage are also covered. Wayman and Singer conclude with a discussion of how these considerations, along with others, affect the larger enterprise of international political research.

The Correlates of War Project has sometimes been seen as too concerned with data and not enough with "theory," and some might view this volume as further confirmation. Yet, every one of these indicators and the resulting data set are theory-driven. Furthermore, if we are ever to develop a reasonable approximation of theory, rather than plausible hunches or elegant speculative formulations, we must first establish valid and reliable indicators and the comprehensive data sets that derive from them. Our hope, then, is that these pioneering efforts will continue to stimulate others to address this challenge. Success in this enterprise may not be sufficient, but it remains an imperative.

Contents

5. Inter-nation Interactions

6. Conclusion

1
Introductory Overview

Variables, Indicators, and Data: The Measurement Problem in Macropolitical Research

J. David Singer

One of the more debilitating digressions in the evolution of the scientific enterprise is the controversy over the relative importance of models and data. Time and again, in every discipline from archaeology to zoology, the issue has reappeared with sufficient force to engage scholarly attention and to generate reams of rhetoric. In the social sciences, as in the biological and physical sciences, we have expended considerable energies on the data versus model (some would say "theory") emphasis, usually to the detriment of scientific advancement.

Worse yet, in the universities and institutes of the scholarly world, students are often reinforced in such a way that they enter into their scientific careers committed to pursuing one or the other activity, rather than both. Some are so persuaded of the primacy of modeling and theorizing that they disdain empirical work, neither reading that of others nor sufficiently mastering the techniques of data acquisition and data analysis to conduct empirical work themselves. And others become so enamored of the concrete, referent world and so suspicious of abstractions and of speculation that they neither read about nor engage in those particular activities. While these are extreme cases, they have been all too visible in most of the social sciences since their inception.

The way this dichotomy is put makes it clear that I consider it as unnecessary as it is dysfunctional, and the hope here is to articulate an intelligently balanced and integrated view. Certainly there are times in the development of a discipline when we have gone so far toward one or the other of these extremes that the cumulative processes of science are seriously jeopardized. Then, of course, it is time to shift our emphasis, attention, and resources in

Reprinted from *Social Science History*, 6, no. 2 (Spring 1982): 181–217. © 1982 Social Science History Association. Reprinted by permission of Duke University Press.

order to redress the imbalance. To put it cybernetically, we have no objections to fluctuations around a relatively stable steady state, but when these perturbations are of appreciable duration and magnitude, they may end up requiring corrective feedback that is too extreme, lasts too long, and costs too dearly.

The Data-Model Connection

One way to reduce the frequency and magnitude of these radical swings in scientific activity is to recognize the critical—and early—role that data play in mediating the continuous interaction between theoretical hunches and empirically testable models. On the basis of all sorts of things, from current folklore and idle fantasy to the hard evidence produced by prior investigations, the researcher formulates speculative schemes that might help to explain the phenomena of interest. But as these schemes take on coherence and plausibility, the social scientist begins to translate them into operational models that can be put to the test and checked out against the "real," referent world. This translation, in turn, rests heavily upon the strategies that will be used to generate the data that represent empirical reality. To put it another way, the concepts that go into the model have to be converted into operational indicators, so called because they make explicit the operations or procedures by which the phenomena of the referent world are expressed in sets of scientifically useful data.

The wide range of processes by which we make this conversion or translation from intellectual construct to machine-readable data set is quite broad, and will be described later. But they rest heavily on what might be thought of as instrumentation: The development of techniques and procedures by which we can observe phenomena that are not visible to the naked eye. The same, of course, has been equally true of the physical and biological sciences; as Clark (1971, 109) noted in his biography of Einstein, "pure" science has always relied on measurement techniques in order to move forward. If we recall Kepler's need for Tycho Brahe's systematic observations and measurements, or Hershel's reliance on a more sensitive thermometer, or Michelson and Morley, whose mercury float and mirrors permitted them to demonstrate that "ether flow" had no effect on the movement of light rays, we find further grounds for concurring with Maxwell's statement that he was "happy in the knowledge of a good instrument maker." We know more about the physical and biological world today, Clark reminds us, "not because we have more imagination, but because we have better instruments." In the social sciences, where many of our explanatory concepts refer to symbolic behavior, intrapersonal processes, and other equally intangible phenomena, we need to be even more creative and diligent in our instrumentation.

All of this is to emphasize that the scientific enterprise—be it carried out in the laboratory, the field setting, or in the reconstruction of history (Singer 1977)—is equally dependent upon the big picture and the precise technique, creative explanation and meticulous description, uninhibited speculation and disciplined measurement. We cannot construct and test models in the scientific sense of the word without data, and we cannot efficiently generate or acquire data without close attention to the models that we now have, and to the theories we hope they will become (Deutsch 1966 and 1969).

Toward a Clarification of Terms

While laymen and dictionaries may accept the proposition that *data* is merely the plural of *datum,* the scientific definition should be somewhat more stringent. That is, any item of factual or existential truth may well be a datum: the Treaty of Versailles took effect in January 1920; the Japanese fleet was victorious in the Battle of Tsushima Straits, and so forth. But a number of such existential statements would not constitute data until we had very clear and explicit coding rules by which we defined the effective date of treaties (relatively simple), victory in naval battles (less simple), and national sovereignty (even less simple). Without such criteria for coding and classifying, we cannot generate a set of data, and therefore cannot make a scientifically useful descriptive statement about some population of treaties, naval battles, or sovereign states.

Second, and closely related, is the matter of quantification. In each of these three examples, we can decide which cases are included or excluded without invoking any quantitative criteria; purely qualitative criteria will often suffice. While an appreciation of this truth often leads to the statement that one need not quantify to do scientific research, such reasoning is flawed. Even though we can assign each particular case, condition, or event to a given category without necessarily quantifying, the moment that we generalize about the set of cases, we must enumerate how many fall into each category. Thus, even if quantification is not essential—and often it is essential—for identifying a datum, it is always essential for describing the data set into which it falls.

While discussing matters definitional, let us also deal with two labels that are sometimes applied to macrosocial data sets. One of these is "aggregate data" which, if taken literally, would apply to sets of data that describe groupings or populations without describing the individuals or small units that constitute the aggregation. These are summed or averaged scores for the aggregation, but not the scores for its individual components, leaving us in the dark as to how the characteristics are distributed within the aggregated population. But since scientists can (in the aggregate!) be as imprecise in their terminology as journalists, public officials, and laymen, we often see the label applied to any data set other than the tabulation of election results or opinion surveys. However, since most of these data sets only have the aggregated results of the election or survey, and nothing on the specific individuals who were involved, it is unsettling to see them set apart and labeled as something distinctly different from aggregate data! There are, of course, important differences between these and other data sets, but rarely does the aggregated/disaggregated dimension capture it. In practice, then, all too many of us use the label to describe a residual category, a nondifferentiated melange. Some lump everything that is not based on the observation of individual human traits or behaviors into the aggregate data category, while still others use it to include quantitative data produced by governmental or commercial organizations for their policy purposes, rather than by social scientists for research purposes.

Another label—more recently coined but equally imprecise—is that of "process-produced" data, by which is usually meant the latter-mentioned type of aggregate data. Since all data sets, by definition, are produced by some sort of intellectual and social process, it is not particularly useful to include corporate earning reports or governmental estimates of unemployment, but to exclude election votes or public opinion distributions. In the paragraphs that follow, we suggest a typology that rests on rather different dimensions, leading, we trust, to a more precise and useful set of categories.

A Proposed Typology of Data

Having rejected some of the more misleading labels and definitions, we should propose some alternatives, and we do this in the context of a proposed typology of social science data. As we see it, a useful typology must deal with at least three dimensions along which the many types of data might be differentiated. The first dimension embraces the type of variable that we hope to describe via our data set or, to put it another way, the concept that is represented by our data. The second is the level of aggregation at which the data-making observations are conducted. And the third is the procedure by which the observation is conducted and the data thereby generated.

To clarify these rather abstract statements, let us reiterate that any effort to describe or explain a social process must begin with a number of concepts (Kerlinger 1973, 28–29). But those are only mental constructs. We can imagine them but we can seldom see, touch, or hold them; few of the variables with which we speak and think can be directly measured or scaled or categorized. Normally, these conditions or events cannot be directly observed because they are too intangible, or because they occurred so long ago or far away as to be out of sight, or are too spread out in time or in space, or comprise too many components to be observed simultaneously. Thus, we often have no choice but to observe carefully those conditions and events that *are* accessible to our direct senses, and then infer from them the value or state of the unobserved phenomenon. In other words, what we do observe is the indicator (or proxy, or representation) of what we would like to observe, and the values or magnitudes manifested in our data serve as indirect indicators of the fluctuating values of the concepts. To put it another way, we think and theorize in terms of concepts, and our data serve as convenient surrogates that represent them and can be subjected to statistical analysis.

Turning, then, to our first dimension—the types of variable that the data set is supposed to represent—we can identify three such types: the attributes of social entities, the relationships between and among entities, and the behaviors that these entities manifest vis-à-vis one another. By *attribute* we mean some property or characteristic of any social entity ranging from a single individual to the global system, and from a loose and transitory band of hunters or coalition of pressure groups, to a formal and meticulously organized corporation or national government. More specifically, any social entity may be described in terms of its physical, structural, or cultural attributes. By physical attributes, we mean the size of a person or group, the age profile of a nation or political party, the racial composition of a province or a professional association, the geography of a continent, the fertility of a nation's soil, the productivity of an industry, the range of a navy's guns, and so forth. While some of these physical attributes may be due to the structural or cultural attributes (or the behavior) of certain groups, the distinction between cause and consequence must always be kept in mind. All too often, a physical attribute such as steel output, for example, is treated as a structural or cultural attribute because it is to a great extent affected by the structure and culture of the nation.

As to structural attributes, we have in mind the institutional and organizational arrangements and patterns by which sociologists, economists, and political scientists might describe a given social entity. Such concepts as social stratification, oligopoly, or bicameralism might be obvious examples; the first two are fairly informal and unofficial attributes of a system, whereas the latter would be formally institutionalized in legal documents. And while many structural attributes of an entity or system are inferred from the relationships and links between and among its component entities or subsystems, this hardly justifies the open-ended use of "structure" that we find in today's social science literature. Some use the word to embrace any set of social relationships among entities; others can mean statistical relationships among variables, recurrent historical patterns, and just about anything else for which no other word comes to mind.

Cultural attributes can also cause confusion inasmuch as the word *culture* has been used to describe virtually every attribute of a social entity, from its beliefs to its behaviors and from its pottery to its agricultural practices. We use it here in the more restricted sense of the distribution of perceptions, preferences, and predictions held by the people who comprise the entity; that is, beliefs about what is or was, what should be, and what will be (Singer 1968b).

With these three sets of attribute dimensions, any social entity can be described, compared with itself across different points in time, and compared with any other entities. To borrow from Gordon Allport's insightful distinction (1955), they permit us to deal with our social entities in terms of both their being and becoming, but not their behaving, to which we will attend after a look at the class of variables that falls between attributes and behavior: that of *relationships* among entities.

Unfortunately, the concept of relationship also has a multitude of meanings, of which only two concern us here. One sense is that of comparison: The relationship between the USSR and the United States in nuclear capabilities is that, for example, the Soviets have about 2,500 strategic delivery vehicles versus 2,000 for the United States, but only 7,000 deliverable warheads versus 9,200. When we are merely making a comparison between or among entities along a given attribute dimension, we will not speak of a relationship but of a *comparison*. The second, more complex meaning—and the one that we will use here—is that of connections, links, bonds, and associations between and among entities. How interdependent, durable, cooperative, open, and so on is or was the relationship between or among some specified population of entities, groups, nations, and the like?

The final class of variables, after the attributes of entities and the relationships among them, is that of *behavior,* which we use in its most literal form. What is a given entity doing, in the verbal or motor sense of the word? For example, is an individual speaking, a group of individuals negotiating, a pair of nations trading, an alliance of nations fighting a war? Note that we do not use behavior to include changes either in the attributes of an entity or in the internal conditions that might account for its behavior. That is, the brain cells may behave and interact when an individual expresses a thought, or individuals may converse prior to a group's acting, or bureaus may interact before an international organization condemns a member, and so forth. But this refers, in each case, to the behavior of a component, and not to the behavior of the entity itself.

We stress all of these distinctions not only because the vocabulary of social science is often imprecise, but because conceptual and semantic precision are essential to valid indicator construction and systematic data generation. When we turn to the connections among concepts, their indicators, and the data sets that emerge from the application of these indicators, it will be clear that semantic idiosyncrasies can lead to considerable mischief and confusion.

So much, then, for the first dimension in our typology of data: the type of social phenomenon (attribute, relationship, or behavior) involved. The second dimension revolves around what is often called the level of analysis, or, more accurately, the level of aggregation. In the above discussion, we have alluded occasionally to the distinction between a social entity and its component units or subentities, and we have inevitably spoken of entities that may range in size and complexity from the single individual up through the global system. Let us now address these distinctions in a more explicit and systematic manner, since they are as central to the validity of our index construction and data acquisition as are the distinctions between and among one's classes of variables (Singer 1961; Moul 1973).

For most social science disciplines, this great variety of social entities can be arranged along a vertical axis, with the individual human being at the lower end and the global system at the upper. In between, and working upward, one thinks of primary groups, such as the family, the face-to-face workgroup, and the friendship clique. At the next level are such secondary groups as the extended family; bureaus of municipal, provincial, or national governments; offices of commercial firms, departments of universities, labor unions, and so forth. At a fourth level are the governments, firms, universities, and labor unions themselves. Next, might be such territorial and subnational entities as provinces or regions, and then nations themselves, followed by international or supranational coalitions, alliances, or formal organizations at the continental or global level. The specific grouping and the specific level of social aggregation are not particularly important for our purposes here, and one's choice of grouping and level will reflect the theoretical question at hand. But, as already intimated, after choosing one's outcome variable and the explanatory variables whose predictive or postdictive power is to be examined, one must be extremely precise in going about the construction of the indicators and the acquisition of the data. To put it in more formal language, the validity of the inferences we make in linking our indicators to our variables will rest heavily upon the appropriateness of the aggregation levels at which each is found, as well as upon the reasoning that lies behind the types of variables (attribute, relationship, or behavior) themselves.

With these preliminary (but by no means trivial) matters of epistemology and terminology behind us, we now turn to our primary assignment: the role of variables, indicators, and data in macropolitical research.

Data Are Made, Not Born

While there are exceptions to the proposition that "data are made, not born," we will ignore them for the moment, on the grounds that the social sciences have paid an exorbitant price by assuming that the only available data are "born data." As McClelland (1972, 36) reminds us, too much social science research has rested on data sets that have been "requisitioned" from some other source. To advance further, he suggests that we will have to go after more difficult data: "needed bodies of facts will have to be quarried by hand out of hard rock." While the metaphor may be overly stark, it emphasizes that we must sift through vast and messy bodies of disparate facts in order to produce neat and tidy data sets. Perhaps the panning of gold—in which the few cherished flakes and nuggets are separated from the abundant gravel and sand in the riverbed—might be an equally appropriate metaphor.

Either way, the point is that we cannot expect the macrosocial sciences to advance if we rely primarily upon requisitioned data that are readily at hand. To the extent that we do follow that strategy—and thus acquiesce in the popular myth that social science is not "really" a science because most of its concepts are not readily measured or already found in quantitative form—we perpetuate our backward condition. We turn, therefore, to the procedures and reasoning that are followed in the making or generating of macropolitical data. Following that, we can briefly identify some of the sources in which we find our data more nearly ready-made.

The Validity of Indicators

In any discussion of indicators and their validity, we often use words like *proxy* and *surrogate,* and thus call attention to the fact that our data are not identical either to our conceptual variables or to real-world phenomena, but are rather detectable traces of the latter and representations of the former. We utilize our data—via our indicators—to infer the presence and strength of our variable in a given real-world, empirical setting. To emphasize the point further, try to imagine directly observing such attributes as the nationalism of an individual, the rationality of a decision unit, the centralization of a political party, the cohesiveness of an alliance, or the power of an international organization. Similarly, how might we directly observe the existence or the strength of relationships such as a marriage between individuals, the hostility between ethnic groups, or the economic interdependence among nations?

Even behavior and interaction—the most visible and audible of our three classes of social phenomena—are seldom directly observable, at least in a scientifically useful sense. That is, we may see or hear reports of a revolution or a diplomatic visit or the making of a trade agreement, and we may witness some part of the event or episode. But even here, we or our informants only see or hear a small fraction of the behaviors and interaction sequences. And, as noted earlier, if these events occurred before we came on the scene, or across a wide area of space or span of time or behind closed doors, we can only piece together certain bits of information and then *infer* the occurrence of certain behaviors (Webb et al. 1966).

The purpose of an indicator, then, is to help us generate a data set from whose magnitudes and values we can validly infer the values of the actual phenomena that interest us. While we suggested earlier that our data provide the observed values from which we infer the values and magnitudes of our unobserved variables, this can occasionally be an overstatement. If, for example, our variable is "severity of war," a perfectly reasonable indicator might be the number of fatalities "caused" by the war, and that should be observable. But a moment's reflection reminds us that, even if we could reliably discriminate between those fatalities that were caused by the war and those that were merely associated with it in time and space, the former number would itself not be directly observable. Rather we would first have to infer it from all sorts of reports and records, and then make the second inference from that number to the conceptual variable called severity.

Similarly, in the electoral behavior field, if our variable is that of voters' attitudes toward the political parties in a campaign, we usually offer the voters the stimulus of a questionnaire, and from their oral responses we infer their opinions about certain attributes of the parties. From those inferred opinions, we go on to infer a general attitude toward the parties, and on occasion we even go to a third inference as to whether they will vote, and if so, for which party. In the social sciences, such examples of our reliance on inferential leaps are numerous, and their frequency—as well as their often heroic proportions—should make us attentive to ways in which we might ascertain the validity of our indicators.

By validity, we mean the extent to which our indicators bridge the gap between the referent world and the observed variable that is purported to represent the referent world: the extent to which they actually measure what we claim to measure (Kerlinger 1973, 457). While most scientists agree that the validity of an indicator is never fully demonstrated, there are four basic tests that help us to estimate how close we have come. First, there is "face validity," by which we mean that most other specialists agree that the indicator seems to get at the concept it allegedly represents. In more refined terms, face validity rests on the plausibility of the reasoning behind the indicator: Why should we expect it to tap the concept we have in mind? A somewhat pretentious label for that reasoning is the "auxiliary theory" (Blalock 1968), but since it would be naive to expect, and costly to construct, a genuine theory to buttress every indicator we use, we prefer to stay with reasoning or rationale.

In addition to this intuitive criterion of face validity, there are three empirical tests that may be involved. The most direct is that of carrying out the operations called for by the indicator and then examining the scores that result. To the extent that they coincide with what we and other specialists expected, the indicator's alleged validity is further enhanced. Next, we can ascertain how strongly the indicator at hand correlates with a well-established alternative indicator of the same phenomenon (Campbell and Fiske 1959). Suppose, for example, one were using the number and rank of officerships in universal intergovernmental organizations (IGOs) as an indicator of a nation's "diplomatic importance," but wanted to go back to 1820, a century prior to the League of Nations. One solution might be to use instead the number and rank of diplomatic missions sent to each nation's capital by all the other nations in the system (Small and Singer 1973). If we found a high correlation between the IGO and the diplomatic scores for most of the nation-years since 1920, we would have greater confidence in the validity of the IGO officership indicator, given the fact that the diplomatic mission indicator not only seems reasonable, but produces scores that also seem reasonable.

But this test also has its weaknesses, one of which is the danger of spurious inference. To take another example, just because there happens to be a strong and positive correlation between total population and other indicators of national power—and there usually is (Russett et al. 1964; Rummel 1972)—one would not argue that population is a valid indicator of the concept. Not only are there many cases in which the correlation is weak, but there are even quite a few nations whose "power score" for certain periods will be *negatively* correlated with their population size. Examples of this pattern include nineteenth- and early twentieth-century China and India, and modern Israel.

A third empirical test of an indicator's validity is its "criterion validity" (Kerlinger 1973, 459), or its performance in the context of a well-supported theoretical model. If the variable that it allegedly taps is, according to the model, supposed to rise or fall in a certain correspondence with another variable (the validity of whose indicator is generally accepted), and it indeed rises and falls as it should, many would consider it quite valid. But given how few solid theories there are in political science (or economics or sociology) this could be a very unsatisfactory test. The chances of the suspect indicator being invalid are certainly no less than the chances of the "theory" itself being wrong. And, of course, the accepted indicators with which the new one is supposed to covary could, themselves, turn out to be less than valid reflectors of the variable they allegedly tap.

The Reliability of Indicators

While social scientists must, of necessity, devote a great deal of attention to the validity of their indicators, and even more to the analysis of the data generated via these indicators, we often tend toward the cavalier when it comes to the quality of the information upon which these more interesting activities must ultimately rest. The problem of "data quality control" (Naroll 1962) is all too often relegated directly to our data collection assistants and indirectly to the historians, archivists, clerks, biographers, and journalists who generated and assembled the raw material from which we begin. This quality problem can be viewed as two subproblems: the reliability of the indicators that convert the facts into data, and the accuracy (and completeness) of the facts to which the indicator's operations are applied.

As to reliability, we mean the extent to which we come up with the same scores when the same procedures are applied by the same coders to the same factual materials over and over, or by different coders at the same or differing times. The former is known as test-retest reliability and the latter as intercoder reliability. Both are primarily a function of the clarity, explicitness, and precision of the coding rules; the less the ambiguity in these rules, the higher will be the reliability of the indicator and the higher the probability that our coders are detecting, selecting, classifying, and recording the facts as intended by those who developed the indicator. To put it another way, the coding rules describe the operations by which the raw recorded traces of empirical reality are converted into scientifically useful data.

Perhaps the most typical procedures for such conversion are those known, somewhat misleadingly, as "content analysis" (Pool 1959; Berelson 1952; Holsti 1969; and North et al. 1963). We say misleading because it is not an analysis procedure at all, but one for generating data. In any event, the procedure is designed to shift through a tremendous body of written materials in order to identify certain patterns that would otherwise remain lost. Without imaginative and rigorous procedures, the empirical "gold" that we seek would remain obscured by all the associated verbiage that is not relevant to the patterns we seek, but within which the rare items are embedded.

The same basic principles are followed when we code and classify events and conditions that unfold in the natural world, or that have already been more impressionistically recorded by historians or on-the-spot observers in years gone by. In any utilization of the content analysis approach, the same principles apply: We articulate our concepts, operationalize them, set up our coding rules, and count the frequency with which indicators of variables appear. The major drawback of this method, especially when applied to large amounts of material, is that it takes a long time. Electronic computers are now used for tabulating and sorting the results via such programs as the General Inquirer (Stone et al. 1966), but the basic assignment of words, phrases, and themes to a given category must still be done by the human eye, mind, and hand. It may be, however, that we will soon have electronic optical scanners, which, when programmed with the coding rules, will be able to "read" thousands of pages very quickly and count—when found in the specified context—the frequencies of the words and phrases that interest us in a particular study.

If, for example, we suspected that a government had gradually become more willing to negotiate an arms reduction agreement without insisting on on-site inspection, but had never explicitly expressed that shift, a careful coding of its articulations might reveal a declining frequency of references to such inspection. Of course, if a decline were found, it could reflect mere carelessness, an effort to engage in tacit bargaining, or perhaps even an attempt to bypass certain domestic elements that might oppose the policy shift, were it made explicit. The need for careful inference always remains.

Alternatively, a subtle and gradual shift in mood could be unwittingly communicated if a political group's statements revealed, via content analysis, a changing ratio of hostile and friendly adverbs and adjectives when dealing with certain other groups. Even more subtle, albeit intended, could be a regime's effort to deemphasize the dangers of radioactive fallout in its domestic press, as a stratagem for preparing its citizens for a resumption of nuclear weapons tests in the atmosphere (Singer 1963b).

The point is that we can use such data-generating procedures to magnify certain information and ignore other information, and to detect certain obscure "signals" that might otherwise be lost in a sea of "noise." And the principle is the same whether we code historical narratives in order to detect certain classes of events (Merritt 1966), newspapers to detect changing reliance on certain political strategies, or legislative debates to detect shifting political values (Namenworth and Lasswell 1970). The procedures and rationale are dealt with more fully in the specialized literature, but enough has been said here to make clear the need for a well-conceived research design and a carefully constructed set of rules by which the coders will detect, classify, and record only what is intended by the researcher. If designed and executed carefully, the content analysis procedure can generate highly reliable data, and thus reduce our reliance on impressionistic or highly selective interpretation of a wide variety of written (and pictorial or graphic) materials. And, as already suggested, the reasoning and procedures are virtually identical, whether we are shifting through official statements in search of certain symbolic themes, through newspaper reports in search of certain economic traces, or through historians' monographs in search of certain behavioral patterns.

The Accuracy of Data Sources

While the political scientist can—through competence, resourcefulness, and diligence—eventually solve most problems connected with indicator reliability, the accuracy of the source materials to which our indicators are applied often lies beyond our control. In those cases, we can only eschew perfection, and adapt to the unpleasant realities in a thoughtful, creative, and frank fashion (Morgenstern 1963). Let us illustrate the problem by reference to certain types of data sources and suggest a few of the strategies for dealing with them.

There would seem to be three basic types of error in the factual materials with which we work, and each calls for a slightly different response. The most serious is the *systematic* distortion of the facts, due either to some fundamental but unintended flaw in the original procedures for observation and reportage or to the desire of the compilers or editors to mislead the potential user. In the former category might be a set of putatively complete trade figures, but with transshipped products omitted, or military personnel figures that exclude national police or border guards without so indicating.

More likely to be intentional would be an official chronology of major power conflicts, in which all the other nations' allies are also included, but not those of the compiler nation, or military budgets in which the compiler includes supplementary appropriations for the other governments but not for his own. These possibilities of systematic distortion, intended or not, remind us of the importance of familiarity with the historical context, the relevant literature, alternative sources, the bookkeeping practices employed, and statistical techniques by which to compare various sets of distributions. Needless to say, the researcher's failure to discern systematic bias in the data sources will produce badly distorted data, and thus highly dubious findings.

The second problem is that of *random* errors, often resulting from carelessness, naiveté, and incompetence at the origin or in the reportage, or in typographical and transcribing errors, or even in efforts to correct for systematic error. Normally referred to in the aggregate as "measurement error," these random inaccuracies often cancel one another out and may even have no discernible effect on the results that emerge from subsequent analyses of the data. More likely, however, there will be some effect, and if the errors are in the sources of the outcome variable data, we will merely get a poorer fit between our theoretical model and the observed regularities. But if the errors lie in data sources on the predictor side, the effect could be somewhat more serious. Random error in the values of these "independent" variables will result in attenuation biases in their coefficients, and the greater this random error, the more nearly will their coefficients approach zero.

A third type of error in the sources to which we turn for data is that of *incomplete* compilations, either because the original observations were incomplete, or because some of them were lost or eliminated later on when the compilations were being made. An illustrative example is that of some class of government expenditure or activity, with certain nations in certain historical periods consistently falling into the "missing" category. Often we cannot tell whether that class of activity just did not occur, or whether it occurred but was not recorded. Another frequent example is the tendency of regimes that are bureaucratically underdeveloped to publish, or report to an international body, figures that are so obviously wide of the mark that they are omitted from any compilation that is undertaken.

Missing facts and estimates need not, however, necessarily lead to the "missing data problem"; there are several strategies for estimating the value of those points that are missing. The simplest is merely to make an "informal estimate," and while this method may well produce an accurate estimate, it rests on something less than a perfectly reproducible algorithm. Equally simple is the arithmetic interpolation or extrapolation, but the virtue of its reproducibility is offset by its neglect of all information other than the trend line along which it is presumed to fall. Slightly more complicated, when working with a cross-temporal series, is to calculate the interpolated or extrapolated entries via simple statistical regression if the trend is linear, and polynomial or logarithmic regression if the trend is more complex. And if there is no clearly visible overall trend, but a fairly high degree of autocorrelation, autoregression models can be used (Nelson 1973). Somewhat more complex, but quite justifiable, is to take another series for which we have a relatively complete set of entries, and with which the incomplete series is highly correlated (positively or negatively), and then use statistical regression procedures to solve for the missing entries.

Other strategies can also be developed for making the estimates as accurate as possible, but regardless of the technique used, we must check its reliability by comparing the results with the values of a well-established data series that might be expected to correlate highly with the one at hand. Also important, if we make extensive use of missing data estimation techniques, is our need to test the sensitivity of the data analysis results to the estimates used. This is readily accomplished by running the analyses with, and then without, the estimated cases, and if there is a discernible difference in the results, it is clear that the missing data estimates need to be reexamined, even if only to identify the systematic bias in the error source. This is not, however, to say that the estimates must be discarded. Since data points that are unavailable usually have more of a systematic bias than those that are available, they really could be deviant in their values and thus should be expected to exercise a clear impact on one's analytic results.

If, despite the three types of inaccuracy (random, systematic, or missing) in a set of raw data, we decide that we have no choice but to use the set nevertheless and then go ahead with one or more of the remedial procedures outlined above, two additional steps may be considered. One is to correct the obtained/estimated values to a lower level of measurement: from ratio to interval, from interval to ordinal, and, in extremis, from ordinal to nominal.

In principle, if the inaccuracies are not too severe, this procedure will generally discard the more erroneous information, but preserve that which is essentially correct.

Similarly, if we are working with time series, we can smooth out the trend line by the use of the moving average. This procedure treats each individual observation as unjustifiably precise in appearance, and hedges by combining it with one or two of the readings just before and just after, using the average of those three or five readings. Needless to say, the moving average solution, while eliminating misplaced precision and giving us a smoother set of values with smaller and fewer perturbations, leads inevitably to a marked increase in the autocorrelation coefficient. As a result, if one were interested in the interobservation differences—such as in arms race analyses or in evaluations of the short-term effects of a policy change—these smoothing procedures would be highly inappropriate.

Before leaving this matter of factual accuracy, there is the unavoidable issue of the so-called confidence interval, and I approach it with some trepidation. Those who have done a fair amount of indicator construction and data generation are often asked to attach some numerical value to the accuracy of the data generated from one or another data source. One possible response might be to provide as honest an estimate as we can, indicating what fraction of the data points fall within each of several error ranges. This would require three distinct calculations. First, how far off could each point in each series possibly be? Second, how probable is that extreme error, and how probable are the descending error ranges as we approach perfect accuracy? And, third, for a given data set, made up of several series, what fraction of the points falls into each of those probable error and/or confidence intervals? If we could intelligently make the first two estimates, it would be a simple matter to combine them into a single index of accuracy, such as the "standard error" of an observation, or perhaps even a Gini-like index. But experience suggests that steps one and two would not only be very time-consuming, but also could result in a misleadingly precise representation of a highly subjective and impressionistic process.

A more modest indicator of the data generator's confidence—adapted from the weapons technology community—might also be worth examining. When a large salvo of missiles is fired, accuracy is expressed in terms of "circular error, probable," indicating the radius of a circle within which half of the missiles could be expected to fall. In the same vein, we could ask how many standard deviations out from the mean of the distribution curve we would have to go to capture half of the points in the series. If either of these methods has been used in the macrosocial sciences, we have not encountered it.

A final point regarding the accuracy of our data, or the factual materials from which they are generated, concerns the uses to which the data will be

put. We noted earlier that a data set based upon moving averages, interpola-
tions, and other smoothing procedures will suppress or eliminate the temporal
fluctuations that could be critical to certain types of investigation. The point is
that every data set that rests upon multiple sources will require certain internal
adjustments, even if only to achieve comparability across actors and observation points on a given dimension. While this should cause no concern to the
social scientist, it could make many data sets quite useless to the historian.
But since the latter usually focus on a limited number of actors or years—
while introducing an impressive number of variables and thus ending up with
a poor N/V ratio (Deutsch, Singer, and Smith 1965)—they are unlikely to
turn to a large data matrix when they need only a few of its cells. They are also
wise in not doing so.

Thus, every data set must be examined closely, along with the coding rules
by which it was generated, prior to its use in systematic analysis. This is not,
however, to agree with the assertion that one must only generate one's data after
formulating the research design. A given data set can—and should—be utilized for an appreciable array of investigations reflecting a diversity of theoretical orientations, and the idea of tailor-made data for each theoretical
problem and orientation is errant nonsense. Not only would (and does) such
practice make for gross inefficiency in the social sciences, but it also drastically
impedes cumulativeness, since each study could end up resting upon a slightly
different data base, making comparison and synthesis highly questionable
(Leng and Singer 1970). Moreover, it would lend support to the suspicion—
already accepted by many of our critics—that we carefully select our data and
tailor our indicators in order to assure the statistical results that accord with our
"theories."

Data Generation via Indicator Construction

In the previous section, we examined the criteria that need to be approxi-
mated—if not fully satisfied—in the construction of indicators, and the way
in which they are used to generate the data that represent the changing values
or magnitudes of a variable. Bearing both activities in mind, let us shift now
from these general considerations to a number of specific data generation
problems. The plan here is to illustrate the wide range of data sources and
data-making procedures in the context of our three types of variables: attributes, relationships, and behaviors.

Indicators of Attributes

We illustrate first with attributes, not only because they are the most familiar
and usually require less in the way of heroic inferences than do indicators of

relationships and behaviors, but also because—paradoxically—constructing indicators of attributes can lead to more problems of conceptual slippage than with those of relationships and behaviors.

To illustrate, suppose that a key attribute in a planned investigation is the "diplomatic importance" of nations, to which we alluded earlier. How might we go about measuring such an attribute in a reliable fashion, and what sort of indicator would be valid for a wide variety of nation types across perhaps a century and a half? The most obvious indicator would probably be one that rests upon the verbal behavior of diplomats, calling for them to rank today's nations in response to certain questionnaire items. But if we wanted to go back in time more than a few years, contemporary diplomats would not be very helpful; in that case, we might turn to the expert judgments of diplomatic historians of the periods and regions of interest.

Leaving aside the cost in time and money for such an opinion survey, it would suffer from the familiar flaws of all intuitive judgments, no matter how carefully stimulated, recorded, and combined. Within the population of respondents, there would be a wide range of criteria as to how the nations' diplomatic importance should be evaluated, with some thinking largely in terms of military or industrial capability, others relying on protocol or conference participation or diplomatic visits, and still others trying to recall which nations most regularly "had their own way" in the various regions and periods. Even if provided with explicit criteria, our respondents would be inclined to reinterpret or modify them between start and finish, either unconsciously or because of their belief that we should not use the same ones for such varying nations or periods. Further, since our historians will normally be truly expert in rather narrow bands of time and space, they will bring highly detailed knowledge to bear only within the intersection of those bands, and considerably less to bear in evaluating or scaling nations in other regions and periods. Yet another source of inconsistency might be the moment at which the interview or questionnaire was used: Has a recently encountered article or document left the strong impression that Austria-Hungary was overrated by the other powers in the 1890s, for example? Would an earlier or later interview produce a different estimate? In sum, threats to consistency across judges and across time, and hence to reliability would, along with the logistical problems, be disabling, even if the researcher's instrument were carefully designed to maximize the validity of the responses.

Wisely rejecting expert opinion as a basis for estimating the diplomatic importance of nations, the researcher might turn to a less expensive and more reliable method: content analysis of a carefully drawn sample of books or monographs on the relevant time-space intersections. With a good library, explicit criteria as to what is meant by the concept of diplomatic importance, precise instructions as to which passages to read and how to classify certain types of statements, and well-trained and thorough coders, this could be a highly satisfactory procedure for generating diplomatic importance scores. The major advantage here is that we secure the more stable judgments of our experts without the trouble and expense of interviewing live subjects merely by going through their writings and systematically recording all of their statements regarding the diplomatic importance of the nations with which they were dealing in each study. If we are trying to generate data reflecting a concept that is widely used and whose definition—however preoperational— is widely shared, the content analysis strategy is surely preferable to that of questionnaires or interviews. But if major time-space domains have been ignored in the literature, or if the concept at hand is neither widely used nor consistently defined, content analysis of scholarly works will not suffice.

A closely related research option might be to content analyze, not the writings of scholars, but the writings of those whose role it is to observe and comment on foreign affairs as they unfold: journalists, columnists, and editors. There are and have been newspapers with good coverage of foreign affairs in every region of the world, and there are copies of these papers going back many decades, if not centuries. Moreover, given the shared perceptions and the inevitable symbiotic relationship between the elite press and the political elites, it is reasonable to infer that the press (especially on the editorial page) will provide, over the long run, a fair expression of the elite consensus in each nation regarding the relative diplomatic importance of most of the nations in the international system.

Yet another possibility might be to code the diplomatic communications among the world's foreign ministries or between the ministries and their embassies and legations, but at least two factors would argue against this source of data. One is that evaluative statements regarding the relative importance of other nations seem to be relatively rare in these communications. The other is that newspaper files are considerably more available and accessible than diplomatic archives, if the written trace is our preferred vehicle.

But as the previous section reminds us, there may be alternative vehicles for getting at our concept, and if they look as if they might be less costly and time-consuming—as well as equally strong on the validity and reliability dimensions—they may be preferable. That we (Small and Singer 1973) so thought when faced with the need to measure diplomatic importance is clear from the fact we indeed selected the bureaucratic-behavioral trace of diplomatic missions. The "auxiliary theory" or line of reasoning is quite simple. For reasons of economy, tradition, personnel limits, and so forth—as well as for policy reasons—the typical government over the last 150 years has established diplomatic missions in only about 45 percent of the world's capital cities, with 55 percent of them ignored. This produces, in effect, an ongoing plebiscite in which all the nations are continuously "voting with their missions" as to which of the others are more or less important to them. While some of the individual decisions may be quixotic, the net effect when all these decisions are aggregated year after year provides us with a collective judgment on the part of those who decide where their nations' primary interests lie.

Although the face validity of this attribute indicator (reflecting both the reasoning behind it and the rankings that it produces) and its correlational validity vis-à-vis the international organization officerships mentioned earlier are reassuring, it is too soon to tell whether its role in a well-founded theory will further enhance our confidence in it. While awaiting that particular test of validity, a reasonable researcher would certainly go ahead and use it, but with the prudence that should accompany the use of any less-than-proven instrument, along with the knowledge that it may well contribute to the very growth of theory that will permit its most demanding tests.

Despite the apparent indirectness of the above indicator, the number of inferential steps from conceptual variable to indicator to data can be even greater. Let us illustrate this via an attribute of the international system's structure, using an indicator that reflects a *distribution of national attributes,* rather than a directly observable attribute of the system per se. In the classical literature, we often find the proposition that peace is preserved by maintaining approximate parity among the major powers, and by avoiding conditions of preponderance. The closer the distribution of capabilities is to perfect equality, the less the likelihood of war, and the closer that distribution is to pure monopoly, the greater the likelihood of war. To test that very plausible proposition, one would first have to develop an indicator of major power capabilities, and then develop an indicator of the extent to which they are concentrated in the hands of a small number of powers. A multidimensional indicator now in use (Singer, Bremer, and Stuckey 1972) and whose validity seems quite adequate, is based upon: population (total and urban); industrial activity (energy consumed and steel produced); and military preparedness (armed forces size and expenditures). First, we have to acquire—requisition would surely underestimate the difficulty—the raw facts for each nation in each year on each of the six dimensions, using national government statistics, summaries prepared by international organizations, commercial yearbooks, scholarly monographs, and (in extremis) unpublished archival materials.

Once these raw facts have been transformed into comparable data series, we convert the absolute values into each nation's percentage share of the total. Thus, if there are five major powers in the system in a given year, and each holds precisely 20 percent of the overall capabilities, the distribution is equal, and the concentration score is therefore zero. Conversely, if one or two of them hold the lion's share, making for something akin to monopoly or duopoly, we would get a very high concentration score. Of course, the pattern usually lies between these extremes, and in any case we calculate the indicator's value using the (Ray and Singer 1973) formula:

$$CON = \sqrt{\frac{(\Sigma S_i^2) - \dfrac{1}{N}}{1 - \dfrac{1}{N}}}$$

Thus, to indicate the magnitude of this particular system attribute at a given moment, we begin with data on each nation's capability attributes, combine and weight them according to one or another theoretically persuasive formula (or perhaps even treat them as equally important), convert those absolute scores into percentage shares of the aggregation's total, and finally convert those shares into a single indicator summarizing the inequality of the distribution for that month or year. This is hardly an observation of a systemic attribute, but that is increasingly true as we move toward more realistic indicators of theoretically sophisticated concepts. Nor is there anything wrong with using such indicators, as long as the line of reasoning is very explicit and the cross-level inferences are empirically and logically justified; illustrative of such indicators of distribution are: Alker and Russett (1964); Cutright (1967); Duncan and Duncan (1955); Greenberg (1956); Hall and Tideman (1967); and Lieberson (1969).

One may also get at certain structural properties of a complex system by using dyadic relationship or bondedness data. Macropolitical investigations rest quite often on notions of cleavage or fragmentation (Rae and Taylor 1970), segregation (Bell 1954), or polarization in the system at hand (Wallace 1973a; Bueno de Mesquita 1975), either as an outcome to be explained or as an explanatory variable that might help account for the variation in some theoretically interesting outcome. In that case, we would first requisition, gather, or generate the data reflecting the presence and magnitude of a certain class of bond or link between each pair of entities that comprise the system at the time of each observation. This could be a relationship as constant and given as geographical distance, or one that reflects a consciously chosen and often changing bond, such as alliance commitments or commercial exchanges.

Here, the data would be entered into an actor-by-actor matrix in which every component entity is given both a row and a column. In the cell marking the intersection between A's row and N's column, the bondedness data are entered for every pair that is bonded on that dimension; for those pairs that have no such bond, a zero is entered. Once these data are entered into our computer files, we use one of a number of matrix (Guttman 1968; Lingoes 1973) or data reduction routines (Harmon 1976) to ascertain the number of discernible clusters or poles, the depth of cleavage between clusters, the strength of the bondedness within them, and so forth. Further, depending on the theoretical question at hand, one may compare the configurations at successive times to measure the direction and rate of change in them, or compare those reflecting two or more different types of bondedness (such as economic interdependence or political alignment) in order to tap the extent to which the different configurations reinforce or counteract one another.

Indicators of Relationships

As already suggested, the word *relationship* in social science can have a multitude of meanings, and two of the possible meanings concern us here. One reflects the similarity of two entities along a given attribute or property dimension: the relationship between entities A and B in terms of their relative size, power, wealth, organizational complexity, cultural homogeneity, and the like. Strictly speaking, we should use such words as comparability or similarity in this connection, reserving "relationship" for links and associations that bond or relate them to one another. Let us do so here, and explore some of the ways in which macropolitical relationships might be ascertained and measured.

While it is true that some attribute or property variables rest upon the relationship among the component units of the entity (and we return to that issue shortly), most of them tend to be more directly observable, or else inferable from data that are observable. But when we try to describe relationships, we are dealing not only with "the two-body problem," but with that most intangible of phenomena, a bond or link or association. Even addressing something as elusive as a cultural attribute (an organization's morale or a political party's credibility), there is some directly observable trace from which reasonable inferences may be drawn, but almost all interentity bonds are beyond direct observation. Unlike the bonds that connect physical or biological entities, those that connect social entities are largely symbolic and intangible.

Illustrative examples are contracts between commercial firms, treaties between nations, multilateral agreements linking international organizations to member governments, and so forth. In these cases, there is at least the written document that describes the bond. But equally important to the student of comparative or international politics are those bonds and links that do not rest upon tangible documents but upon inherited or arranged understandings, or even upon historical concatenations that were never intended. For example, two nations may be found in the same grouping or cluster based on the fact that their diplomatic missions are in virtually the same capitals, or on their tendency to belong to the same international organizations. On the other hand, their membership in a given alliance cluster would not only be the result of more conscious choice, but also be a condition of which its elites could hardly be unaware.

The above-mentioned relationships would normally be inferred from the close scanning of a bondedness matrix, in which every entity is listed in both a column and a row of the type of matrix described earlier, with the presence, absence, or strength of the bond connecting each pair shown in the cell marking the intersection of one's column with the other's row. Once the raw data reflecting these bonds had been acquired or generated and entered into the matrix, we could use one of the several computerized decomposition algorithms to ascertain which entities clustered together on that type of bond at that particular moment.

Yet another type of data that can be used for inferring relationships is that of interaction. While, as suggested earlier, there is often a failure to discriminate between these two classes of variable, conceptual precision in our data making—and thus our theory building—requires it to be made. By relationship, of course, we mean the sorts of bonds and associations referred to above, and by interaction, we mean behaviors that are directed toward, and responsive to, one another. While a relationship may affect interaction patterns (partners in a coalition government, for example, are likely to vote with the government on a confidence measure) and interactions may affect relationships (courtship leading to marriage, negotiation leading to a formal agreement, trade leading to a common market), they are clearly not the same phenomenon. Further, we may predict interaction patterns from a relationship (exchanging military plans on the basis of a defense pact) and a relationship from observed interaction (membership in opposing coalitions on the basis of conflictive behaviors). And, of course, we may infer the existence of a relationship from observed interactions (a most favored nation agreement from the mutual reduction of tariff levels). Bearing these distinctions in mind, we turn to our third type of indicator: that reflecting behavior and/or interaction.

Indicators of Behavior and Interaction

We suggested earlier that these phenomena are generally more visible than attributes or relationships, but this does not mean that it is necessarily easier to observe and measure them in the scientific sense. One reason for the difficulty in observation is that behavioral events occur rapidly, and if the observer is not on the scene at the precise moment, the action will be missed. And if they happen to occur very slowly, one would require a sequence of observers to relieve one another (Alger 1966). Also problematical are behavior and interactions that occur across so wide a swath of space that they are beyond our capacity to see, or otherwise sense. Thus, despite their tangibility (unless carried out in secrecy), interactions require us to develop particularly ingenious indicators and sensitive strategies for picking up their traces.

The traces that are left by the behaviors and interaction of political entities can be sought in a variety of places. For nations vis-à-vis other nations, these might be the memoirs of, or (if our interest is in relatively recent events) interviews with, the participants or close observers; diplomatic archives; foreign ministry chronologies; official records of international organizations; newspaper accounts; and the standard narrative monographs by historians working from these other sources. For legislative bodies, government ministries, political parties, or interest groups, the sources will not be that different: memoirs, interviews, newspaper accounts, official documents, and so forth.

Again, however, knowing where to look for the traces (or recollections) left by behavioral phenomena is only part of the game. Once the raw material has been located—if at all—the problem remains of converting what is essentially an undifferentiated welter of facts and impressions into scientifically usable data sets. In addition to the issues discussed under basic procedures for the generation and extraction of data, there are two particular problems.

First, there is the conceptual distinction between behavior and interaction, and while it is seldom noted, our failure to do so can lead to some foolish interpretations. The most dramatic example would be that of conflict escalation, in which there is a strong tendency for the observer to assume that all belligerent moves by one party are directed toward, or are in response to, the self-evident opponent or adversary. Just as nations in an arms race may well be arming vis-à-vis third and fourth parties (Moll 1974)—not to mention vis-à-vis a variety of domestic actors—all political actors attend to several others simultaneously. Thus, rather than make an easy inference from the separate behaviors of an "obviously" interacting pair, it is essential that we begin by coding each party's behaviors separately, and only then ascertain the degree to which they constitute interaction. The existence of an obvious relationship is insufficient evidence, as is the mere temporal or geographical proximity of their separate behavior sequences. Usually, it is necessary to examine one facet or another of the respective decision processes prior to concluding that the behavior patterns constitute a literal interaction process.

The second problem with behavioral and interactional data sets is that we are never certain that the full population of events has been identified. Those who have tried to generalize about behavioral regularities only to discover that their generalizations rested upon an incomplete and highly skewed set of cases can appreciate this problem, but there seldom is any ironclad procedure for assuring a complete universe. When we deal with such behaviors as legislative roll-call votes or the cases before a court during a given session, the danger of missing any of the events is very low. But if our concern is with behavior that occurs in a less fully institutionalized environment, the probability of missing some of the cases can be all too high. This is particularly true if the researcher is only interested in a subset of the population, such as only those internation disputes in which military force was mobilized or deployed. In such a situation, how do we know whether the chroniclers, journalists, or historians might have omitted some or most of those qualifying cases because "nothing important" came of them? The standard solution here, when secondary materials are the only data source available, is to code several of them, written from different perspectives in time as well as place and culture.

Conclusion: Some Modest Proposals

Of all the skills that go into the growth of social science knowledge, the least developed is that of data generation. While data generation and index construction—like model building and data analysis—are not sufficient in themselves, they are absolutely necessary to the scientific enterprise. Yet college and graduate school curricula seldom include courses on the subject, journal articles on it are extremely rare, there seem to be fewer than ten texts on the subject in English, and worst of all, most of the scores of texts on social science methods provide only a superficial glance at the problems and strategies associated with the generation of data. Further, whereas the philosophers of science have turned out reams on the ways in which to interpret observed patterns, they have virtually ignored the processes by which the observations themselves might be carried out and recorded.

We might speculate as to the sources of this unfortunate asymmetry. Do we consider the acquisition of data so simple and obvious a task that anyone can do it? Or do we assume that it is best left to the historians? Or if the past holds no key to knowledge about the future, that journalists and bureaucrats and librarians can do the job for us? Perhaps we are all "closet theorists," persuaded that logic, elegance, and imagination are all we need to understand social phenomena. Or, to invoke a football metaphor, with the quarterback basking in the limelight, why become a guard? The possibilities are nearly endless, but far from reassuring.

Several solutions, in addition to those implied above, come to mind, and an article on political research methods is surely the appropriate place to suggest a few of them. Despite a plethora of discouraging tendencies in the macrosocial sciences today—ranging from such gimmickry as "evaluation research" and "futurology," to increasing faith in pure cerebration, to perpetuation of the dubious fact-values dichotomy—there are several encouraging ones. Among these is the increasing interaction between social scientists and historians, reflected in the establishment of the Social Science History Association. The central objective, as we understand it, is to help social scientists become more longitudinal and historians to become more scientific. In our view, this convergence holds considerable promise for both sets of disciplines, and perhaps even for an ultimately integrated science of human behavior. More particularly, political scientists, economists, and sociologists can profit by taking a more retrospective view of the phenomena that engage them, and can become more familiar with a greater diversity of cases from which to generalize. But most germane here is a third possibility: that we will learn from them how to get at and then evaluate the incredibly rich variety of traces left to us by earlier generations. The interaction will, we hope, also lead historians to think nomothetically, both in the formulation of explanations and in the gathering of facts. Just as the social scientist needs to be more attentive to the intricacies of single episodes and the hidden secrets of half-forgotten artifacts, historians can become sensitive to the need for comparability in their facts and generality in their explanations.

Another possibility, also institutional, might be the establishment of a journal or annual (preferably multilingual) devoted to data generation and index construction in cross-national and international politics. Such a journal could help to educate those who are unfamiliar with the methods and results in this sector, and help the more avant garde to expand their repertoires. And it could signal the discipline's recognition that models without empirical evidence may be good fun, but incomplete science. Perhaps most importantly, it could create incentives, rewards, and legitimacy for those who might otherwise continue in the comfortable ways of waiting for the other fellow's data set, or of theorizing without data entirely. Another possibility, involving the foundations, comes to mind. Rather than continue to invest largely in research that is neither reproducible nor cumulative, perhaps one or two of these quasi-public institutions might be persuaded to establish a few centers whose primary task might be the generation, maintenance, and diffusion of data sets of potentially wide applicability. Such units as the International Relations Archive of the Inter-University Consortium for Political and Social Research have intermittently considered and even entered into such activities, but none has yet done so in a vigorous and sustained fashion because of the financial constraints, the difficulty of deciding which data sets would most be worth producing, and the absence of strong demand. Despite these constraints, and the lack of strong institutional support, we have nevertheless turned out a number of data collections, ranging widely in both substantive focus and scientific quality; among these are: Banks (1971), Banks and Textor (1963), Morrison et al. (1972), Russett et al. (1964), Singer and Small (1972), and Taylor and Hudson (1972); an excellent critique of several of them is Gurr (1974).

Finally, those of us who teach and do research in the macrosocial sciences stand in need of some modest reforms. First, we can set a better example by increasing the inductive element in our own research mix, and by investing in the generation of more ambitious data sets. Second, when we write up our results, we can describe and justify our data-making procedures, eschewing the tendency to treat those activities as somehow too trivial to mention. Third, as teachers, we can break away from the stereotyping behavior that has kept us so data-poor: the early classification of our students, especially at the graduate level, as either "brilliant and creative theorists" or "competent, but plodding empiricists." This sort of practice discourages our most capable people from taking on the important and challenging work in indicator construction and data generation. Worse yet, it virtually assures the perpetuation of our peculiar two-culture problem, and makes it quite unlikely that we will begin to turn out what the discipline and the world need most: the complete social scientist.

2
National Attributes

The Diplomatic Importance of States, 1816–1970: An Extension and Refinement of the Indicator

Melvin Small and J. David Singer

In an earlier article, we presented our findings on the composition of the interstate system, along with the diplomatic importance or "status" attributed to each member by the others in the system (Singer and Small 1966a). Covering the period between the Napoleonic Wars and the onset of World War II, we set out both to calculate the ranking of the states every 5 years during those 125 years, and to make explicit the criteria by which system membership and status ranks were established. Our major motivation was to identify the empirical domain within which our own research would go forth and to develop certain indicators that were relevant to the Correlates of War Project; it also seemed likely that these data might be of use to others in the scholarly community (see, for example, Wallace 1973b).

In extending the project beyond World War II and up to a more recent date, we faced not only the requirement to gather additional diplomatic representation data, but also the opportunity to reconsider some of our original indicators. In this supplementary report, therefore, we will not only present the additional data, but will also use the occasion as an opportunity to recapitulate (and where necessary, modify) the procedures and rationale behind our proposed index of diplomatic importance. Worth noting at the outset is the fact that we are not the only ones with certain reservations about the index. A number of our colleagues have, in spoken (if not written) word, raised some questions about its validity. Some of the criticisms can only be termed foolish, but most of them have struck us as eminently reasonable. In the opening section, we will address ourselves to the question of validity; in later sections we will summarize our revised procedures, compare them to those originally employed, and then follow with a recapitulation of the resulting indicator values.

Reprinted from *World Politics* 25 (1973): 577–99. Reprinted with permission of Princeton University Press.

Diplomatic Representation as an Indicator
of Importance

In the original study we argued that the relative importance that the states in the system attributed to one another could be inferred from the number and rank of the diplomatic missions accredited and dispatched to each of their capitals. The reasoning was that the decision to locate, maintain, or abolish a mission of any particular rank in any foreign capital reflected a wide variety of considerations within and between the several governments, and that the sum total of such missions would represent some consensus as to how important the recipient state was to all the others in the system. In other words, we treated the numerous and continuing decisions of whether or not to send diplomatic missions to foreign capitals as a sort of running sociogram, illuminating each state's relative diplomatic importance to the membership of the system at large. The resulting scores seemed, in our judgment, generally to vindicate that assumption, and to reflect the changing—as well as the stable—fortunes of the system's members over the nineteenth and twentieth centuries.

On the other hand, the problem of face validity remained far from solved. Not only were we somewhat dissatisfied with some of the rankings, but we also concluded that the reasoning behind the index needed to be stated in more detailed and vigorous fashion. One of the purposes of this paper is to do exactly that; but before doing so, a few words as to the utility of such an indicator might be helpful.

What can one do with an adequate measure of diplomatic importance? At its simplest, such an index would help to distinguish between states with high, medium, and low diplomatic involvement vis-à-vis the others in the system, and thus differentiate between central and peripheral subsystems. Second, such an index would permit us to test a variety of hypotheses regarding the relationship between the diplomatic importance of a state and its foreign policy behavior, interaction, and relationship patterns. A third type of use might be to measure the discrepancy between a state's diplomatic importance and its capabilities—in order to test hypotheses, for example, which relate status discrepancies to foreign policy actions. Other uses come to mind, and are being followed in the Correlates of War Project, but enough has been said to indicate that our interests are not merely antiquarian or encyclopedic.

Aside from the question of utility, what are the probabilities of constructing a valid and reliable index of diplomatic importance? A useful point of departure is to note that every effort to "measure" some social phenomenon requires us to infer back from what we *can* observe to what we cannot—or do not—observe in any direct fashion. We use words, numbers, and pictures as representations of the referent ("real") world, and make inferences about the referent world phenomenon on the basis of the symbols we use to represent it. What we seek here is a rather general reflection of the relative importance of each state member to the others in the system during a given half-decade. One way to clarify the limitations of the proposed indicator is to spell out some of the things we are *not* trying to measure. First, we are not trying to measure power, capability, or influence. These characteristics of a state will certainly affect its diplomatic importance, but they are not identical with it. And, as suggested above, the very magnitude of the difference between importance and these other attributes remains a critical area of inquiry. Second, we are not proposing to measure "relative acceptance" or any other deviation in a country's score between what it *does* receive and what it *should* receive, given its geographical centrality, size, power base, or other intrinsic attribute.[1] Third, we are not (at least for the time being) interested in measuring the importance of one particular state to another particular state. To measure a specific dyadic relationship with sufficient precision would require much more evidence than will be offered here. Thus, no inferences should be—or can be—made about China's importance to the United States from the absence of their respective embassies in Peking and Washington (an example that is often suggested by critics of our proposed indicator). To extend that point a bit further, we are not trying to measure a state's importance in a particular region or in the context of a specific substantive problem. The index is intended to be *general* as to place and context, not specific. Nor are we interested here in measuring the short-run fluctuations in a state's diplomatic importance. Rather, the objective is to estimate the more slow-moving importance scores as they rise and decline in response to gross and general trends in international politics.

Further, we are not trying to measure the precise interval between two states that fall close to one another in our rank orderings. Even though we compute and present the raw and normalized interval-scale scores of the states, we urge users not to interpret these scores too literally. To emphasize the imprecision of these values, we eschew the convention which shows a tie by giving the equal scorers a fractional rank position, such as 7.5 for those which tie for seventh place in a given period. Rather, we rank them as seven and eight arbitrarily, by their state code number. For the same reason, we also convert those two sets of interval scores into grouped ordinal scores, dividing the membership of the system into quintiles, each of which contains approximately one-fifth of the members in the given observation year.

---

1. For an application of that strategy to data on international trade, see Alker and Puchala (1968).

Returning, then, to what we *do* seek to measure, we reason as follows: first, most governments do not establish diplomatic missions in the capital (or principal) cities of *all* other sovereign members of the system. They send missions to only a fraction of the other states; as a matter of fact, that fraction has been a rather consistent figure, ranging from a low of 37 percent in 1849 to a high of 60 percent in 1827 when the system was considerably smaller. This means that, over the past 155 years, we usually find missions from only about 45 percent of the other states in the capital of the average state.

What accounts for this deviation from universality? We begin with the awareness that each government has a given propensity to exchange missions with each of the others in the system, in accordance with its judgment of their relative importance to its own state. Reflecting geographical and logistical distance, economic interdependence, cultural affinities, alternative modes of intercourse via third-party nations or organizations, and so forth, that set of judgments will at the very outset, assure a less than universal exchange of missions. On top of this original estimate of importance, each government must also contend with a variety of resource limitations. These would include: a perceived limitation of funds and personnel in general; a lack of diplomats familiar with the language, culture, etc. of a possible diplomatic partner; and the reluctance of diplomats to accept certain posts on grounds of remoteness, climate, housing, cuisine, servants, and ambiance. These limitations require that governments husband their scarce personnel and funds, and thus further reduce the likelihood that all will have missions in all. If the decision to exchange missions were simply a function of perceived relative importance in the context of limited resources, we *could* interpret our indicator as reflecting the relative importance of each state to every other state, and thus make reasonable inferences at the *dyadic* level.

But intervening between the judgment of another state's relative importance and the dispatch of a mission, there is a second set of inputs into the prospective sender's decision process. We refer to political constraints and incentives, some of which can occasionally be potent enough to outweigh the original judgment. These could include not only the political eagerness or reluctance of the potential partner, but: (a) domestic pressures favoring or opposing the establishment or perpetuation of a given bond; or (b) the urgings of other influential governments favoring or opposing such a bond. Although we would not argue that our original judgments as to the relative importance of a given state are completely apolitical, they are usually made within the context of the foreign ministry, and thus normally reflect a degree of detached expertise. But when special interest groups or foreign governments intrude into the process, we can expect an occasional deviation from what the bureaucratic consensus would have been.

Although it is often suggested that such "political" incentives or constraints are a twentieth-century innovation, the precedent goes back at least to the 1820s and 1830s. As the South American revolutions of that period succeeded in replacing monarchies with republics, the United States was eager to see the legitimization of the new governments. The more autocratic regimes of Europe (particularly Russia, Austria, and Prussia) were quite opposed, however, and such states as Britain and Holland found themselves caught between the two sets of pressures. And while many Europeans did eventually exchange missions with many of the American states, the Holy Alliance was able to slow down the rate of recognition. To some extent, such political pressures were again generated following the revolutions of 1848, but not to the extent found in the current century with the rise of the Communist regimes. This time, however, the United States has been on the other side, urging—with appreciable success—the *withholding* of recognition from the USSR in the 1920s and 1930s, and from China in the 1950s and 1960s, to take the more dramatic examples. Even in 1970, with missions in 87 percent of the system's members, the United States (and many of its allies) withheld official recognition from Albania and Mongolia—as well as China—on political grounds.

The effects of such extranormal pressures will usually lead to depressed importance scores for the states whose isolation is sought by one or another of the major powers. Whether these "lower-than-expected" scores can be thought of as valid indicators of the holders' diplomatic importance depends upon the reasoning behind the measure, and this leads to the second part of the causal inference loop that we see as linking the indicator with the concept and with the referent world. One interpretation would have it that the recipient's score has been contaminated by extraneous considerations and that we therefore have a threat to our indicator's validity. Another interpretation—and the one which informs the argument at hand—is that the net score *does* reflect the recipient's importance. In one way or another, every government is faced periodically with the need to estimate, or re-estimate, how "important" it is to exchange missions with every other one in the system. That relative importance is reflected in its willingness to: (*a*) allocate limited resources to a given diplomatic bond, (*b*) incur the costs of overcoming domestic or foreign opposition to such a bond, and (*c*) sacrifice one set of attractive bonds in order to maintain or establish another set of more or less equally attractive ones.

We might think of those recurrent national choices as constituting a slowly changing and ongoing plebiscite among all the system's members, in which the separate governments must weigh myriad considerations in determining how important it is for them to have or not have a formal and reciprocated diplomatic presence in each of the other world capitals. To put it another way, the number (and/or rank) of missions in each state is a resultant of all the decisions concerning relative importance that have been made in the months and years preceding each observation year. Those several decisions, which cannot be reliably or economically observed, predict to (or "cause") the total number of ambassadors, ministers, and chargés d'affaires accredited to a given state in any half-decade.

Carrying the argument a step further, the importance indicator may also be interpreted in a predictive, as well as a postdictive fashion. In that case, our causal inference is that the diplomatic importance of a state will be high if it has diplomatic bonds with many other states and low if it has few such bonds. While the essentiality of such missions may decline with the improvement in communications technology, or the increase in multilateral contacts via the IGOs, or shifts from bureaucratic to summit diplomacy, the relative ability of states to be important to others at a given time will clearly be a function, inter alia, of their place in the global communication network. If we consider diplomatic bonds as channels in such a network, and each capital as a node, a node into which a great many channels flow will be more critical and salient to the overall network than a node at which very few such channels intersect. That, too, is diplomatic importance.

In sum, then, our measurement argument is that the number of diplomatic missions found in a given national capital at t_1 will be both a *consequence* of the relative importance attached to that nation by the others in the system at t_0, and a *cause* of its relative importance at t_2.

Modifying the Indicator

In the original report, we spelled out our measurement and coding procedures in considerable detail, carrying the reader step-by-step from data acquisition through the varieties of index construction. Here, we will recapitulate the general procedures briefly, going into detail only where modifications or clarifications seem to be in order. On the basis of our own experience with the indicator (in its several forms) plus the comments offered by others, we find three sets of problems that call for further explication. These are: (*a*) the post-1945 inflationary trend toward greater use of ambassadors and the relative decline in the numbers of ministers and envoys, (*b*) the degree to which diplomatic missions are exchanged in a purely reciprocal and symmetric fashion, and (*c*) the extent to which the indicator should reflect the importance of the states from whom the missions are sent. Let us examine these three problems in that order, and then summarize our revised coding and scaling procedures.

The Problem of Post-1945 Inflation

The original scores, it will be recalled, were computed in several ways. The first of these was the composite score, and it reflected not only the *number* of

TABLE 1. Percentage Distribution of Diplomatic Ranks Received in Sample Capitals, 1816–1965

	1816	1844	1874	1904	1930	1950	1965
Ambassador	15.0	7.8	10.3	14.8	17.5	42.5	88.2
Minister	72.4	69.8	80.2	80.2	72.6	53.4	5.5
Chargé	12.6	22.4	9.5	5.0	9.9	4.1	6.3

Note: The eleven states in the sample, all members of the central system, were Britain, France, Prussia or Germany, Sardinia or Italy, Holland, Belgium, Austria, Switzerland, Denmark, Sweden, and the United States.

accredited missions in the recipient nation, but the *ranks* of those missions. Adhering to the *règlements* of Vienna (1815) and Aix-la-Chapelle (1818), we divided the missions into three ranks: ambassador, envoy or minister (whether accredited to the head of state or the foreign ministry), and chargé d'affaires; consular officials were not counted. The host state received three points for each ambassador, two for each minister, and one for each chargé. Such a scheme makes perfect sense as long as there is considerable differentiation, and the post-Napoleonic pattern did indeed hold for about 130 years. But on the eve of World War II we already had some signs that the pattern was breaking down. By 1950, as table 1 indicates, diplomatic "inflation" had clearly begun to take its toll. If more and more governments replaced ministers with ambassadors, scores based on the rank of the missions would begin to lose their discriminatory power. Examining eleven states representing the middle and major powers that have been in the system since its inception, we find that the ambassadorial rank accounted for about 15 percent of their diplomatic missions until the 1930s. But on the heels of World War II, that figure rose sharply, and by 1965 it approached the 90 percent level.[2]

Faced with this situation, we considered and tried several alternative measures (including budget share, proportions of secretariat personnel, and elected officerships in various intergovernmental organizations) and found them quite invalid on their face; the reasons will be obvious to students of international organization and need not be reiterated here. Similarly, we quickly discarded the idea of weighting missions according to their staff size, their budget, or the value of their buildings.[3] Following those brief experi-

---

2. Writing in 1946, diplomat-historian Harold Nicholson noted this inflationary trend when he wrote that "the Vienna *Règlement* (of 1815) did in fact settle the precedence problem for more than a hundred years. It may well be that some future Congress will find itself obliged, in view of the multiplicity of Embassies which have since been created, to adopt a further *Règlement* under which Ambassadors are classified as the first, second, or third category. This, it is to be expected, will provoke a most invidious discussion."

3. For an analysis based upon size of mission in the post–World War II era, see Alger and Brams (1967).

ments, we returned to our raw data to see if it really made any difference whether we included the diplomatic rank of each mission received. With a mixture of chagrin and relief, we found that such a refinement made almost no difference in the rank orderings of the states. The smaller states, having originally received more low-ranking than high-ranking diplomats, suffer little by this change in coding rules. And the "top dogs," having so many missions of all ranks, lose little by the modification; only such states as Turkey, which often receive fewer missions than such middle powers as Holland or Denmark, but those frequently at the ambassadorial level, sustain any appreciable loss. As a matter of fact, the rank correlation between the weighted and unweighted scores for the period of 1816–1940 was .99, suggesting that we had invested considerably more time and money in data acquisition and computation than were necessary. The empirical lesson is that one's indicators can be too refined as well as too crude.

The Problem of Asymmetric Representation

A second problem came to light once our data were all in and assembled into a machine-readable, nation-by-nation matrix. We found that about 10 percent of our dyadic diplomatic bonds were asymmetrical. That is, while X may have sent an envoy to Y, Y was reported as not having reciprocated; the asymmetric pattern was coded accordingly.

The problem is, first, to identify the various ways in which such reported asymmetries can come about, and second, to settle upon a reasonable scheme for coping with them. In principle, there should be no such asymmetries, since the formal rules and established procedures make it clear that negotiations on the granting of diplomatic recognition should ultimately lead to an exchange of diplomatic missions. But there are several ways in which deviations can and do occur.

First, on some occasions, one of the parties will be embarrassed by a shortage of funds or personnel, and will accredit one minister or ambassador to two or even three governments. He or she will reside in only one of these capitals, but will have a staff in the other(s) and will visit on a regular basis. In both the original coding and here, we score on the basis of missions established and staffed, regardless of whether the head of the mission is responsible for missions in additional neighboring states. That source of reported asymmetries, then, is of no consequence here. Second, the logistics and bureaucratic politics within governments could be such as to make for lengthy delays in the dispatch of a representative. This is usually true of only one party, and we no longer assume an asymmetry, but code Y's mission as if it were already in X once X's has been established in Y. At worst, this coding convention could lead to a slight acceleration of the date at which X picks up an additional point. Given the temporal imprecision of our index, the effect of this change is inconsequential. Third, diplomatic lists are usually prepared by the protocol office in a foreign ministry and then made available to governmental and nongovernmental users of those lists, including those who collate and publish them. Somewhere along that tenuous administrative chain, occasional errors of omission (and commission) would not be surprising. Under the revised procedures, we explicitly recognize that such errors can occur, and again utilize the assumption of perfect symmetry.

A fourth source of asymmetry could, however, be quite real: a government could intentionally delay the dispatch of its representative, or recall him for an appreciable period of time. In very rare instances, the political realities might even lead to an *agreed* temporary asymmetry. But given the brevity of such possible periods of asymmetry in almost all of these cases, we are again justified in coding as if the bond were reciprocal at all times. A fifth possible source comes to mind, but it need not be seriously considered: the unilateral decision of one government to establish a mission in another's capital city without benefit of either negotiation or reciprocity. We have heard suggestions that the more aggressive states might engage in this practice as an indirect way of gaining visibility, influence, or importance, but we find no evidence of that practice now or in the past century and a half.

To summarize, then, we now treat all the asymmetries that turn up in the historical record as irrelevant, recognizing that they are either temporary aberrations or the consequence of reportorial errors. The effect of this modification is to rectify the slightly understated scores of those states which were at the disadvantaged end of the reported asymmetries. How do the scores generated by these slightly different sets of coding criteria compare? The mean *tau* value for the correlation between the presymmetrized and the revised rankings is .83; it would be even higher were it not for the first three observation periods, whose data inadequacies produce rank-order coefficients of .63, .53, and .60, respectively. Notwithstanding the similarity in the original and revised rank scores, we are persuaded that the revision, calling for an assumed reciprocity throughout, provides us with an indicator whose validity is appreciably enhanced.

The Problem of Differentiating among Senders

A third problem looks most serious, but turns out to be negligible in historical fact. One of the more credible threats to the face validity of our index is that it assigns one point to the recipient state, regardless of whether the embassy or legation has been set up by Burma or Britain, Yemen or Yugoslavia. The alert critic might then suggest that we remedy this obvious deficiency by weighting each mission—not by its rank on the ambassador-minister-chargé ladder—but by the diplomatic importance of the sending government. This is readily accomplished by a simple iterative procedure, in which the computer is programmed not merely to count the number of entries alongside each state's name in the state-by-state matrix for each observation year, but to multiply each such entry by the number of missions found in each sending state's row. Thus, for 1950, Argentina would receive 40 points for the Spanish mission and 70 for the United States' mission in Buenos Aires, rather than just one point for each. Consequently, the states that are highly valued by those with the higher diplomatic importance scores will themselves receive a higher score than if most of their partners were middle- and low-ranking.

As suggested at the opening of this section, this procedure might indeed appear to make "more sense," but empirically it makes virtually no difference. The distribution of missions around the globe is, and has been, such that the nonweighted and weighted scores never show a rank correlation lower than .90 (1840); for 1935 the *tau* value is .96, and the mean for our thirty-one sets of observations is .94. The only discernible result of weighting is to raise slightly the scores of the states that exchange fewer missions, but to try to make them "count" by concentrating on the top-ranked system members. Thus, we can repeat a conclusion that we stated in the original article: the iterative weighting scheme adds virtually nothing to the validity of our index, but raises its computation cost considerably.[4]

Scoring Procedures Summarized

Having discussed the three major problems encountered in trying to devise a valid measure of diplomatic importance, let us now briefly summarize the coding procedures. For each diplomatic bond, as manifested by the exchange of missions at the chargé level or above, the host state receives one point. (Mere recognition, which may precede the dispatch or exchange of missions by several years, is not sufficient.) These observations are taken once per half-decade, producing thirty-one sets of readings when the compilation is updated to 1970. Given the generally slow rate of change in the scores, the researcher who is working with annual data may either use the same score for each of the four following years or, better still, interpolate, with little cause for concern. As long as the missions are at the rank of chargé d'affaires or higher, the host state receives one point; as reported above, differentiating among the three standard ranks makes virtually no difference up through the 1940s, and by

---

4. One indication of how closely the original and the revised indices converge is the magnitude of the coefficient of concordance. The minimum value of Kendall's W when the asymmetric, the weighted, and the non-weighted symmetric scores are correlated is .83 (for 1824); the maximum is .99 (for 1935); and the mean is .96.

1950 almost all missions are at the embassy rank. For similar reasons, we find it neither necessary nor economical to differentiate according to the importance score of the sender.[5]

Once the total number of missions in each system member's capital has been recorded for each observation year, we have that state's raw importance score. To permit comparability across the years, in view of the rather steady increase in the size of the system, we normalize those scores by converting them into percentage form. Thus, the normalized score for each state is simply determined by ascertaining what percentage of the rest of the system's members have established diplomatic bonds with it in each half-decade. The top figure can range from 1.00 for several periods in the nineteenth century to a low of 0.82 for Italy in 1920; the lowest score is 0.00, for Rhodesia in 1970.

Finally, to reemphasize our earlier point that neither of these interval-scale figures be taken too literally, we also aggregate the states into quintile groupings for each observation year. That is, even though we compute and present cardinal and ordinal scores, the user must understand that such numbers offer only an approximate indication of each state's position; we are not suggesting, for example, that India, having two more bonds than Canada in 1965, is exactly two points (or 0.017) more "important" than the latter. Even the quintile scores must not be overinterpreted; our intention here is merely to provide one possible measure of the states' gradual ascents and declines in importance over the past century-and-a-half.

Data Sources

A generally accepted rule of thumb concerning quantification in the macrosocial sciences is that the further back in time one goes in search of reliable data, the more difficult the problem becomes. The United Nations Secretariat, for example, and that of the League before it, have systematically compiled a large body of statistical information by which their member states might be described and compared along a wide variety of dimensions. National governments, industrial firms, and business associations have likewise begun the

---

5. One other minor detail concerns the special case of the eight German and five Italian states which, prior to 1870, did not qualify for inclusion in the central system. Because the states in these two groupings had close dynastic ties, and were thus expected to exchange missions with their sister states, we excluded such missions in the original computation of each of their scores. In retrospect, that ad hoc rule seems both arbitrary and unnecessary; many groups of nations were in the same position of almost inevitably having to exchange missions. Furthermore, the effect of these more or less automatic missions is a minor one, raising the mean Italian score in 1859, for example, from 11.0 to 14.2, and that of the lesser German states from 8.63 to 13.75. Our data set, which is available at the International Relations Archive of the Inter-University Consortium for Political Research at the University of Michigan, now reflects this revision.

systematic compilation and publication of all sorts of figures in the past several decades. Unfortunately, what holds for certain economic and social data does not necessarily hold for diplomatic data, even if we leave aside matters of reliability and validity. The problem of ascertaining the presence or absence of diplomatic representation in national capitals for the sample years since 1945 has turned out, surprisingly, to be almost as acute as it was for the previous 130 years. As pages 251–52 and footnote 22 of the original article indicate, we were able to find most of the needed information for the earlier period in the *Almanach de Gotha,* and the gaps were filled without too much difficulty by recourse to fewer than a dozen additional sources. Since World War II, however, things have not been quite as simple.

Although many foreign ministries do publish one or more lists per year showing the state in which their government maintains an embassy, legation, etc., or from which they receive such missions, one can readily appreciate the effort of assembling over one hundred such lists for each sample year and then comparing and collating the information. Thus, we felt it would be more economical to find one or more single sources from which the missions sent by or received in a large number of states might be ascertained.

Unfortunately, the *Almanach de Gotha,* which had weathered everything from Napoleon to World War I, did not survive the Nazi era and ceased publishing in 1940. In 1951, the *Diplomatic Year-Book* and *World Diplomatic Directory and World Diplomatic Biography* were published which offered detailed lists of the representatives accredited to each government, but, for reasons unknown to us, publication ceased in 1952, making it necessary to find alternate sources for 1955, 1960, 1965, and 1970. (Of course, our task was eased immeasurably once we decided to abandon inter-rank discrimination and to score solely on the presence or absence of missions.)

For these four data points we used the *Europa Year-Book, The Statesman's Year-Book,* and the *Code Diplomatique.* For the earlier years, the first of these proved to be the most useful, since *The Statesman's Year-Book* did not provide relatively complete listings until the mid-sixties. In addition, we corresponded with a number of foreign ministries and were thus able to fill some of the gaps in these three publications. Finally, we were able to compare our results with those provided by East, who has collated all the separate listings from several of the postwar editions of *The Statesman's Year-Book.* Despite the diversity of our sources, however, we feel as confident about our figures for the post–World War II period as we did about those for the earlier span.

Identifying Interstate System Members

So much for coding procedures, data sources, and the rationale behind the measures. Let us turn now to the equally critical matter of identifying those national political entities that constituted the interstate system during the period under study, and whose diplomatic importance we seek to measure. Since the criteria for inclusion in the system were carefully spelled out in the original paper and updated in Russett et al. (1968), they will here be dealt with only briefly. From 1816 to 1920, a state was considered a member of the system if it had a population of at least 500,000 and recognition from our two "legitimizers," England and France. From 1920 to the present, a state qualified for membership if it had the requisite 500,000 population and recognition from any two major powers, or if it was a member of the League of Nations or the United Nations, for however brief a period.

There were, however, the inevitable exceptions. Thus, even though they lacked the diplomatic recognition or membership in international organizations, five states were nevertheless classified as members of the system: Nepal from 1920, Mongolia from 1921, Yemen from 1926, Saudi Arabia from 1927, and Rhodesia from 1966. On the other hand, five states that did meet our criteria were not classed as independent members of the system. India, despite her membership in the League, was excluded until 1947; Byelorussia and the Ukraine were excluded, since their membership in the United Nations was merely the result of a political bargain arranged at Yalta; and Manchoukuo and Slovakia clearly failed on the grounds that they exercised virtually no control over their foreign policies.[6]

The Results: Diplomatic Importance Scores

In table 2 we show the diplomatic importance scores of all members of the system for the post–World War II period. Given the exceedingly unsettled state of the world during the war and immediately after its termination, we do not show any figures for 1945; thus we move from 1940, the final reading in the original paper, to 1950 as the first meaningful set of data for the period under study here. For each of the years (1950, 1955, 1960, 1965, and 1970), we divide the states into quintiles, as before, and show the total number of diplomatic bonds for each state. In addition, we have again controlled for change in the size of the system to permit comparison across time; this normalization is achieved by dividing each state's total score by the size of the system, less one, that year. Therefore, a score of 1.00 would mean that all the others in the system had missions in that state's capital that year; the U.S. score for 1950 means that 93 percent of them had missions in Washington that year. Rounding to two places (with decimal points removed) frequently creates the appearance of tied scores, but we have retained the rank positions

---

6. Space limitations preclude the listing here of the fluctuating system membership that emerges from the application of these coding criteria; the resulting lists may be found in tables 2.1 and 2.2 of Singer and Small (1972).

TABLE 2. Diplomatic Importance Ranks and Scores by Half-Decade, 1950–70

1950

Rank	Missions Received	Normal-ized Score	Rank	Missions Received	Normal-ized Score
1 United States	70	93	39 Guatemala	25	33
2 France	70	93	40 Costa Rica	25	33
3 United Kingdom	67	89	41 Rumania	25	33
4 Belgium	62	83	42 Bolivia	24	32
5 Italy	61	81	43 Hungary	24	32
6 Holland	58	77	44 Nicaragua	22	29
7 Denmark	54	72	45 Australia	22	29
8 Argentina	51	68			
9 Norway	51	68	46 Haiti	21	28
10 Switzerland	50	67	47 Honduras	21	28
11 Sweden	50	67	48 Bulgaria	21	28
12 USSR	45	60	49 South Africa	21	28
13 Chile	44	59	50 Iraq	21	28
14 Brazil	43	57	51 Pakistan	21	28
15 Egypt/U.A.R.	42	56	52 Paraguay	20	27
			53 Syria	20	27
16 Mexico	41	55	54 Luxemburg	19	25
17 Spain	40	53	55 Afghanistan	17	23
18 Czechoslovakia	39	52	56 Saudi Arabia	16	21
19 Cuba	38	51	57 Iceland	15	20
20 Turkey	38	51	58 Israel	15	20
21 Poland	36	48	59 China	15	20
22 India	35	47	60 Ireland	14	19
23 Canada	34	45	61 Thailand	14	19
24 Venezuela	34	45			
25 Portugal	34	45	62 New Zealand	13	17
26 Dominican Rep.	33	44	63 Ethiopia	12	16
27 Ecuador	33	44	64 Jordan	12	16
28 Colombia	32	43	65 Philippines	12	16
29 Peru	32	43	66 Liberia	10	13
30 Finland	32	43	67 Albania	9	12
31 Iran	32	43	68 Burma	8	11
			69 Indonesia	8	11
32 Greece	30	40	70 Ceylon	7	9
33 Panama	29	39	71 Nepal	4	5
34 Uruguay	29	39	72 North Korea	3	4
35 Lebanon	29	39	73 South Korea	3	4
36 Yugoslavia	28	37	74 Mongolia	2	3
37 Salvador	26	35	75 Yemen Arab Rep.	1	1
38 Taiwan	26	35			

TABLE 2—Continued

1955

Rank	Missions Received	Normalized Score	Rank	Missions Received	Normalized Score
1 United Kingdom	77	92	43 Colombia	33	39
2 United States	76	90	44 Guatemala	32	38
3 Italy	76	90	45 Bolivia	32	38
4 France	74	88	46 Hungary	32	38
5 Holland	68	81	47 Bulgaria	32	38
6 Sweden	65	77	48 Panama	31	37
7 Belgium	63	75	49 Paraguay	31	37
8 West Germany	63	75	50 Rumania	31	37
9 Denmark	63	75	51 Thailand	30	36
10 Switzerland	62	74			
11 Spain	61	73	52 Honduras	29	35
12 Norway	60	71	53 Salvador	29	35
13 Argentina	58	69	54 Philippines	29	35
14 Austria	58	69	55 Iraq	28	33
15 Brazil	55	65	56 Costa Rica	27	32
16 India	55	65	57 Luxemburg	27	32
17 Mexico	54	64	58 Afghanistan	27	32
18 USSR	54	64	59 Haiti	26	31
			60 Nicaragua	26	31
19 Yugoslavia	52	62	61 Ethiopia	26	31
20 Japan	52	62	62 South Africa	26	31
21 Chile	51	61	63 China	25	30
22 Poland	51	61	64 Taiwan	25	30
23 Canada	50	60	65 Burma	24	29
24 Egypt/U.A.R.	50	60	66 Iceland	23	27
25 Turkey	49	58	67 Saudi Arabia	22	26
26 Pakistan	49	58	68 Ireland	21	25
27 Czechoslovakia	48	57	69 Jordan	21	25
28 Venezuela	44	52	70 Ceylon	21	25
29 Iran	44	52			
30 Portugal	43	51	71 Libya	19	23
31 Finland	43	51	72 New Zealand	19	23
32 Cuba	41	49	73 Liberia	12	14
33 Indonesia	41	49	74 Yemen Arab Rep.	12	14
34 Greece	40	48	75 Albania	11	13
			76 East Germany	10	12
35 Peru	38	45	77 South Vietnam	9	11
36 Lebanon	38	45	78 Cambodia	8	10
37 Ecuador	36	43	79 Mongolia	7	8
38 Uruguay	36	43	80 North Korea	7	8
39 Dominican Rep.	35	42	81 Nepal	7	8
40 Syria	35	42	82 Laos	6	7
41 Israel	35	42	83 North Vietnam	5	6
42 Australia	35	42	84 South Korea	3	4

(continued)

TABLE 2—*Continued*

1960

Rank		Missions Received	Normal-ized Score	Rank		Missions Received	Normal-ized Score
1	Italy	82	92	46	Equador	37	42
2	United States	80	90	47	Afghanistan	36	40
3	United Kingdom	80	90	48	Salvador	35	39
4	Holland	77	87	49	Iraq	35	39
5	France	75	84	50	Guatemala	34	38
6	Sweden	73	82	51	Haiti	33	37
7	Austria	71	80	52	Costa Rica	33	37
8	Denmark	71	80	53	Bolivia	33	37
9	West Germany	69	78	54	Burma	33	37
10	Belgium	67	75	55	Philippines	33	37
11	Japan	65	73	56	Australia	33	37
12	Yugoslavia	63	71				
13	Switzerland	62	70	57	Panama	32	36
14	Spain	62	70	58	Paraguay	32	36
15	Norway	62	70	59	Sudan	32	36
16	India	61	69	60	Ethiopia	31	35
17	Argentina	60	67	61	Tunisia	31	35
18	Czechoslovakia	58	65	62	Honduras	30	34
19	Egypt/U.A.R.	58	65	63	Bulgaria	29	33
				64	Jordan	29	33
20	Brazil	56	63	65	Nicaragua	28	31
21	Poland	55	62	66	Luxemburg	27	30
22	USSR	55	62	67	Saudi Arabia	27	30
23	Finland	55	62	68	China	27	30
24	Cuba	54	61	69	Iceland	26	29
25	Turkey	54	61	70	Morocco	26	29
26	Israel	53	60	71	Cambodia	24	27
27	Mexico	52	58	72	Ghana	23	26
28	Portugal	52	58				
29	Canada	51	57	73	New Zealand	22	25
30	Greece	50	56	74	Ireland	20	22
31	Pakistan	50	56	75	South Africa	20	22
32	Chile	49	55	76	Nepal	20	22
33	Venezuela	47	53	77	Libya	19	21
34	Iran	47	53	78	Malaysia	18	20
35	Indonesia	47	53	79	Albania	17	19
36	Lebanon	45	51	80	Liberia	16	18
37	Thailand	45	51	81	Laos	15	17
				82	South Vietnam	15	17
38	Uruguay	43	48	83	South Korea	14	16
39	Rumania	43	48	84	East Germany	12	13
40	Taiwan	42	47	85	Mongolia	10	11
41	Hungary	40	45	86	Yemen Arab Rep.	8	9
42	Colombia	39	44	87	North Korea	8	9
43	Peru	39	44	88	North Vietnam	8	9
44	Ceylon	39	44	89	Guinea	5	6
45	Dominican Rep.	38	43				

TABLE 2—Continued

1965

Rank		Missions Received	Normal- ized Score	Rank		Missions Received	Normal- ized Score
1	United States	112	93	45	Bulgaria	51	42
2	United Kingdom	112	93	46	Thailand	51	42
3	France	111	92	47	Venezuela	49	40
4	Holland	109	90	48	Peru	49	40
5	West Germany	102	84	49	Uruguay	49	40
6	Sweden	102	84	50	Tunisia	49	40
7	Italy	101	83	51	Syria	49	40
8	Belgium	95	79	52	Ceylon	49	40
9	Japan	95	79				
10	India	89	74	53	Jordan	46	38
11	Canada	87	72	54	Saudi Arabia	46	38
12	Switzerland	87	72	55	China	46	38
13	Israel	85	70	56	Ethiopia	45	37
14	Austria	84	69	57	Afghanistan	45	37
15	USSR	83	69	58	Guinea	44	36
16	Egypt/U.A.R.	83	69	59	Colombia	42	35
17	Denmark	82	68	60	Mali	42	35
18	Norway	79	65	61	Australia	42	35
19	Yugoslavia	76	63	62	Philippines	40	33
20	Lebanon	75	62	63	Senegal	39	32
21	Pakistan	75	62	64	Guatemala	38	31
22	Poland	74	61	65	South Vietnam	38	31
23	Spain	71	59	66	Ecuador	37	31
24	Czechoslovakia	70	58	67	Luxemburg	37	31
25	Brazil	69	57	68	Taiwan	37	31
				69	Haiti	36	30
26	Finland	67	55	70	Dominican Rep.	36	30
27	Argentina	66	55	71	Salvador	36	30
28	Sudan	66	55	72	Panama	36	30
29	Turkey	65	54	73	Libya	36	30
30	Greece	64	53	74	Burma	36	30
31	Ghana	62	51	75	Laos	36	30
32	Indonesia	62	51				
33	Iraq	61	50	76	Bolivia	35	29
34	Hungary	59	49	77	Zaire	35	29
35	South Korea	59	49	78	Nicaragua	34	28
36	Mexico	57	47	79	Costa Rica	34	28
37	Portugal	57	47	80	Paraguay	33	27
38	Rumania	57	47	81	Liberia	33	27
39	Chile	55	45	82	Cameroon	33	27
40	Nigeria	55	45	83	Iceland	32	26
41	Morocco	55	45	84	Malaysia	32	26
42	Cuba	54	45	85	Honduras	31	26
43	Algeria	53	44	86	Dahomey	31	26
44	Iran	52	43	87	Cambodia	31	26

(*continued*)

TABLE 2—Continued

1965

Rank	Missions Received	Normalized Score	Rank	Missions Received	Normalized Score
88 Ireland	30	25	105 Somalia	19	16
89 Ivory Coast	28	23	106 Uganda	18	15
90 New Zealand	28	23	107 Mauritania	17	14
91 Cyprus	27	22	108 Malagasy	17	14
92 Nepal	26	21	109 East Germany	16	13
93 Togo	24	20	110 Chad	16	13
94 Tanzania	24	20	111 Kuwait	16	13
95 Niger	23	19	112 North Vietnam	16	13
96 Upper Volta	23	19	113 Zambia	13	11
97 Sierra Leone	23	19	114 North Korea	13	11
98 Congo	23	19	115 Central African R.	12	10
99 South Africa	23	19	116 Rwanda	12	10
100 Yemen Arab Rep.	22	18	117 Burundi	10	8
			118 Jamaica	9	7
101 Albania	21	17	119 Trinidad-Tobago	9	7
102 Gabon	21	17	120 Malawi	9	7
103 Kenya	21	17	121 Malta	2	2
104 Mongolia	21	17			

1970

Rank	Missions Received	Normalized Score	Rank	Missions Received	Normalized Score
1 United Kingdom	122	92	23 Israel	85	64
2 Holland	119	89	24 Poland	83	62
3 France	119	89	25 Czechoslovakia	80	60
4 Belgium	117	88	26 Finland	80	60
5 Switzerland	117	88	27 Bulgaria	78	59
6 United States	115	86			
7 Sweden	114	86	28 Brazil	75	56
8 Canada	113	85	29 Turkey	72	54
9 Italy	110	83	30 South Korea	71	53
10 West Germany	106	80	31 Greece	68	51
11 Japan	103	77	32 Sudan	68	51
12 India	103	77	33 Algeria	67	50
13 Austria	98	74	34 Lebanon	67	50
14 Denmark	97	73	35 Ethiopia	66	50
15 Pakistan	96	72	36 Hungary	64	48
16 Yugoslavia	95	71	37 Morocco	63	47
17 USSR	92	69	38 Mexico	62	47
18 Norway	92	69	39 Ghana	62	47
19 Rumania	91	68	40 Nigeria	60	45
20 Spain	88	66	41 Indonesia	60	45
21 Egypt/U.A.R.	86	65	42 Chile	59	44
22 Argentina	85	64	43 Tunisia	59	44

TABLE 2—*Continued*

1970

Rank	Missions Received	Normal- ized Score	Rank	Missions Received	Normal- ized Score
44 Australia	58	44	88 Laos	37	28
45 Venezuela	55	41	89 Iceland	36	27
46 Mali	55	41	90 Mongolia	36	27
47 Iran	54	41	91 Cambodia	36	27
48 Thailand	53	40	92 Mauritania	35	26
49 Guinea	52	39	93 Singapore	35	26
50 Syria	52	39	94 New Zealand	35	26
51 Ceylon	52	39	95 Haiti	34	26
52 Peru	50	38	96 Honduras	34	26
53 Uruguay	50	38	97 Malta	34	26
54 Senegal	50	38	98 Zambia	34	26
55 Kenya	50	38	99 Nepal	34	26
			100 South Vietnam	34	26
56 Portugal	49	37	101 Somalia	33	25
57 Afghanistan	49	37	102 Congo	31	23
58 Taiwan	49	37	103 North Korea	31	23
59 Jordan	48	36	104 Upper Volta	30	23
60 Cuba	47	35	105 Niger	29	22
61 Tanzania	47	35	106 Sierra Leone	28	21
62 Iraq	47	35	107 Togo	28	21
63 China	47	35	108 Chad	28	21
64 Malaysia	47	35			
65 Zaire	46	35	109 Malagasy	26	20
66 Colombia	45	34	110 Albania	25	19
67 Saudi Arabia	45	34	111 Central African R.	25	19
68 Ivory Coast	43	32	112 North Vietnam	25	19
69 Kuwait	43	32	113 Ireland	24	18
70 Philippines	43	32	114 South Africa	24	18
71 Luxemburg	42	32	115 Gabon	23	17
72 Cameroun	42	32	116 Burundi	23	17
73 Libya	42	32	117 Yemen Arab Rep.	23	17
74 Panama	41	31	118 Malawi	22	17
75 Dominican Rep.	40	30	119 Jamaica	21	16
76 Salvador	40	30	120 Trinidad-Tobago	20	15
77 Ecuador	40	30	121 Rwanda	18	14
78 Burma	40	30	122 Botswana	17	13
79 Guatemala	39	29	123 East Germany	16	12
80 Paraguay	39	29	124 Barbados	15	11
81 Liberia	39	29	125 Guyana	14	11
82 Uganda	39	29	126 Lesotho	13	10
			127 Mauritius	13	10
			128 Gambia	12	9
83 Costa Rica	38	29	129 Yemen People's R.	12	9
84 Cyprus	38	29	130 Equatorial Guinea	11	8
85 Dahomey	38	29	131 Swaziland	5	4
86 Nicaragua	37	28	132 Maldive Islands	3	2
87 Bolivia	37	28	133 Rhodesia	0	0

reflected by the three-place figures. These scores are based on the state of affairs at the beginning of the half-decade; thus the seventeen new states that entered the system during 1960 and the three states that entered the system during 1965 are not included in our tabulation or used in computing normalized scores until the following observation years.

The data in table 2, plus those found in the earlier paper, permit one to ascertain which states were in which approximate position vis-à-vis others in any given half-decade since the Congress of Vienna. For some theoretical purposes, such cross-sectional pictures of the system's hierarchy can be quite useful; but for others, it would be more valuable to have a longitudinal picture, and were space available, such a table would be presented.

Conclusion

The general impression, as one scrutinizes the scores and rankings in table 2, is that we have come fairly close to "tapping" the concept of diplomatic importance. By and large, the major powers always cluster at the top; the "pariah" states and their satellites score somewhat lower than their better-established opposite numbers; the nonaligned states outrank their NATO and Warsaw Pact counterparts; the smaller but centrally placed states show up higher than might be expected; and the more peripheral actors systematically fall into the lower quintiles. Further, the longitudinal picture is quite satisfactory: the peripheral states move up on the diplomatic importance scores as they industrialize and/or seek an increasingly active role in the system; those which suffer defeat (or great damage) in war show the expected decline and vice versa; and the newly independent states begin near the bottom of the listing but move up as their potential is developed and recognized.

On the other hand, the index does produce some readings that might seem out of place, and they also merit attention. One apparent anomaly is the tendency of certain smaller states of Western Europe to hover near or at the top of the rankings during most of the post–World War II period, above the USSR, China, India, or Japan. Partly, this is due to the reluctance of governments to sever long-established ties, and partly to the fact that the interstate system is still centered in Europe. In addition, Belgium, Holland, and Switzerland are major trading states as well as hosts to a variety of international organizations, while Italy also provides the seat of the Vatican, making it an important focal point for the Catholic countries of the world. The position of Soviet Russia, then, below these smaller Western states, should come as no surprise.

Further, as we have already emphasized, we are not trying to measure size, military capability, or industrial potential, even though such factors will affect the scores. Moreover, as a revolutionary (and therefore pariah) state in a conservative and capitalist-dominated system, the Soviet Union's score will inevitably reflect the fear and hostility of other members of the system, plus the systematic efforts of the major Western powers to keep her in isolation. The same may be said, but more forcefully, of the People's Republic of China. Not only are her capabilities considerably fewer than the Western press suggests, and her energies largely directed toward internal development, but the United States has, until very recently, systematically discriminated against and tried to isolate this latest challenger to the old diplomatic order.

Having noted these possible discrepancies between the computed scores and what might have been "expected," we remind the reader that, as a first systematic attempt, any index such as this will certainly have some deficiencies. More important, there will be disagreement as to whether deviations from the expected are indeed discrepancies. That disagreement will, in turn, depend upon both the folklore out of which our expectations arise and the clarity and face validity of the reasoning behind the measuring procedures. Though there is little we can do about the former, we hope that our performance on the latter is adequate. In any event, we regard the argument made here to be considerably more rigorous and explicit than that found in the original paper.

Finally, some may feel that we have taken on an impossible task: trying to reflect, in a single indicator, a complex state of affairs which emerges from a variety of background factors. It is clear that we have not produced a simple proxy indicator, with a one-to-one association between the observed phenomenon and some single unobserved condition in the empirical world. But the very diversity of the factors that affect the measure and the very complexity of the decision processes that produce the outcome may well be viewed as an asset. When we can, by parsimoniously observing a single set of traces, tap the resultant of a very complex set of interactions, we have progressed on the measurement front. And what holds for the GNP of a nation, the IQ of a schoolboy, the earned-run average of a baseball pitcher, or the force of a moving object would seem to hold for the diplomatic importance of a state.

We realize, however, that such single-index measures of complex phenomena are never fully satisfactory in reliability and validity, and that they usually undergo improvement as they are put into use and their inadequacies become evident. As the science of world politics develops, we trust that the measure at hand will not only prove useful to many researchers, but will experience whatever improvements and refinements turn out to be necessary.

Reconstructing the Correlates of War Data Set on Material Capabilities of States, 1816–1985

J. David Singer

Introduction

This essay examines some of the more crucial issues in the construction of an indicator of material capabilities, discusses the implications of the various options, and then indicates the decisions taken in the Correlates of War Project. As will be evident, few of these decisions are optimal, the trade-offs are difficult, and we thus remain open to further advice—but not for long, given the Data Development for International Research (DDIR) research schedule. Equally evident is the fact that the enterprise did not need to start from scratch. Competent and creative historians, social scientists, physical scientists, military analysts, and operations researchers have all examined the idea of power base, national strength, and capabilities, and, as our bibliography will make clear, about two dozen have tried to develop—and generate the data for—indicators of these national attributes.

We have profited greatly from these prior efforts, be they speculative, empirical, or both, and while some of this literature has been of positive assistance, most of its value was to illuminate the dead ends and alert us to those myriad strategies that we would do well to avoid.

General Considerations

Before turning to the specific dimensions in any detail, certain general considerations might be noted. First and foremost is that of comparability, across a long time-period (1816 to the present), a staggering variety of territorial states, peoples, cultures, and institutions, at radically different points in their economic, social, and political development at a given moment. Thus an

---

Reprinted from *International Interactions* 14 (1988): 115–32. Reprinted with permission from Gordon and Breach Science Publishers S.A.

indicator that might validly compare a group of European states in 1960 could easily be useless in comparing one of them to a North African state in the same year, no less than in 1930 or 1870.

A second consideration is that of available estimates. While most of the indicators used in the COW Project are generated by the application of operational criteria and coding rules to the rather soft and ambiguous "traces" of history (such as the onset of war or outcome of a militarized dispute) and about whose validity and reliability we can be quite confident, here we are reliant upon apparently precise numerical traces recorded by others at earlier times, for different reasons, and in accord with coding and scaling criteria that can range from unknown to inconsistent. Despite these sources of possible error, we have no choice but to identify, select, and combine numerical estimates of evidence ranging from army size to energy consumption, hoping that we have recognized and taken account of differing criteria. One must do the best one can with the figures handed down. That is, we have been unable to develop a set of procedures for reconstructing the GDP or GNP of most societies for any adequate length of time, and, even were such reconstructed figures available, their validity as an indicator of national strength would be most dubious. To take the more obvious problems, one might ask rhetorically how much a state's material capabilities are either enhanced by or reflected in the wages paid to paper shufflers in the Kremlin or advertising moguls on Madison Avenue.

This leads, then, to a brief consideration of some other dimensions and indicators of capability, and a summary of which were rejected, which accepted, and why. Worth noting here is the intention to tap the scholarly consensus as to the major components of general capabilities, and not to develop the most robust predictor of success in diplomacy, crisis, or war. The extent to which these capabilities do account for such success, and thus covary with "power" is, of course, an empirical question, and there is mounting evidence that the two differ in frequent and important ways.

Basic Dimensions

Why only demographic, industrial, and military indicators of national capabilities? Why not geography of location, or terrain, or natural resources, all of which clearly affect material capabilities? For example, location in several senses could be important: insular and peninsular states tend to be more able to trade with a larger fraction of the others, to be somewhat more defensible against invasion, to emphasize sea power over land power and thus appear less threatening as a potential invader, and to have fewer close neighbors with whom to quarrel. Landlocked states typically are more restricted in their choice of trading partners, can be more vulnerable to invasion, occupation, or annexation (mitigated of course by less passable terrain), have more immediate neighbors, and "require" greater land forces that could appear threatening. All these facets could enhance or detract from a state's capabilities, but they seem too idiosyncratic, state-specific, and dyad-specific to permit valid comparisons across space or across time with the attendant changes in technology and culture.

As to such natural resources as arable land, climate, and resource availability, we have not only the low probabilities of valid comparison, but by the same token these factors are reflected to a considerable extent in the indicators that *are* used.

Then, of course, there is the whole question of effective political institutions, citizen competence, regime legitimacy, and the professional adequacy of the national security elites. While these are far from negligible, they are, as suggested earlier, contributory to national power and the efficiency with which the basic material capabilities are utilized, but they are not a component of such capabilities.

A final and major point regarding alternative indicators of our three major dimensions is their feasibility. That is, most researchers would grant that the demographic, industrial, and military dimensions are three of the most central components of material strength, but would nevertheless quarrel either with (1) the specific subcomponents or (2) the decision to stay with them throughout the 170 years under study. Let us deal with these issues in their specific context.

Each dimension rests on two subdimensions, as follows: For the demographic dimension, we use the total population of the society that the state controls (with greater or lesser success) plus the number of people living in "urban agglomerations" as defined by the regime at that time. Were we interested in a measure of "development"—and while this is often strongly correlated with capabilities—we would find "percent urban" more useful, but our object here is to estimate the number of people who are most readily mobilized to produce the "sinews of war" and other elements of physical prowess.

While the decisions on the demographic components were relatively clear-cut (and space limitations preclude fuller treatment of some of the conceptual and observation problems concerning even this, the simplest of our three dimensions), those for the other two dimensions were not. For the industrial capabilities, we now use: (1) industrial energy consumption, converted into coal-ton equivalents from such diverse sources as coke, coal, hydroelectric, and nuclear power; and (2) iron and steel production, with iron excluded after 1890. Why not use indicators more appropriate to the historical and technological characteristics of each period, such as petrochemicals in the post-1920 period, aviation production or use from 1946 through perhaps

1970, and electronics manufacture since then? The answer is obvious, and yet not fully persuasive. First, different groups of states go through these development stages at different times, and shifting indicators would preclude cross-national comparisons for a given year or decade. Second, every shift for a single state would put an abrupt halt to any effort to measure industrial growth rates and compare, for example, a pair of nations in an enduring rivalry. Let me say that, while we are not fully content with these decisions, none of a more compelling sort has turned up, despite considerable effort on our part and a steady flow of constructive suggestions from others.

Of the alternatives, one with which we are now experimenting is the equivalent of an "industrial production index," several of which are found in the literature on economic cycles. The virtue of such an indicator is its composite, multidimensional nature, reflecting those components making up the industrial "basket" of certain groups of states in certain periods. But the comparability problem appears to remain. A related opinion is that of providing briefer series alongside our disaggregated sets, for the appropriate periods, leaving individual users free to aggregate to the extent they see fit. Suggestions are particularly welcome on these issues.

Turning to the military dimension, the issues are equally vexing. Our decision was to go with: (1) military personnel on active duty, thus excluding reserves as well as many but not all paramilitary forces; and (2) military expenditures over the previous five years. The objections to both are reasonable and numerous. For example, reserves that are well-trained and quickly mobilizable have been and continue to be crucial on occasion. The Prussians of 1870 and the Israelis of today are prime—but nevertheless rare—illustrations. Another objection is that military expenditures reflect, at best, the input of resources into a process that varies markedly in efficiency and honesty across states and times. It is thus unlikely systematically to reflect output in terms of trained and organized personnel equipped with effective, reliable, and appropriate hardware. The objections and alternatives are myriad, and will be discussed in full in the handbook that emerges from this enterprise.

Validation vis-à-vis Other Indicators

In the methodological literature of the social sciences one finds an overwhelming imbalance between the treatment of data *analysis* on the one hand and the *generation* of data on the other. But within the limited body of work on the latter, there is appreciable concern with the validation of the indicators that emerge from the data-generation process. One of the more frequently noted—and perhaps most compelling—of these procedures is comparison with other indicators that allegedly tap the same phenomenon.

We have relied heavily on this criterion in two different ways. First, we have attended to the extent to which each of our six individual indicators and three pairs of indicators covaries with the others. While it is important to ascertain that this combination serves to tap the different components of material capabilities, we would nevertheless expect a modest convergence among them. The results seem intuitively reasonable, confirming that while some states score high in large part on the basis of large populations, large armed forces, and perhaps high iron and steel production, others score high on the basis of urban population, energy consumption, and military expenditures. In this connection, we have experimented with a number of combinatory procedures such as Smallest Space Analysis (SSA-II) to see what changes occur in the rankings when we discount aggregated scores that rest too heavily on only one or two of the six components. This reflects the assumption that a "strong" state must have a solid balance of all the capability components, and indeed it does lead to some modest and reasonable rearrangements in rank-orders for some groups of states in some historical periods.

Second, and just as important, is the covariation between each of our six, three, and other combinations and aggregations on the one hand and, on the other, alternative indicators. As the data will show, the convergence is relatively strong, but not disconcertingly so.

Capabilities, Importance, and Major Power Status

Another perspective on the validation problem examines the covariation between one's indicators of capabilities and certain theoretically similar concepts. Here, of course, we do not look for particularly high correlations, but rather examine both the convergences and the divergences and try to be reasonably confident that both can be explained.

In the Correlates of War Project, we looked at two such hierarchical patterns: (1) attributed diplomatic importance, and (2) major power status. One indicator of attributed diplomatic importance is based on the number (and sometimes the rank) of diplomatic missions in each state's capital. Naturally enough, the industrial or military strength of a state alone will not be sufficient to attract missions from a large fraction of the system's members. For example, such revolutionary regimes as those in France in the 1850s, Russia in the 1920s and 1930s, and China in the 1950s and 1960s will typically be treated as pariahs and were in fact low in the number of diplomatic missions sent and received. (The figures of missions sent and received are almost always identical, following the well-established—if now deteriorating—principle of reciprocity.) Similarly, some weaker states in some periods have scores of importance considerably higher than would be expected on the basis of physical strength. The classic example is Spain from the mid-nineteenth century to the post–World

War I period, thanks to its strong cultural bonds with the twenty-odd Latin American states. Our data show a good many other apparent anomalies, but in each case we find ample empirical grounds for not being surprised.

As to major power status, we encounter a more complex issue, given the dominance of what might be called the "primitive realist" school. Some scholars even go so far as to use "big" and "major" interchangeably, or to equate the latter with "hegemonic," whatever that ambiguous concept implies in its more recent incarnation.

In the COW context, we use "major" in the same sense as most diplomatic historians, and, from 1816 through the early 1960s, there is an impressive convergence, regardless of the nationality or theoretic predilections of the scholar. The criteria are largely nonquantitative, *unlike* the diplomatic importance indicator, but *like* the latter, they reflect the aggregated or collective judgment of the system membership. That is, a major power in any period is a state that is regarded by others—especially the other and typically more well-established majors—one of that small "oligarchy," to use Schwarzenberger's expression, that dominates not only in the region of each member, but globally as well. These states have taken on global "interests" and do a fair job of defending them. Implicit in this, of course, is the frequent possibility of a division of interests within the oligarchy, and that state of affairs is typically a precursor to wars of substantial severity and magnitude.

A less-than-perfect rank-order correlation exists between our material capabilities indicators and inclusion in the major power category. For example, by the end of its Civil War, the United States was among the top two or three in the total system on such capabilities, but not until the United States had: established itself as a key actor in Asia, the Pacific, and the Caribbean; become increasingly involved in the affairs of the European states; defeated the Spanish in two oceans; and played a key role in negotiating the end of the Russo-Japanese War, was it treated as a full-fledged major power by other states, and so classified by the historical profession.

At the other end of the spectrum is the case of Austria-Hungary. Its empire was in disarray and material capabilities in serious decline by the turn of the century, yet historians and statesmen treated it as a major power until the defeat of the Central Powers in World War I. Two other examples are contemporary Germany and Japan. The latter has been, for better than two decades, a central and dominant figure in industrial production, technological innovation, and the international trade and monetary sector. Yet Japan is still not included when the other major powers conduct a wide variety of activities—not only vis-à-vis the Middle East, Europe, Central America, and Africa, but even in the Pacific and in South and Southeast Asia. This is, of course, partially a policy choice on the part of Japan's elites, and partially a function of its still negligible military capabilities in a global system in transition. In this changing global system the traditional criteria of major power status are still taken seriously by the elites of the current major powers: the United States, Soviet Union, Great Britain, France, and China (all of whom, it might be noted, are holders of permanent seats in the United Nations Security Council as well as equipped with the most modern version of the crown jewels, a nuclear arsenal). Much of what has been said of Japan applies to West Germany, but more dramatically, given the impressive conventional weapon capabilities of the Federal Republic and (in my view) its de facto control over nuclear weapons as well.

Conclusions

Most observers of world politics today are persuaded that many relevant characteristics of the system are in the process of rapid and radical change. Foremost among these changes are the bases of state power, the decreasing utility of military forces, the end of unconditional viability (to use Boulding's phrase) for the major powers, changing criteria of political legitimacy, and the rising importance of economic instruments of interstate influence. Thus, even as we recall the regularity with which each generation of scholars and practitioners has made the same claim over the centuries, there is a good chance that today's changes are indeed more dramatic than those of the past 170 years. This is largely an empirical question, and we shall continue to address it both as a part of our DDIR obligation and in the larger context of a research enterprise that is as committed to observing pattern and continuity as it is to observing and explaining system breaks and parameter changes as they impinge on the probability that the human race will still exist as we know it in the new century that is fast approaching.

**Appendix. National Capability Data Set:
A Partial and Selected Bibliography**

The National Capability Dataset was constructed from a variety of nationally and internationally based sources, of which a small fraction is listed here. That is, in addition to those found here, we have consulted well over a thousand books, monographs, articles, reports, and archival documents to ascertain the best estimates for nearly 200 different members of the international system, over the period of nearly two centuries, covering six different indicators, and a number of subindicators from which the former could be aggregated. Thus we provide here, for the use of our DDIR colleagues and others, a very limited and selected bibliography. As we continue to upgrade, update, extend, correct, and evaluate this particular COW data set, the full bibliography (already over sixty pages) will become available.

The bibliography is divided according to subject:

A. General (sources providing data on more than one set of indicators)
B. Demographic
C. Military: currency conversion
D. Military: personnel, expenditures
E. Industrial.

Each division is separated into "most useful" and "less useful" sections. This distinction is based on indispensability (accuracy, coverage, comparability, etc.) rather than quantity of data contained in any particular source. As a result, many of the works included in the "most useful" sections may contain only a few small bits of information, but such that we could not find them elsewhere. By the same token, some sources in the "less useful" sections are almanacs and compendia that we rarely used because most of their information was more reliably available elsewhere.

A.1. General: Most Useful

Almanac de Gotha. 1764–1942. *Almanac de Gotha: Annuaire Généalogique, Diplomatique et Statistique.* Gotha: Justus Perthes.

France, Institut National de la Statistique et des Études Économiques. 1878–. *Statistique Générale: Annuaire Statistique de la France.* Paris: Imprimerie Nationale.

France, Ministére du Commerce. 1835–. *Documents Statistiques sur la France.* Paris: Imprimerie Royale.

Germany, Statistisches Reichsamt. 1880–. *Statistisches Jahrbuch für das Deutsche Reich.* Berlin: R. Hobbing.

Great Britain, Board of Trade, Statistical Department. 1874–1914. *Statistical Abstract for the Principal and Other Foreign Countries.* . . . London: H. M. Stationary Office.

League of Nations, Secretariat. 1927–42. *Annuaire Statistique de la Société des Nations.* Geneva: League of Nations.

Martin, Frederick. 1854–. *The Statesman's Year-book: Statistical, Genealogical, and Historical Annual of the States and Sovereigns of the Civilized World.* London: Macmillan.

Mitchell, Brian R. 1962. *Abstract of British Historical Statistics.* Cambridge: Cambridge University Press.

Mulhall, Michael G. 1881. *Balance Sheet of the World for Ten Years, 1870–1880.* London: E. Stanford.

———. 1887. *Fifty Years of National Progress, 1837–1887.* London: G. Routledge.

———. 1899. *The Dictionary of Statistics.* 4th rev. ed. London: G. Routledge.

Sweden, Statistiska Centralbyrån (1955, 1959, 1960) *Historisk Statistik für Sverige.* 3 vols. Stockholm: Statens Reproduktionsanstalt.

United Nations, Department of International Economic and Social Affairs, Statistical Office. 1948–. *Statistical Yearbook.* New York: United Nations.

United States, Bureau of the Census. 1949. *Historical Statistics of the United States 1789–1945: A Supplement to the Statistical Abstract of the United States.* Washington: U.S. Government Printing Office.

Webb, Augustus D. 1911. *New Dictionary of Statistics: A Complement to the Fourth Edition of Mulhall's "Dictionary of Statistics."* New York: E. P. Dutton.

Woytinsky, Wladimer S. 1925–28. *Die Welt in Zahlen.* 7 vols. Berlin: Rudolf Mosse Buchverlag.
———. 1955. *World Commerce and Government: Trends and Outlook.* New York: Twentieth Century Fund.
———, and Emma S. Woytinsky. 1953. *World Population and Production: Trends and Outlook.* New York: Twentieth Century Fund.

A.2. General: Less Useful

Canada, Department of Trade and Commerce, Bureau of Statistics. 1930. *The Canada Yearbook.* Ottawa: Canadian Government Publishing Centre.
Financial Reform Association. 1965. *The Financial Reform Almanack.* Liverpool: Financial Reform Association.
France, Bureau de la Statistique Général. 1835–73. *Statistique de la France: Résultants Statistiques du Dénombrement.* Paris: Imprimerie Royale.
Greece, National Statistical Service 1964–. *Statistical Yearbook of Greece.* Athens: National Printing Office.
Keesing's Contemporary Archives: Weekly Diary of World Events. 1931–. London: Keesing's Ltd.
Moreau de Jonnés, Alexandre César. 1837–38. *Statistique de la Grande-Bretagne et de l'Irlande.* Paris: Imprimerie de Bourgogne et Martinet.
Mulhall, Michael G. 1896. *Industries and Wealth of Nations.* London: Longmans, Green & Co.
New York Tribune. 1838–1914. *Tribune Almanac and Political Registrar.* New York: New York Tribune.
New York World-Telegram. 1868–. *World Almanac and Book of Facts.* New York: New York World-Telegram.
Prussia, Königliches Statistisches Landesamt. 1845. *Die statistischen Tabellen des Preussischen Staats nach der amtlichen Aufnahme des Jahres 1843.* Berlin: Nicolai'schen Buchhandlung.
———. 1869. *Jahrbuch für die Amtliche Statistik des Preussischen Staats.* Berlin: Königliches Statistiches Landesamt.
Union of South Africa, Office of Census and Statistics. 1918–. *Official Yearbook of the Union of South Africa.* Pretoria: The Government Printing and Stationery Office.
Weber, Friedrich Benedict. 1830. *Blicke in die Zeit, in Hinsicht auf National-Industrie und Staatswirtschaft mit besonderer Berücksichtigung Deutschlands und vornehmlich des Preussischen Staats.* Berlin: Nicolai'schen Buchhandlung.
Whitaker, Joseph. 1969–. *An Almanack for the Year of Our Lord . . . .* International ed. esp. 1913. London: Whitaker's Almanack.

B.1. Demographic: Most Useful

Durand, John D. 1960. "The population statistics of China, A.D. 2–1953." *Population Studies* 13(3): 209–56.
Flora, Peter, et al. 1983. *State, Economy, and Society in Western Europe, 1815–1975: A Data Handbook in Two Volumes,* Frankfurt am Main: Campus Verlag.

Issawi, Charles, ed. 1966. *An Economic History of the Middle East, 1800–1914: A Book of Readings*. Chicago: The University of Chicago Press.

———. 1971. *The Economic History of Iran, 1800–1914*. Chicago: The University of Chicago Press.

———. 1980. *The Economic History of Turkey, 1800–1914*. Chicago: The University of Chicago Press.

Italy, Direzione Generale della Statistica. 1878–. *Annuario Statistico Italiano*. Rome.

Leacy, F. H. 1983. *Historical Statistics of Canada*. 2d ed. Ottawa: Canadian Government Publishing Centre.

Mitchell, Brian R. 1962. *Abstracts of British Historical Statistics*. Cambridge: Cambridge University Press.

———. 1975. *International Historical Statistics: Euorpean Historical Statistics, 1750–1970*. New York: Columbia University Press.

———. 1982. *International Historical Statistics: Africa and Asia*. New York: New York University Press.

———. 1983. *International Historical Statistics: The Americas and Australia*. New York: New York University Press.

United Nations, Department of International Economic and Social Affairs, Statistical Office. 1948–. *Demographic Yearbook*. New York: United Nations.

United States, Bureau of the Census. 1976. *The Statistical History of the United States: From Colonial Times to the Present*. New York: Basic Books.

Weber, Adna Ferrin. [1899] 1963. *The Growth of Cities in the Nineteenth Century: A Study in Statistics*. Reprint. Ithaca, N.Y.: Cornell University Press.

Wilkie, James. 1980. *Statistical Abstract of Latin America*. Vol. 20 plus earlier volumes. Los Angeles: University of California at Los Angeles, Latin American Center Publications.

B.2. Demographic: Less Useful

Banks, Arthur S. 1971. *Cross-Polity Time-Series Data*. Cambridge, Mass.: The MIT Press.

Belgium, Ministère de l'Intérieur. 1841–70. *Statistique Générale*. Bruxelles: Ministère de l'intérieur.

———. 1870–1920. *Annuaire Statistique de la Belgique et de Congo Belge*. Bruxelles: Ministère de l'Intérieur.

Beyer, R. E. *Urbanization in Nineteenth Century Latin America: Statistics and Sources*.

Bogue, Donald J. 1985. *The Population of the United States: Historical Trends and Future Projections*. New York: Free Press.

Chandler, Tertius, and Gerald Fox. 1974. *Three Thousand Years of Urban Growth*. New York: Academic Press.

Denmark, Statistiske Departement. 1886–1972. *Statistisk Aarbog*. Copenhagen: Statens Statistiske Bureau.

Genealogisch-Historisch-Statistischer Almanach für das Jahr. . . . 1824–48. Weimar: Verlag des Landes-industrie-comptoirs.

Germany, Statistisches Reichsamt. 1892. *Stand und Bewegung der Bevölkerung des Deutschen Reichs und fremder Staaten in den Jahren 1841 bis 1886*. Berlin: Puttkammer und Muhlbrecht.

Germany, Federal Republic, Statistisches Bundesamt. 1972. *Bevölkerung und Wirtschaft, 1872–1972*. Stuttgart: W. Kohlhammer Verlag.

Great Britain, Central Statistical Office. 1840–. *Annual Abstract of Statistics*. London: H. M. Stationary Office.

Ho, Ping-ti. 1959. *Studies on the Population of China, 1368–1953*. Cambridge, Mass.: Harvard University Press.

Japan, Office of the Prime Minister, Bureau of Statistics. 1949–. *Japan Statistical Yearbook*. Tokyo.

Keyser, Erich. 1957. *Hessissches Städtebuch*. Stuttgart: W. Kohlkammer Verlag.

_____. 1959. *Badisches Stätedbuch*. Stuttgart: W. Kohlkammer Verlag.

_____. 1962a. *Bayerisches Städtebuch*. 2 vols. Stuttgart: W. Kholkammer Verlag.

_____. 1962b. *Württembergisches Städtebuch*. Stuttgart: W. Kohlkammer Verlag.

_____. 1964. *Städtebuch Rheinland-Pfalz und Saarland*. Stuttgart: W. Kohlkammer Verlag.

Kurian, George Thomas, ed. 1982. *Encyclopedia of the Third World*. Rev. ed., 3 vols. New York: Facts on File.

London, Greater London Council. 1966–. *Annual Abstract of Greater London Statistics*. London: Greater London Council.

Lorimer, Frank. 1946. *The Population of the Soviet Union: History and Prospects*. Geneva: League of Nations.

Mexico, Secretarias de la Economia Nacional. 1938–. *Anuario Estadistico*. Mexico City.

Norway, Statistisk Sentralbyrå. 1800–. *Statistisk Arbok för Norge*. Oslo: H. Aschehoug.

Prussia, Statistisches Landesamt. 1845. *Die Statistischen Tabellen des Preussischen Staats*. Berlin: Nicolai'schen Verlag.

_____. 1851–55. *Tabellen und amtlichen Nachrichten über den Preussischen Staat für das Jahr 1849*. 6 vols. Berlin: A. W. Hayn-Verlag.

Romania, Directiunea Statisticei Generale a Finanteior. 1904–. *Anuaral Statistic*. Bucharest.

Spain, Instituto Nacional de Estadistica. 1912–34, 1942–. *Anuario Estadistico de España*. Madrid.

Sweden, Statistiska Centralbryån 1914. *Statistisk Årsbok för Sverige*. Stockholm: Statens Reproduktionsanstalt.

Taiwan, Department of Civil Affairs. 1951–. *Statistical Yearbook of the Republic of China*. Taipei.

Turkey, Devlet Istatistik Enstitüsü. 1928–. *Türkiye Istatistik Yilligi* [Statistical Yearbook of Turkey]. Ankara.

United Nations, Statistical Office. 1980. *Patterns of Urban and Rural Population Growth*. New York: United Nations.

United States, Bureau of the Census. 1878–. *Statistical Abstract of the United States*. Washington: U.S. Government Printing Office.

United States, Central Intelligence Agency, National Foreign Assessment Center. 1979. *China, A Statistical Compendium: A Reference Aid*. Washington: U.S. Government Printing Office.

Venezuela, Dirección General de Estadistica y Censos Nacionales. 1877. *Anuario Estadistico de Venezuela*. Caracas.

C.1. Military (Currency Conversion): Most Useful

Benoit, Emile, and Harold Lubell. 1967. "The World Burden of National Defense." In *Disarmament and World Economic Interdependence*, ed. Emile Benoit, 29–59. New York: Columbia University Press.

Davis, L. E., and J. R. T. Hughes. 1960. "A Dollar-Sterling Exchange 1803–1895." *The Economic History Review* 13(1): 52–78.

Deutsch, Henry. 1910. *Arbitrage in Bullion, Coins, Bills, Stocks, Shares and Options.* 2d ed. London: E. Wilson.

Einzig, Paul. 1962. *The History of Foreign Exchange.* New York: St. Martin's Press.

International Monetary Fund. 1948–. *International Financial Statistics.* Washington: International Monetary Fund.

Kelly, Patrick. 1821. *The Universal Cambist and Commercial Instructor.* 2d ed., 2 vols. London.

Keynes, John Maynard. 1923. *A Tract on Monetary Reform.* London: Macmillan.

League of Nations. 1944. *The International Currency Experience.* Princeton, N.J.

Lee, William. 1976. "Soviet Defense Expenditures." In *Arms, Men, and Military Budgets 1977,* ed. William Schneider and F. S. Hoeber. New York: Crane Russak and Company.

Norman, John Henry. 1892. *Complete Guide to the World's 29 Metal Monetary Systems.* New York: G. P. Putnam.

Posthumus, Nicolaas Wilhelmus. 1946. *Inquiry into the History of the Prices in Holland.* Leiden: E. J. Brill.

Subercasseaux, G. 1920. *Le Papier-monnaie.* Paris: M. Giard & E. Brière.

The Times. 1816–1914. London: various issues used to get foreign exchange rates.

Vere, Charles. 1836. *The Pocket Cambist, Containing Tables of Monies of the Principal Cities in all Parts of the World.* London: Simpkin, Marshall & Co.

C.2. Military (Currency Conversion): Less Useful

Bell, Philip W. 1956. *The Sterling Area in Postwar World: Internal Mechanism and Cohesion.* Oxford: Claredon Press.

Bloch, Marc. 1954. *Esquisse d'une Histoire Monétaire de l'Europe.* Paris: A. Colin.

Bratter, Herbert. 1939. *Foreign Exchange Control in Latin America.* New York: Foreign Policy Association.

Brorowing, G. 1834. *Domestic and Financial Conditions of Great Britain.* London.

Cassel, Gustav. 1922. *Money and Foreign Exchanges After 1914.* London: Constable & Co.

Clare, George. 1893. *The ABC of the Foreign Exchanges.* New York: Macmillan.

Copeland, Elisha. 1834. *Tables for Receiving and Paying Gold Coins of the United States, Great Britain, France, Spain, Portugal, Brazil, Mexico, and Columbia, and also some of the Gold Coins of Russia, Prussia, and Holland.* Boston: Jonathon Howe.

Coussis, Demosthenes. 1932. *Die Griechische Währung von 1828 bis 1928.* Athens: L. Lambropoulos.

Crawford, William H. [1820] 1879. "Report on Currency." In *The Proceedings of the*

International Monetary Conference of Paris, 1878. Washington: U.S. Government Printing Office.

Easton, Harry T. 1813–1908. *Tate's Modern Cambist: A Manual of Foreign Exchanges and Bullion,* numerous editions, esp. 1831 and 1908. London: E. Wilson.

Gregory, Theodor Emanuel. 1922. *Foreign Exchange Before, During, and After the War.* London: H. Milford.

Harris, Seymour E. 1930. *The Assignats.* Cambridge, Mass.: Harvard University Press.

Helfferich, Karl Theodor. [1903] 1928. *Money.* London: The Adelphi Company.

Margraff, Anthony W. 1904. *International Exchange: Its Terms, Parts, Operations, and Scope.* 2d ed. Chicago: International Exchange.

Mitchell, Wesley C. 1903. *A History of the Greenbacks: With Special Reference to the Economic Consequences of Their Issue, 1862–65.* Chicago: The University of Chicago Press.

New York Reform Club, Second Currency Committee. 1891–. *Second Currency: A Compendium of Accurate and Timely Information on Currency Questions.* New York: New York Reform Club Second Currency Committee.

Seyd, Ernest. 1886. *Bullion and Foreign Exchanges Theoretically and Practically Considered.* London: Effingham Royal Exchange.

Thompson, Williams. 1914–. *Dictionary of Banking.* London, several editions.

Walré de Bordes, J. 1924. *The Austrian Crown: Its Depreciation and Stabilization.* London: P. S. King & Son.

D.1. Military (Personnel, Expenditures): Most Useful

Australia, Parliament. 1914. *Naval Expenditures of the Principal Naval Powers.* Command paper, 27 November.

Becker, Abraham. 1963. *The Soviet National Income and Product in 1965: The Goal of the Seven-Year Plan.* Santa Monica, Calif.: Rand Corporation.

Belgium, Ministère des Finances, Chambre des Représentants. 1840. *Compte Rendu des Recettes et Dépenses du Royaume pendant l'Année 1838.* Bruxelles: M. Hayez, Imprimeur de l'Acadamie Royale.

———. 1889. *Statistique Générale des Recettes et des Dépenses du Royaume de Belgique 1840–1885.* Bruxelles: M. Hayez, Imprimeur de l'Acadamie Royale.

Bogart, Ernest L. 1919. *Direct and Indirect Costs of the Great World War.* New York: Oxford University Press.

Bornstein, Morris. 1959. "A Comparison of Soviet and United States National Product." In *Comparisons of the United States and Soviet Economies,* ed. U.S. Congress Joint Economic Committee, 377–95. Washington, D.C.: U.S. Government Printing Office.

Carrias, Eugene. 1960. *La Pensée Militaire Francais.* Paris: Presses Universitaires de France.

Chalmin, Pierre. 1957. *L'Officier Francais de 1815 à 1870.* Paris: M. Riviére.

Clode, Charles M. 1869. Vol. 1 of *The Military Forces of the Crown: Their Administration and Government.* London: John Murray.

Clowes, Sir William. 1897–1903. *The Royal Navy: A History from Earliest Times to the Present.* 7 vols. Boston: Little, Brown.

Curtiss, John Shelton. 1965. *The Russian Army under Nicholas I, 1825–1855.* Durham, N.C.: Duke University Press.

DeGaulle, Charles. 1945. *La France et son Armée.* Paris: Plon; Berger Levrault.

Dernberger, Robert. 1975. "Evaluation of Existing Estimates for China's Military Costs and Preliminary Illustration of the 'Best' Available Method for Making New Estimates." University of Michigan. Typescript.

Dupuy, Trevor N. 1970–80. *The Almanac of World Military Power.* Dunn Loring, Va.: T. N. Dupuy Associates.

Erickson, John. 1962. *The Soviet High Command: A Military-Political History, 1918–1941.* New York: St. Martin's Press.

Ermarth, Fritz. 1964. *Economic Factors and Soviet Arms Control Policy: The Economic Burden of Soviet Defense Effort.* Cambridge, Mass.: Massachusetts Institute of Technology, Center for International Studies, Arms Control Project.

The Europa Yearbook. 1960–. 2 vols. London: Europa Publications.

Foot, Michael Richard Daniel. 1961. *Men in Uniform: Military Manpower in Modern Industrial Societies.* New York: Praeger.

France. 1838. *Compte Général de l'Administration des Finances rendu pour l'Année 1837.* Paris: Imprimerie Royale.

————, Institut National de la Statistique et des Études Économiques. 1845–99. *Annuaire Économie Politique,* no. 25. Paris.

France, Ministère des Finances. 1823. *Propositions de Lois Relatives à l'Ouverture de Credits Extraordinaires pour le Service de 1823 et à la Fixation du Budget des Dépenses et des Recettes de 1824.* Paris: Imprimerie Royale.

Fujiwara, Akiva. 1961. *Gunjishi: The History of Military Affairs in Japan.* Tokyo.

Genealogisch-historisch-statistischer Almanach fur das Jahr . . . (1824–48) Weimar: Verlag des Landes-industrie-comptoirs.

Genealogischer und Statistischer Almanach für Zeitungsleser (1859). Weimar.

Gerlach, A. J. A. *Fastes Militares des Indes-Orientales Néerlandaises.* Paris: C. Borrani.

Germany. 1862. *Zur finanziellen Seite der Militärfrage.* Berlin: Verlag der Königlichen Geheimen Ober-Hofbuchdruckerei.

Gittings, John. 1967. *The Role of the Chinese Army.* New York: Oxford University Press.

Godaire, J. G. 1962. "The Claim of the Soviet Military Establishment." In *Dimensions of Soviet Economic Power,* ed. U.S. Congress, Joint Economic Committee, 33–46. Washington, D.C.: U.S. Government Printing Office.

Great Britain, Board of Trade, Statistical Department. 1874–1914. *Statistical Abstract for the Principal and Other Foreign Countries.* London: H. M. Stationery Office.

Great Britain, Central Statistical Office. 1840–1938, 1946–. *Annual Abstract of Statistics.* London: H. M. Stationery Office.

Guichi, Ono. 1922. *War and Armament Expenditure of Japan.* Concord, Mass.: Carnegie Endowment for International Peace.

Hislam, Percival. 1908. *Admiralty of the Atlantic: An Enquiry into the Development of German Sea Power, Past, Present, and Prospective.* London: Longmans, Green and Co.

Howard, Michael. 1961. *The Franco-Prussian War: The Germans Invasion of France, 1870–71.* New York: Macmillan.

International Institute for Strategic Studies. 1959–. *The Military Balance.* London: International Institute for Strategic Studies.

———. 1962. *Communist Bloc and the Western Alliances: The Military Balance 1962–1963.* London: International Institute for Strategic Studies.

Italy, Direzione Generale della Statistica. 1878–. *Annuario Statistico Italiano.* Rome.

Japan, Office of the Prime Minister, Bureau of Statistics. 1960. *Japan Statistical Yearbook.* Tokyo.

Khromov, Pavel A. 1950. *Ekonomicheskoe Razvitie Rossii V XIX-XX Vekakh 1800–1910* [Economic Development of Russia in the 19th and 20th Centuries]. Moscow: Goszda Polititicheskoi Literatury.

Klein, Burton H. 1959. *Germany's Economic Preparations for War.* Cambridge, Mass.: Harvard University Press.

La Gorce, Paule Marie de. 1963. *La République et son Armée.* Paris: Fayard.

League of Nations. 1926–41. *League of Nations Armaments Yearbook: General and Statistical Information.* Geneva: League of Nations.

Lee, William. 1977. *The Estimation of Soviet Defense Expenditures 1955–1975: An Unconventional Approach.* New York: Praeger.

Liu, Frederick Fu. 1956. *A Military History of Modern China, 1924–1949.* Princeton, N.J.: Princeton University Press.

Löbell, Henrich von. 1874–1906. *Jahresberichte über die Veränderungen und Fortschritte im Militärwesen.* Berlin: E. S. Mittler & Sohn.

Loftus, Joseph. 1968. *Latin America Defense Expenditures 1838–1965.* Santa Monica, Calif.: Rand Corporation.

Malchus, C. A. Freiherr von. 1830. *Handbuch der Finanzwissenschaft und Finanzverwaltung.* Stuttgart und Tübingen: J. G. Cotta'schen Buchhandlung.

Monteilhet, Joseph. 1932. *Les Institutions Militaires de la France, 1814–1932: de la Paix Armée à la Paix Désarmée.* Paris: Libraire Felix Alcan.

Naikoko, Tokeikyoku. 1967. *Meiji Hya Kunen Shiryo* [Statistical Data for the Hundred Years since Meiji]. Tokyo.

New York Times. 1947–49. "Military Surveys." May 12, 1947, May 16, 1948, and March 27, 1949.

Ogawa, Gotaro. 1923. *Expenditures of the Russo-Japanese War.* Cambridge: Oxford University Press.

Powell, Ralph L. 1955. *The Rise of Chinese Military Power, 1895–1912.* Princeton, N.J.: Princeton University Press.

Prussia, Statistisches Landesamt. 1851–55. *Tabellen und amtliche Nachrichten über den Preussischen Staat für das Jahr 1849.* 6 vols. Berlin: A. W. Hayn Verlag.

Quetelet, Lambert Adophe J. 1829. *Recherches Statistiques sur le Royaume des Pays-Bas.* Bruxelles: M. Hayez.

Romanones, Alvaro Figueroa y Torres, Conde de. 1924. *Las Responsabilidades Politicas del Antiguo Régimen de 1875 a 1923.* Madrid: Renacimiento.

Romero, Matias. 1898. *Geographical and Statistical Notes on Mexico.* New York: G. P. Putnam's Sons.

Rüstow, Wilhelm von 1867. *Die Russische Armee.* Vienna: A. Hilberg.

Schneider, William, and F. S. Hoeber, eds. 1976. *Arms, Men, and Military Budgets.* New York: Crane, Russak, and Co.

Sellers, Robert C., ed. 1966–77. *Reference Handbook of the Armed Forces of the World.* Washington, D.C.: Robert Sellers Associates.

Sivard, Ruth Leger. 1979–. *World Military and Social Expenditures.* Leesburg, Va.: WMSE Publications.

Stockholm International Peace Research Institute. 1969–. *SIPRI Yearbook of World Armaments and Disarmament.* New York: Humanities Press.

Taylor, Charles L., and David A. Jodice. 1983. *World Handbook of Political and Social Indicators.* 3d ed. New Haven, Conn.: Yale University Press.

United Nations, Department of International Economic and Social Affairs, Statistical Office. 1948–. *Statistical Yearbook.* New York: United Nations.

United Nations, Office of the Secretary General. 1962. *Economic and Social Consequences of Disarmament: Replies of Governments and Communications from International Organizations.* New York: United Nations.

United States, Arms Control and Disarmament Agency. 1964–. *World Military Expenditures and Arms Transfers.* Washington: U.S. Government Printing Office.

United States, Office of Naval Intelligence. 1911. *Information Concerning Some of the Principal Navies of the World.* Washington: U.S. Government Printing Office.

United States, War Department, Military Commission to Europe. 1861. *The Armies of Europe.* Philadelphia.

Upton, John. 1878. *The Armies of Asia and Europe.* New York: D. Appleton and Company.

Wanty, Emile. 1957. *Le Milieu Militaire Belge de 1831 à 1914.* Bruxelles: Palais des Académies.

Whiting, Kenneth R. 1966. *The Development of the Soviet Armed Forces, 1917–1966.* Maxwell Airforce Base, Ala.: Air University.

D.2. Military (Personnel, Expenditures): Less Useful

Appleman, Roy E. 1961. *The United States Army in the Korean War.* Vol. 1 of *South to the Naktong, North to the Yalu.* Washington: U.S. Department of the Army, Office of the Chief of Military History.

Austria, K. K. Statistische Central Commission. 1828–71. *Tafeln zur Statistik der Österreichischen Monarchie.* Vienna: Statistische Central Commission.

———. 1863–. *Statistiches Jahrbuch der Österreichischen Monarchie.* Vienna: K. K. Hofund Staatsdruckerie.

———. 1893. *Österreichisches Statistiches Handbuch für die im Reichsrathe vertetenen Königreiche und Länder.* Vol. 12. Vienna: C. Gerhold und Sohn.

Belgium, Ministère de l'Intérieur. 1838–40. *Documents Statistiques sur le Royaume de Belgique.* Bruxelles: Van Dooren Freres.

———. 1907. *Statistique générale de la Belgique: Exposé de la Situation du Royaume de 1876 à 1900.* Bruxelles: Imprimerie Becquart-Arien.

Block, Maurice. 1860. *Statistique de la France Comparée avec les Autres États de l'Europe.* 2 vols. Paris: Amyot.

Booth, Richard. 1970. *The Armed Forces of African States, 1970*. London: Institute for Strategic Studies, Adelphi Papers no. 67.

Carlson, Evans F. 1940. *The Chinese Army: Its Organization and Military Efficiency*. New York: International Secretariat, Institute of Pacific Relations.

Cohn, Stanley H. 1962. "The Gross National Product in the Soviet Union: Comparative Growth Rates." *Dimensions of Soviet Economic Power*, ed. U.S. Congress, Joint Economic Committee, 67–89. Washington: U.S. Government Printing Office.

Dupuy, Richard Ernest. 1839. *The World in Arms: A Study in Military Geography*. Harrisburg, Pa.: The Military Service Publishing Co.

Encyclopaedia Britannica. 1910. 11th ed. Cambridge: Cambridge University Press.

Fuller, J. F. C. 1946. *Armament and History*. London: Eyre and Spottiswoode.

Hume, Martin A. S. 1900. *Modern Spain 1786–1898*. New York: G. P. Putnam's Sons.

Kieran, John, ed. 1947–. *Information Please Almanac, Atlas, and Yearbook*. New York: Simon and Schuster.

Löbell, Henrich von. 1874–1906. *Jahresberichte über die Veränderungen und Fortschritte im Militärwesen*. Berlin: E. S. Mittler & Sohn.

Morgan, John Hartman. 1946. *Assize of Arms: The Disarmament of Germany and Her Rearmament 1919–1939*. New York: Oxford University Press.

Nimitz, Nancy. 1952. *Soviet National Income and Product*. Santa Monica, Calif.: Rand Corporation.

Prussia, Kriegsministerium. 1909. *Das Königliche Preussische Kriegministerium 1809–1. März 1909*. Berlin: Kommissions-Verlag Invalidenbank.

Ropp, Theodore. 1959. *War in the Modern World*. Durham, N.C.: Duke University Press.

United Nations, Statistical Office. 1957–. *Yearbook of National Account Statistics*. New York: United Nations.

United States, War Department, General Staff, War College Division No. 17. 1911. *Strength and Organization of the Armies of France, Germany, Austria, Russia, England, Italy, Mexico, and Japan*. Washington: U.S. Government Printing Office.

Vagts, Alfred. 1937. *A History of Militarism: Romance and Realities of a Profession*. New York: W. W. Norton.

Wilkie, James. 1961–80. *Statistical Abstract of Latin America*. Los Angeles: University of California at Los Angeles, Latin American Center Publications.

Wood, David. 1968. *Conflicts in the Twentieth Century*. London: The Institute for Strategic Studies, Adelphi Papers no. 48.

E.1. Industrial: Most Useful

American Iron and Steel Association. 1868, 1871–1911. *Statistics of the American and Foreign Iron Trades*. Philadelphia: American Iron and Steel Association.

Barrows, Gordon Hensley. 1965. *International Petroleum Industry*. New York: International Petroleum Institute.

Burnham, Thomas Hall. 1943. *Iron and Steel in Britain, 1870–1930.* London: G. Allen and Unwin.

Darmstadter, Joel, et al. 1971. *Energy in the World Economy: A Statistical Review of Trends in Output, Trade, and Consumption Since 1925.* Baltimore, Md.: Johns Hopkins Press.

Ehlers, Joseph H. 1929. *The Production of Iron and Steel in Japan.* Washington: U.S. Government Printing Office.

Foster, G. 1918. *Die Türkische Berghan.* Weimar.

France, Institut National de la Statistique et des Études Économiques. 1845–99. *Annuaire de l'Économie Politique.* Paris; various issues.

Great Britain, Board of Trade, Statistical and Commercial Department. 1874–1914. *Statistical Abstract for the United Kingdom in Each of the Last Fifteen Years.* London: H. M. Stationery Office.

Great Britain, Commonwealth Energy Committee. 1966. *Sources of Energy.* London.

Great Britain, Overseas Geological Surveys, Mineral Resources Division. 1921. *Mineral Industry of Great Britain: Foreign Countries, Statistical Summary.* London: H. M. Stationery Office.

————. 1923–48. *The Mineral Industry of the British Empire and Foreign Countries: Statistical Summary.* London: H. M. Stationery Office.

————. 1948–72. *Statistical Summary of the Mineral Industry: Production, Exports, Imports.* London: H. M. Stationery Office.

Khromov, P. A. 1950. *Economic Development of Russia in the 19th and 20th Centuries.* Moscow.

League of Nations. 1927. *Memorandum on Coal.* Geneva: League of Nations.

————. 1927–40. *International Statistical Yearbook.* Geneva: League of Nations.

————. 1929. *The Problem of the Coal Industry.* Geneva: League of Nations.

Putnam, Palmer C. 1953. *Energy in the Future.* New York: D. Van Nostrand.

Smith, Harry B. Allin. 1922. *Statistical Record of the British Iron and Steel Industry.* Washington: U.S. Government Printing Office.

United Nations. 1952. *World Energy Supplies in Selected Years, 1929–1950.* New York: United Nations Statistical Office.

————, Department of International Economic and Social Affairs, Statistical Office. 1948–. *Statistical Yearbook.* New York: United Nations Statistical Office.

United States, Bureau of the Census. 1883–86. *Statistical Abstract of the United States.* Washington: U.S. Government Printing Office.

World Power Conferences. 1936–60. *Statistical Yearbook of World Power Conferences.* London: The Central Office of the World Power Conference.

E.2. Industrial: Less Useful

Barger, Harold, and Samuel H. Schurr. 1944. *The Mining Industries, 1899–1939: A Study of Output, Employment, and Productivity.* New York: National Bureau of Economic Research.

Bornstein, Morris. 1959. "A Comparison of Soviet and United States National Product." *Comparisons of the United States and Soviet Economies,* ed. U.S. Congress, Joint Economic Committee, 377–95. Washington: U.S. Government Printing Office.

Burn, Duncan Lyall. 1940. *The Economic History of Steelmaking, 1867–1939: A Study in Competition.* Cambridge: The University Press.

Cheng, Yu-kluei. 1956. *Foreign Trade and Industrial Development of China: A Historical and Integrated Analysis Through 1948.* Washington: University Press of Washington, D.C.

France, Institut National de la Statistique et des Études Économiques. 1845–99. *Annuaire Économie Politique.* Paris.

Garcia, José A. 1970. *Los Mineros Mexicanos.* Mexico City.

Habakkuk, H. J., and M. Postan, eds. 1965. *The Cambridge Economic History of Europe.* 2d ed. Vol. 6: *The Industrial Revolutions and After: Incomes, Populations, and Technological Change* (two parts). Cambridge: Cambridge University Press.

Issawi, Charles, ed. 1966. *An Economic History of the Middle East, 1800–1914: A Book of Readings.* Chicago: University of Chicago Press.

———. 1971. *The Economic History of Iran, 1800–1914.* Chicago: University of Chicago Press.

———. 1980. *The Economic History of Turkey, 1800–1914.* Chicago: University of Chicago Press.

Kuznets, Simon, Wilbert E. Moore, and Joseph J. Spengler, eds. 1950. *Economic Growth: Brazil, India, Japan.* Durham, N.C.: Duke University Press.

Okawa, Kazushi. 1957. *The Growth Rate of the Japanese Economy Since 1878.* Tokyo: Kinokuniya Bookstore Co.

UNESCO. 1957. *World Sources and Consumption of Energy, Paper No. 2: Energy in the Service of Man.* Paris: UNESCO.

Union of the Soviet Socialist Republics. 1956–. *National Economy of the USSR: Statistical Yearbook.* Moscow.

Usher, Abbott Payson, et al. 1937. *Economic History of Europe Since 1750.* New York: American Book Co.

Measuring Military Allocations:
A Comparison of Different Approaches

Gary Goertz and Paul F. Diehl

In principle (and surely in propaganda), military establishments exist in order to protect a nation-state from its enemies. All nations, with the possible exception of Costa Rica and Iceland, have some level of military preparedness. In order to maintain that preparedness, economic resources, be they human or capital, must be allocated to the military. Accompanying this allocation to the military are certain opportunity costs and possibly harmful economic side effects. Our goal is not to make a contribution to the existing literature on the domestic consequences of military spending, but rather to analyze and evaluate various operational measures of that allocation.

Measurement approaches in the social sciences are inherently theoretically based and vary according to the purposes and preconceptions of the individual researcher. Rather than assess all possible measurement approaches for military allocations, we chose to concentrate on those that relate to the study of conflict. By making such a choice, we bypass those indicators of military allocations designed to assess economic costs (that is, those that consider domestic economic effects; for example, see Russett 1982). We focus instead on indicators that have actually been used to identify the magnitude of military allocations and to study their impact on conflict escalation (for example, military expenditures divided by GNP).

This is not simply a methodological exercise. The implications for the study of conflict are potentially great. Military allocations are thought to play a prominent role in national decisions for war. First, high military allocations may be an early warning indicator of conflict escalation. Nations may be reluctant to fight unless they have adequate military preparations. High military allocations are indicative of this preparedness and, perhaps, also of the willingness to use military force.

Reprinted from *Journal of Conflict Resolution* 30, no. 3 (September 1986): 553–81. © 1986 Sage Publications, Inc. Reprinted by permission of Sage Publications, Inc.

Second, military allocations might also provide a link in the causal chain for war. High allocations could indicate the influence that military officials have in government decision making. In addition, high allocations could foster the growth of militarized movements or strengthen their public appeal (Noel-Baker 1958). For these reasons, the use of force might be a more likely policy choice during a serious confrontation. The probability of war may also be affected if one nation seeks to bring its opponent's economy "to its knees" through protracted arms competition. Some argue that a strategy of increasing military allocations to unacceptable levels could lead one side to back down and avoid conflict. Another school of thought states that the overallocated protagonist could launch a preventive war before it falls behind its less encumbered foe in the future.

Whatever their effects, military allocations have been seen as an important factor in accounting for the outbreak of war by a variety of scholars. Prior empirical research on military allocations and conflict, using a variety of different indicators, has yielded varied and often inconsistent results (Weede 1981). Newcombe and Wert (1973) discovered a positive relationship between high allocations and conflict involvement. Rummel's (1972) work shows similar findings, but the relationship is much weaker. In contrast, Kegley et al. (1978) find high allocations positively associated with external conflict only in the relative absence of domestic conflict. Choucri and North (1975) report wide variation in the military allocation ratios of the major powers prior to World War I.

Although some of this inconsistency in results undoubtedly can be traced to differences in the spatial-temporal domain, the variation in indicators could also be responsible. Before any further theoretical models are constructed or empirical analyses using military allocations performed, it might be useful to step back and consider the different indicators of military allocations. We can perhaps account for some of the differences among previous studies by identifying the effects of using different indicators. More important, the identification of the strengths and weaknesses of each indicator will enable a more informed choice of indicators in the future, hence greater validity and a better understanding of how military allocations affect the likelihood of war.

In considering different indicators of military allocations, we wish to appraise the face, convergent, discriminant, and predictive validity of each measure. In the first section, we specify a number of face validity criteria for the construction of a "good" indicator of military allocations. Next, we describe each measurement approach and evaluate it along those criteria, detailing its advantages and shortcomings. We then specify a set of empirical criteria and proceed to conduct various statistical tests in order to assess the other forms of validity for each indicator. We end with a study of militarized confrontations and the role of military allocations. The latter includes separate analyses for each indicator in order to permit a comparison of the results. In the conclusion, we hope to be able to evaluate each military allocation indicator and provide a guide to those contemplating research on military allocations and conflict. A note of caution to the reader is appropriate at the outset. A "good" indicator of any concept is more than a function of its ability to pass a series of statistical tests. The choice of indicator should also be dependent on the theoretical framework used and should be appropriate for the model tested. Our analysis is meant only to investigate the issues of comparability and empirical validity and not those related to the appropriate theoretical approach, which can vary greatly.

Criteria for Indicator Construction

Before conducting extensive empirical analyses, we believe a good indicator of military allocations must pass at least four tests:

(1) Is the indicator valid over space and time? A good military allocation indicator should be applicable to a wide range of countries. When dealing with a large spatial domain, the indicator must be valid for both large and small countries, making allowances, if necessary, to insure comparability. Because economic data are frequently used in indicator construction, the approach must guarantee that the indicator will permit valid comparisons between countries across the spectrum from capitalist to socialist economies and from developed to underdeveloped countries.

Equally important, the indicator must be useful throughout the long temporal domain that many conflict studies analyze. Standardization of measures across different historical epochs, however, is often problematic. There must be a balance between choosing a valid indicator for a particular historical period and insuring comparability across periods.

(2) Does the measurement approach produce a baseline by which abnormal allocations to the military can be detected? A major emphasis in conflict studies is the hypothesized relationship between high military allocations and nation-state behavior. It seems to us, then, that a good military allocation indicator should provide the scholar with a means of determining what is a "normal" or "average" military allocation and by implication what is an "overallocation."[1] This becomes particularly important in light of the third criterion. Most desirable would be a method that can identify "overallocating nations," and "underallocating nations," while still permitting subsequent interval level data analysis.

---

1. It could be argued that an explicit method for determining "overallocation" is not necessary for a good indicator of military allocations. Nevertheless, if such controls are not introduced, the problem of parameter instability arises, as noted in the third criterion. This problem has plagued a great deal of conflict research. For example, some of the Correlates of War research shows that estimated parameters are often different for the nineteenth and the twentieth centuries. For elaboration on this and related issues, see Goertz (1984).

(3) Can the measurement approach adjust for changes in the baseline over time? More than validity over a long period of time, the indicator should be able to adjust for changes over time in the baseline for normal allocations. Russett (1970) noted a "ratchet" effect in military personnel allocations for the United States following participation in a war. In fact, normal military allocations for all major powers have risen dramatically since the Congress of Vienna (Diehl and Goertz 1985). What may be a normal military allocation in one period could be an overallocation and a burden in an earlier epoch. Thus, a good indicator must be sensitive to changes in the norm for military allocations, lest it label all nations in the most recent time period as "over-allocators" and all those in earlier periods as "underallocators."

(4) Are the data needed for the indicator available? Expediency in data collection is a poor justification for choosing one measurement approach over another, but even an indicator meeting all the above criteria is useless if the data required are unavailable. The lack of data may force a scholar to narrow the spatial-temporal domain of a proposed study, thereby limiting the level of generalization possible.

Given these criteria, we now turn to a description and evaluation of the various measurement approaches.

Measurement Approaches

A comparison of some portion of a nation's resource base with the resources devoted to the military is most often used to measure military allocations in conflict research. Most studies use military expenditures to represent resources devoted to the military. The variation in measurement approaches tends to center on the choice of indicator for a nation's resource base and the technique of comparison.

With respect to techniques currently used, approaches to measuring military allocations can be roughly divided into two categories: those based on a simple ratio and those that are regression-based. The former use a measure of military appropriation and divide it by an indicator of a nation's resource base. The latter use regression analyses to obtain a predicted or normal military allocation (as a function of the resource base) and then compare the actual allocation with the predicted allocation.

The first measurement approach to be considered has variations that encompass both of these basic techniques.

Military Expenditures and Gross National Product

Perhaps the most common indicator of military allocations is a simple ratio of a nation's military expenditures to its Gross National Product, ME:GNP (Russett 1964 and 1970; Weede 1977; Kegley et al. 1978; Reisinger 1983). The rationale for this approach is that GNP is the best indicator of a nation's total available resources. Consistent with most other measures of military allocations, military expenditures are believed to be the best available measure of resources appropriated to the military. Military expenditure figures generally include a wide range of items (from research and development to military hardware) and therefore are more accurate in defining what is actually allocated to a nation's military establishment.

A more sophisticated, regression-based measurement approach (Newcombe 1969; Newcombe et al. 1973 and 1974) uses GNP and military expenditures in a different manner. The size of a nation's military establishment is postulated to be, to a large extent, a function of the size of its economic base. Therefore, military expenditures are regressed on GNP for a large number of nations over a three-year period. After the regression equation is derived, it is applied to yearly GNP figures for each country to obtain a predicted value for that state's military expenditures. The observed (actual) expenditures are then divided by the predicted values and multiplied by 100, the product being called a "tensiometer." Scores that deviate significantly from 100 indicate over- or underallocation to the military relative to other countries in the period studied.

The Newcombe approach has the advantage of establishing a baseline by which to compare different nations' military allocations. The simple ME:GNP ratio, however, provides no systematic method of defining which nations are over- or underallocating. In addition, the foreign policies of minor powers have a narrower scope, and those nations may spend proportionately less on the military than major powers (Weede 1977). Some minor powers (for example, Japan) are protected by alliances and may feel little need to maintain a large military establishment, whereas others receive a great deal of external military aid. By including a wide range of countries in the regression baseline (most of which are small countries), the tensiometer might identify major powers to be overallocating, whereas their minor power counterparts would appear to be below the average. Thus, the tensiometer does not distinguish between the potentially different norms of military allocations for major and minor powers.

There are a number of problems with using GNP in either the ratio- or regression-based technique. First, GNP is a relatively new concept, dating only to the inception of Keynesian economics. There are serious data problems in a longitudinal study extending before World War I. Estimates of GNP are available (often only at ten-year intervals) for the nineteenth century, but they must always be used with a great deal of caution.

More than just data availability problems complicate the utility of GNP; its validity over space and time must be questioned. A high GNP in recent times may be, in large part, the result of a rapidly expanding service sector instead of industrial strength, giving a false indication of the resources that can be converted to military purposes. Thus, a nation may have a growing GNP, but still experience increasing strain from its military allocations because of declining industrial production, increased military spending, or both. GNP is also a statistic that is heavily biased toward capitalist economies. Gross National Product figures are hard to calculate for centrally planned economies; estimates are often made, but these can be misleading, if not wholly inaccurate (for instance, note the widely varying estimates of Soviet GNP). In addition, production not exchanged in markets is not included or crude estimates are made (for example, China).

Finally, neither of the GNP approaches describes a distinct method for ascertaining possible changes over time. Comparing military allocation ratios of nations in the nineteenth century with those in the twentieth century could be deceiving; the normal level of allocations may have risen considerably over time.

Overall, the GNP approach is simple enough and relies on military expenditure data that are both available and comparable across a broad spatial-temporal domain. Nevertheless, GNP itself has validity and data availability problems that can be quite severe, and even the Newcombe variation, which does provide a baseline for determining overallocation, does not attempt to detect changes in that baseline.[2]

Military Expenditures and National Income

Another approach to measuring military allocations substitutes national income (NI) for GNP as an indicator of a nation's resource base, ME:NI (Nincic 1983). The advantage of national income relative to GNP is that NI does not include indirect business taxes and allows for a capital consumption allowance. Thus, NI is able to present a more accurate picture of the actual amount of national resources available.

The national income indicator suffers from the same drawbacks as the GNP-based indicator. Service sector distortions are still present, and NI data for centrally planned economies are suspect. GNP and NI are highly correlated, as they share the same components, except for the two noted above. Consequently, we will not undertake separate analyses for the national income indicator in the remainder of the study.

---

2. Problems with Newcombe's approach would be particularly evident when comparing pre– and post–World War II epochs. The tremendous increase in the number of sovereign states during the postwar period could have dramatic effects on the baseline.

Military Expenditures and Government Budgets

Another variation of measuring military allocations consists of taking military expenditures as a percentage of government budget (Rummel 1972; Haas 1974; Choucri and North 1975; Cusack and Ward 1981). Here, the assumption is that the only resources actually available for military purposes are those available to a national government.

Government budgets have the advantage of being a readily available data item for an extended period of time (the data, however, are sporadic for certain closed societies, such as the People's Republic of China). Nevertheless, there are important limitations to the military expenditures/government budget indicator. Government budgets are not sufficiently comparable, given the great range of items that is found in different types of economies. Socialist economies tend to channel a greater share of their resources through government budgets than do market economies, thereby making military allocations of socialist nations appear smaller than those in which the governmental role is more modest. This difficulty will also arise when comparing mid- to late twentieth-century governments, in which the role of government in society is relatively great, with their eighteenth and nineteenth century predecessors, which maintained a smaller presence. In the absence of any method to control for historical changes in the scope of government budgets and considering that change occurs at different rates in different countries, the risk of distortion and misconception is great; the lack of a specified baseline for determining normal allocations compounds this problem.

In summary, the government budget approach offers the minor advantage of data availability over the previously cited measurement approaches, while presenting similar or more difficult problems and disadvantages.

Military Personnel and Total Population

Rather than focus on capital resources allocated to the military, another approach to measuring military allocations concentrates on human resources devoted to the military. Andreski (1968) developed the idea of a "military participation ratio" to signify the proportion of individuals in the population used by the military. In conflict research, this has been operationally defined as the number of military personnel of a nation divided by its population (Stoll and Champion 1977; Rummel 1972; Russett 1964). The reasoning behind this indicator is that those individuals in military service are unable to contribute to a nation's production of goods and services and, therefore, are a burden on the economy. Benoit and Lubbell (1967) carry this one step further operationally: they multiply the number of personnel in the armed forces by the average civilian wage or salary, labeling the result "lost production" from military service.

Data availability problems with this indicator are all but nonexistent, but its validity can be challenged. The significance of manpower for military preparedness has declined greatly over the last century probably as a result of a shift in emphasis from labor-intensive to capital-intensive warfare. Success in combat has become more dependent on weaponry than sheer manpower. Accordingly, new resources are being channeled into weapons development and procurement, rather than into increases in troop strength. Thus, the number of military personnel in a nation probably no longer adequately reflects the economic investment in its military. The most technologically advanced nations might have the lowest scores on this measure, even though they may allocate the greatest proportion of financial and industrial resources to the military. The validity of this approach over time is, therefore, in doubt.

In addition, the approach provides no baseline for comparing normal and abnormal allocations. Exacerbating this difficulty is a notable change in the pattern of human resource allocations to the military. Following World War II, virtually all of the major powers maintain large standing armies, regardless of the size of their population. Unfortunately, the present approach cannot adjust for this change.

Overall, the military personnel-based measure may be an adequate indicator of military allocations for the preindustrial age, but its ignorance of the changing structure of appropriations makes it less valid in the modern era.

Comparative Shares of Industrial Capability and Military Expenditure Using System Percentages

A recent approach (Wayman et al. 1983) relies, in part, on industrial indicators of resource capability, rather than aggregate GNP or national income figures. Iron/steel production and energy consumption are used to represent a nation's industrial strength and, in turn, its capacity for military production and supply.

Wayman et al. begin by calculating the major power subsystem totals for military expenditures and the two industrial indicators. Then, they determine the percentage of the total system capabilities that each major power has on each of the three dimensions.[3] The underlying assumption of their next set of transformations is that a nation should have approximately the same percentage of the system's military capabilities as it does for industrial capabilities.

---

3. The rationale and procedure for calculating system capabilities is laid out in Singer, Bremer, and Stuckey (1972).

For example, if nation *A* has 10 percent of the industrial capabilities in the subsystem, it should also be expected to have 10 percent of the military capabilities. This assumption provides an a priori norm for military allocations and as such is not empirically confirmed. This approach calls for dividing the percentage figures (military expenditures by each industrial indicator), with values over one signifying overallocation to the military.

This approach has some attractive features. It establishes a baseline by which the researcher is able to identify military allocations in excess of the norm, thus permitting analyses of the effects of overallocation. The baseline is defined a priori, and there is, therefore, no problem with it changing over time, as potentially exists with empirical baselines. The indicator permits comparisons across many different kinds of national economies throughout a broad time frame. By using percentage shares instead of raw data, the approach is not subject to problems from inflation. Finally, the data required are readily available, and the authors were able to conduct a set of analyses extending back to 1816.[4]

One potential problem is that the indicator is relative and based on single-year capability figures. Thus, a finding that all major powers are overallocating simultaneously is impossible. A nation may be severely strained by its military spending, but this approach will show it to be underallocating if its peers are allocating more heavily to their militaries. In addition, large concurrent increases in military expenditure for all major powers are not adequately reflected by this approach. Each nation could triple its military spending without any increase in industrial capability and yet retain the same military allocation score.

This method has the potential to be applied to minor as well as major powers, although some allowance must be made for the large number of small countries that do not produce any steel. This approach has shown that it fulfills that criteria better than previous attempts, yet it still has some drawbacks for use in conflict research.

Predicted Military Expenditures and Actual Military Expenditures Stratified by Epochs

This approach assumes that military personnel are more significant than other aspects of the military in determining military effectiveness for the early and mid-nineteenth century. Thus, the focus is on the relationship between military personnel and total population until 1860. Citing the problems with GNP,

---

4. One data limitation of their analysis was the unavailability of energy consumption figures prior to 1860.

national income, and government budgets, the analysis centers on military expenditures and the two industrial indicators of Wayman and his colleagues for the post-1860 period (Diehl 1985).

It is hypothesized that the size of a nation's army and its military budget are a function of the human and capital resources, respectively, available to that nation, and an empirical analysis confirmed this point. To establish a baseline, a variation of the Newcombe and Wert (1973) technique is employed. For the period 1816–60, military personnel are regressed on total population. For the period after 1860, military expenditures are the outcome variable and the two industrial indicators (energy consumption and iron/steel production) serve as separate predictor variables. The post-1860 regressions are stratified by historical epochs (1861–1913, 1919–38, and 1946–80) corresponding to observed changes in the baseline.

The observed yearly population and industrial figures are applied to the equations obtained from the four regressions and provide expected values for military personnel and military expenditures. The actual personnel and expenditure values are then divided by the predicted values and the quotient is multiplied by 100. The scores of the industrial indicators are averaged to form a composite score. A score of 100 indicates the average or "normal" number of troops or military expenditure for a nation of its particular size.

This approach has the advantages of adjusting for parameter changes over time; thus, different historical epochs can be easily compared with each other. Furthermore, the measurement approach seems valid over space and time, using different indicators for the pre- and post-1860 period as well as employing comparable measures (military personnel, energy consumption, and so on) throughout. Data availability is not a significant problem and different baselines for each epoch, empirically derived, are important by-products of the approach.

As to the limitations of this approach, the relationship between military spending and resource capability may be strong over a 165-year period, but it is noticeably weaker if confined to the 1919–38 epoch. Because the "fit" of the regression line is rather imperfect for this period, the discrepancy between predicted and actual expenditures is quite large, leading to greater variation in the military allocation scores for this period than other epochs. The outlying scores (particularly the highest ones) exaggerate the actual allocations of countries and distort the results when used in analyses on conflict. (It should be noted that the 1919–38 period is extremely conflict ridden and includes a number of cases in which conflicts escalated to war.)

This approach has been attempted thus far only on major powers, and its applicability to minor powers is uncertain. It appears that some adjustments relating to the technological development of minor powers and military aid would be necessary before the measure can be useful in this domain. Finally, there is a serious problem when attempting to chart military allocations over time by analyzing the slopes and intercepts of the regression lines. Because the dependent variable is monetary (for the post-1860 period), inflation will exaggerate the actual "ratchet" effect or changes occurring across epochs; this problem can be solved if suitable deflators are found.

These are the main approaches to measuring military allocations in the conflict literature; by no means is this an exhaustive list of the possible measurement approaches, although this is almost an exhaustive list of actual approaches. Table 1 gives a summary of the different approaches along with an evaluation of their validity on the criteria given above. Scholars may wish to combine different techniques with various indicators of resource capability. Techniques and indicators beyond those mentioned here are also options for future study.

Developing Some Empirical Criteria

Having established a number of criteria for face validity and evaluated each measurement approach according to those criteria, we can now consider different indicators' validity based on empirical tests. We investigate three kinds of validity as they relate to each measurement approach: convergent, discriminant, and predictive validity (Campbell and Fiske 1959; Ghiselli et al. 1981).

(1) *Convergent validity* requires agreement between scores obtained with two or more indicators presumably measuring the same construct. To investigate this, we will run simple intercorrelation analyses, with special attention to measures that yield the highest coefficients. The greater the correlation of a measure to all others, the more validity that measure has in terms of capturing the same concept.

The reader and the investigators must be careful in assessing the intercorrelations. Similarities index construction or data may account for some portion of a high correlation coefficient, and thereby give a false indication of the convergent validity of the measures in question.

(2) *Discriminant validity* requires disagreement between indicators measuring different constructs. This insures that the indicator is actually measuring what it purports to, rather than some other phenomena. Because we are interested in indicators used in conflict research, we have chosen to run correlations between each military allocation indicator and an indicator of the intensity of a nation's arms buildup. This also provides for a comparison of a static measure (military allocations) and a dynamic one (a military buildup). There should be some positive correlation between the allocation measures and the arms buildup indicator; in fact, a nation's allocation ratio often increases when that nation rapidly increases its weapons acquisition. Nevertheless, the relationship is far from a perfect one. An increase in arms is not

TABLE 1. Summary of Military Allocation Indicators and Their Attributes

Indicator	Military Resources	Resource Base	Technique of Construction	"Norm" or Baseline	System Change Sensitivity	Data Availability	Applicability over Space and Time	Sample Citation
1. System percentage	military expenditures	energy iron/steel	ratio of system percentage shares	yes (a priori)	yes	good	good	Wayman, Singer, and Goertz 1983
2. Stratified epochs	military expenditures	energy iron/steel	regression	yes (empirical)	yes	good	good	Diehl 1985
3. Budget	military expenditures	government budget	ratio	no	no	fair	poor	Rummel 1972
4. GNP	military expenditure	GNP	ratio	no	no	fair	poor	Weede 1977
5. Personnel	military personnel	total population	ratio	no	no	good	poor	Stoll and Champion 1977

always translated into an increase in the allocation ratio because a nation's resource base may concurrently increase, leaving the allocation ratio approximately the same, even after a significant increase in weapons stocks. A high allocation ratio may also persist long after the termination of an arms buildup, reflecting the impact of prior increases in arms acquisition.

Therefore, we might expect some positive correlation between the rate of increase in arms acquisition and the indicators of military allocations, but that correlation should not be very high. A negative or a high, positive correlation for any of our measures would call into question the validity of that indicator.

(3) *Predictive validity* is an evaluation of an indicator's utility in predicting or postdicting a given outcome, according to some theoretical model. In assessing predictive validity, there is the inherent risk of choosing an incorrect model on which the analysis is based. As a consequence, one must be cautious when interpreting results. The failure to confirm a hypothesis may result from a faulty model rather than from an invalid indicator.

In this study, each measure will be assessed to determine its ability to predict escalation to war, according to the hypothesis that high military allocations increase the risk of a conflict escalating to full-scale war. We will analyze a set of militarized disputes and their outcomes, using each allocation measure as the independent variable. Those measures that yield the strongest results can be said to have the greatest validity on this dimension. These tests should also reveal the extent to which results differ according to the measurement approach used. This could be an important exercise in reconciling divergent findings in the literature, as well as a valuable piece of information for scholars contemplating work in this area.

In empirically assessing the various measures of military allocations, we focus on major power nations in the years 1861–1980.[5] The Correlates of War Project provided data for military expenditures, military personnel, energy consumption, iron and steel production, and total population. Government expenditure data are taken primarily from Banks (1971), supplemented by Mitchell (1981) and the Arms Control and Disarmament Agency (1983). Gross National Product figures were primarily taken from Bairoch (1974), who also graciously provided some unpublished estimates. Because the GNP data are given at ten-year intervals, a polynomial regression was run for each country (all r^2 values are over .99) in order to obtain yearly estimates. It must

---

5. The major powers for this study are those identified by Small and Singer (1982): United States (1899–1980), the United Kingdom (1861–1980), France (1861–1940 and 1945–1980), Austria-Hungary (1861–1918), Germany (1861–1918 and 1925–1945); Russia (1861–1917), Soviet Union (1922–80), China (1950–80), Italy (1861–1943), and Japan (1895–1945). Inasmuch as the participants' military allocations during major power wars are all but impossible to measure when economies are fully devoted to the war effort, we bypass analysis for the World War I and World War II years (1914–18 and 1939–45).

be pointed out that estimates represent basic trends and do not reflect fluctuations due to the business cycle; thus, there is some error associated with them. Additional GNP data were taken, when necessary, from the World Bank (1983), U.S. Bureau of the Census (1975), Arms Control and Disarmament Agency (1983), and the International Monetary Fund (1982).[6] "Missing data" are a problem, particularly for government expenditures in the case of China and, to a lesser extent, Germany and the Soviet Union.[7] All monetary data are converted to a common currency, according to Correlates of War Project conversion rates, in order to permit comparability.[8]

For the analysis of discriminant validity, we use a measure of military buildup intensity that is an exponentially weighted average of military expenditure increases over a five-year period (Diehl 1985).

In the analysis of predictive validity, we concentrate on "militarized disputes" and their outcomes. Militarized disputes are "a set of interactions between or among states involving threats to use military force, displays of military force, or actual use of military force . . . these acts must be explicit, overt, nonaccidental, and government sanctioned" (Gochman and Maoz 1984, 587). In determining the outcome of these disputes, we code all disputes that resulted in 1,000 or more battle-related fatalities as a "war" (Small and Singer 1982). All those not satisfying this criterion are labeled as "no war." A list of major power militarized disputes and their outcomes is taken from the files of the Correlates of War Project.

Analysis of Convergent Validity

The simplest and most straightforward way to compare our measures is by correlating them; the correlations are presented in table 2.

For indicators purporting to measure the same thing, one is struck by the low correlations; only two coefficients are greater than .40. This is surprising in that four of the five indicators use military expenditures and differ only in

---

6. Banks (1971) supplied government expenditure data for all years except: 1966–70 (Mitchell 1981), 1971–80 (Arms Control and Disarmament Agency 1983), and 1929–33 for Germany and the Soviet Union (Mitchell 1981). Bairoch (1974) provided all data on GNP except: 1929–79 for the United States (U.S. Bureau of the Census 1975), 1950–80 for China (World Bank 1983), and 1971–80 (Arms Control and Disarmament Agency 1983). Other scattered missing values were filled in by data from the International Monetary Fund (1982). In all cases where data from different sources were combined, we undertook a careful effort to make sure that the figures formed a consistent pattern. Where the data exhibited no consistent pattern or were contradictory, we coded those years as "missing data."

7. "Missing data" for government expenditures included 1861–1970 and 1934–38 for Germany and 1934–38 for the Soviet Union. In addition, there are "missing data" for Chinese government expenditures and GNP for many years between 1950 and 1980.

8. Monetary data are measured in U.S. dollars.

TABLE 2.   Correlations of Military Allocation Indicators

	1. System Percentage	2. Stratified Epochs	3. Budget	4. GNP	5. Personnel
1. System percentage	1.00	−0.09	−0.19	−0.15	−0.05
2. Stratified epochs	−0.09	1.00	0.02	0.05	0.13
3. Budget	−0.19	0.02	1.00	0.65	0.27
4. GNP	−0.15	0.05	0.65	1.00	0.41
5. Personnel	−0.05	0.13	0.27	0.41	1.00

Note: All coefficients are Pearson's *r* coefficients.

the measure of economic resources and the technique of construction. The importance of the technique of construction can be seen in the fact that the system percentage method (Wayman et al. 1983) is virtually uncorrelated with the stratified epochs method (Diehl 1985), despite using exactly the same data (military expenditures, iron and steel production, and energy consumption). The popular GNP method (Russett 1970 and others) is not highly correlated with either of those two indicators, but is highly associated with indicators using the government budget (Rummel 1972 and others) and military personnel (Stoll and Champion 1977) methods. Indeed, the GNP method yields the highest average correlation with the other indicators, but the coefficient is still quite low (.24).[9]

One possible explanation for the low correlations with the stratified epochs approach is that for each epoch (1861–1913, 1919–38, and 1946–80), a different regression line is used to calculate the indicator. Using this hint, correlations were calculated for each epoch separately, and the results are given in table 3.

A quick glance will reveal that the correlations are much higher for the epochs individually than for the whole 120-year period. A broad overview of the results for the three periods seems to indicate that World War II is a watershed in that the correlations are significantly lower (except for military personnel) in the pre–World War II period. Once again, the GNP-based indicator yields the highest average correlations with the other indicators; it had the highest average correlation in the first two epochs and finished second best to the system percentage method in the third epoch.[10]

---

9. The average correlations for each indicator with all others are as follows: system percentages (−.12), stratified epochs (.03), budget (.19), GNP (.24), and personnel (.19).

10. The average correlations for each indicator with all others, stratified by the epochs 1861–1914, 1919–39, and 1945–80 are: system percentages (−.06; .29; .56), stratified epochs (.15; .34; .44), budget (.13; .35; .3), GNP (.39; .56; .52), and personnel (.31; .20; .37).

If one examines the changes over time in the various coefficients, it becomes quite clear why the correlations in table 2 are so low. The evolution of the indicators over time with respect to one another is nonlinear. For example, the correlations between GNP and government budget indicators go from .23 in 1861–1913, to .66 in 1919–38, to .18 in 1946–80; the correlations between indicators based on the system percentage and stratified epochs approaches go from −.22, to .00, to .76 over the three time periods. Thus, the relations between indicators are changing over time in various nonlinear ways.

Another possible explanation for why the overall correlations are so low is that certain indicators are dependent on the composition of the major power

TABLE 3. Correlations of Military Allocation Indicators, Stratified by Epochs

Indicator	1. System Percentage	2. Stratified Epochs	3. Budget	4. GNP	5. Personnel
		1861–1913			
1. System per-centage	1.00	−0.22	−0.14	0.13	−0.03
2. Stratified epochs	−0.22	1.00	0.27	0.36	0.21
3. Budget	−0.14	0.27	1.00	0.23	0.16
4. GNP	0.13	0.36	0.23	1.00	0.87
5. Personnel	−0.03	0.21	0.16	0.87	1.00
		1919–38			
1. System per-centage	1.00	0.00	0.45	0.39	0.33
2. Stratified epochs	0.00	1.00	0.44	0.78	0.14
3. Budget	0.45	0.44	1.00	0.66	−0.04
4. GNP	0.39	0.78	0.66	1.00	0.40
5. Personnel	0.33	0.14	−0.04	0.40	1.00
		1946–80			
1. System per-centage	1.00	0.76	0.31	0.75	0.44
2. Stratified epochs	0.76	1.00	0.37	0.52	0.09
3. Budget	0.31	0.37	1.00	0.17	0.32
4. GNP	0.75	0.52	0.17	1.00	0.65
5. Personnel	0.44	0.09	0.32	0.65	1.00

Note: All coefficients are Pearson's r coefficients.

subsystem (the system percentage and stratified epochs methods), whereas others (personnel, GNP, and government budget methods) are unaffected by the composition of that subsystem and its changes. In the former, the baseline used to calculate the indicator will change when countries enter and depart the major power subsystem; the latter are constructed with data for each country only and hence are not influenced by such changes. The cutoff points that we have chosen are the World War I and II years when some dramatic changes occurred in the composition of the major power subsystem.

One way to examine if the values of nonsystem dependent indicators are changing fundamentally over time is to see if the average values of these ratios increase or decrease dramatically over the three epochs. To investigate this possibility, we use an ANOVA (although technically not all of its assumptions are met here), which tests to see if the means of the three epochs are equal; these results are given in table 4.

The average value for each indicator has increased over time (the F-statistic is significant at .0001 in each case, except the military personnel indicator, and the follow-up tests between individual means are significant at .01), although the rates of increase are different in each case. This, incidentally, supports a finding reported elsewhere (Diehl and Goertz 1985) that the major subsystem is becoming increasingly militarized over time.

A less stringent comparison of the five indicators is a rank-order correlation that gives the degree to which the indicators rank the countries concerned in the same order. Given the variability in the sources of data, measures of economic resources, and techniques of construction, if (despite relatively low Pearson's *r* coefficients) they were to agree on the same ordering, it would still be an indication that they are tapping related concepts.

As table 5 indicates, the convergence among the indicators signifies that, on a grosser level, there is more agreement, but still not the high correlations one would expect from indicators of the same phenomenon (although there

TABLE 4. Mean Values of Nonsystem Dependent Indicators, Stratified by Epochs

	Epochs		
Indicator	1861–1913	1919–38	1946–80
3. Budget	.07	.20	.31
	(.05)	(.16)	(.16)
4. GNP	.01	.04	.11
	(.003)	(.05)	(.08)
5. Personnel	.009	.007	.01
	(.006)	(.005)	(.006)

Note: Standard errors are in parentheses.

appears to be quite close convergence on the ranking of major powers following World War II). The GNP method is again the one with the highest average correlation among the indicators.

When attempting to determine if various indicators are measuring the same concept, one is usually concerned with central tendencies, and hence the use of correlational techniques is quite normal. The situation under investigation here is somewhat different in that researchers have been particularly concerned with countries that are spending abnormally large amounts on the military; in statistical terms, they have been interested in outliers. The previous analyses focused on the degree to which these indicators have the same central tendencies. We now move to a discussion of the degree to which they agree on which states are "over-" or "underspenders."

In this analysis, each state's military allocation, according to each indicator, was classified as either "high," "average," or "low." As we noted above, some indicators inherently define normal levels of allocations and some do not. For those that do not, the mean value for the epoch was classified as "normal" (as we have determined above, an overall mean would be invalid). A definition of "low" or "high" allocations was based on being more than 0.5 to 1.0 standard deviations away from the mean (this varied according to the epoch and the indicator, because in some cases outlying values distorted the variance). Each pair of indicators was then compared in a contingency table analysis in order to test the similarity of their classifications of military allocations; the tau-beta values in table 6 give a summary of the test results.

The agreement between indicators on the outlying values is clearly higher than their agreement on central tendency (compare with table 2). This is particularly the case between indicators using military expenditure data. Again,

TABLE 5. Rank-Order Correlations of Military Allocation Indicators

Indicator	1. System Percentage	2. Stratified Epochs	3. Budget	4. GNP	5. Personnel
1. System per-centage	1.00	0.26 (0.22)	−0.12 (0.09)	0.57 (0.44)	0.31 (0.24)
2. Stratified epochs	0.26 (0.22)	1.00	0.44 (0.33)	0.59 (0.49)	0.50 (0.40)
3. Budget	−0.12 (0.09)	0.44 (0.33)	1.00	0.23 (0.18)	0.25 (0.20)
4. GNP	0.57 (0.44)	0.59 (0.49)	0.23 (0.18)	1.00	0.62 (0.50)
5. Personnel	0.31 (0.24)	0.50 (0.40)	0.25 (0.20)	0.62 (0.50)	1.00

Note: Correlations given are Spearman's rho coefficients; those in parentheses are the more conservative coefficients of tau-beta.

TABLE 6. Cross-Classification Agreement Among Military Allocation Indicators

Indicator	1. System Percentage	2. Stratified Epochs	3. Budget	4. GNP	5. Personnel
1. System percentage	1.00	0.23	−0.04	0.40	0.20
2. Stratified epochs	0.23	1.00	0.32	0.46	0.10
3. Budget	−0.04	0.32	1.00	0.33	0.02[a]
4. GNP	0.40	0.46	0.33	1.00	0.38
5. Personnel	0.20	0.10	0.02[a]	0.38	1.00

Note: Correlations are tau-beta coefficients. Chi-square values are not given, but were calculated for each pair and were significant in all cases at .001, except where noted.
[a]Significant at .05.

the GNP method yielded the best results, although even under the simplified conditions of only three categories, none of the relationships is particularly strong. As in previous analyses, the tests were repeated for the three historical epochs separately; in contrast to the results reported above, we did not find a regular increase over time in the level of agreement between the different measures.

In summary, our analysis of convergent validity yielded somewhat disappointing results. All forms of analysis revealed only weak congruence between the five indicators, although there was greater agreement when rank ordering countries and identifying outliers. Overall, the GNP method was slightly better than the others on most tests, yet on an absolute level, its performance was less than impressive. We also discovered that increases in the norm or average allocation occurred over time.

Analysis of Discriminant Validity

Another test of an indicator is its ability to differentiate itself from indicators of other phenomena. Here, we test the ability of each of the five measures of the military allocations indicator to differentiate itself from an indicator of arms buildup intensity. Earlier, we stated our belief that the correlations between the buildup indicator and the allocation indicators should be positive, but not dramatically high. Table 7 gives the results of our correlational analysis.[11]

The stratified epochs approach and the GNP method perform in the

---

11. In this analysis, outlying scores (> 20) on the arms buildup intensity indicator are eliminated from consideration so as not to distort the results. Including those cases in the analysis yields correlations of less than .10 for all indicators, none of them significant at .01.

TABLE 7. Correlation Between Indicators of Military Allocation and Arms Buildup Intensity

Military Allocation Indicator	Arms Buildup Intensity
1. System percentage	.004
2. Stratified epochs	.22
3. Budget	.11
4. GNP	.21
5. Personnel	.05

Note: All correlations are Pearson's *r* coefficients, outliers (>20.0) on the arms buildup variable are eliminated from consideration.

manner desired for discriminant validity. Both indicators exhibit a positive correlation (just above .20), but no so high as to suggest that the same phenomenon is being measured. The other measurement approaches yield very weak correlations, suggesting that different concepts are being measured (this is desirable), but the indicators appear unable to reflect situations in which military buildups increase the military allocations of a nation.

We now move to our final set of analyses, concerning each indicator's ability to predict conflict escalation.

Analysis of Predictive Validity

In looking through the literature that uses these indicators, the majority of it is concerned with the problem of war and the question of whether "high-allocating" nations are more prone to war than those allocating at more normal levels. Although the indicators considered here do not have high intercorrelations, it remains to be seen whether they produce the same results in the kind of analysis in which they are commonly used.

In order to conduct these exploratory tests, each state in each year was categorized as an "average" (including "low" allocations) or "high" al-locator, in the same manner as described in our earlier analysis. Two-by-two contingency tables were constructed with the allocation level as the predictor variable,[12] and the war/no war outcome of militarized disputes (described above) as the outcome variable. The analyses were performed for: (1) the initiator of the dispute (that nation committing the first act involving military force) and (2) the target of the dispute (the victim of the first act). In addition, a third analysis used the ratio of the allocation levels of the initiator and the

---

12. Military allocation values in this analysis are taken from the year before the militarized dispute, in order to insure that the resources allocated are actually available at the time of the confrontation and to eliminate any distortions from allocations that were reactive to the dispute.

target as the predictor variable. In that test, the two categories were "equality" $(.67A < B < 1.5A)$ and "inequality" $(B < .67A$ or $B > 1.5A)$. A summary of all the results is given in table 8.

In considering the results, the stratified epochs approach is the only one that strongly and consistently associates high allocations with disputes that escalate to war; the chi-square and tau-beta values are significant at .01 under all three testing conditions. The tau-betas for the GNP method are significant in two instances, but at quite low levels.

The remaining three indicators turn in a poor performance in predicting the onset of war. One reason the system percentage method fared so poorly was its inability to reflect large concurrent increases in military allocations. The system percentage indicator remains unchanged if all or most nations in the major power subsystem increase their allocations prior to a war; in fact, the indicator is capable only of reflecting differences in the growth rates of allocations and not the growth itself. One can apply the same line of reasoning to the government budget indicator. As military expenditures increase, so usually do government budgets, and although the indicator will reflect some of the military increase, it still dampens the full impact.

That the personnel indicator is not strongly associated with war is not surprising, as this indicator showed the least variation of all those considered, and one might suspect that drastic changes in troop levels occur after, rather than before, the war has begun (Mullins 1975). In addition, by the Franco-Prussian War of 1870, industrial power was becoming a more important factor in warfare than the number of men that could be put on the field of battle.

Considering our analysis here, it is not surprising that past research has produced a diversity of findings on the effects of high military allocations on conflict. A large portion of this disparity apparently can be traced to the different indicators employed by various scholars. Only the stratified epochs approach performs well in this analysis of predictive validity. The GNP method

TABLE 8. Comparative Performance of Military Allocation Indicators in Predicting Escalation to War

	Initiator		Target		Ratio	
Indicator	χ^2	Tβ	χ^2	Tβ	χ^2	Tβ
1. System percentage	0.00	.01	0.01	.01	3.63	$-.20**$
2. Stratified epochs	8.33**	.31**	9.78**	.33**	9.00**	.32**
3. Budget	0.10	$-.04$	0.08	.03	0.43	.09
4. GNP	1.29	.13**	4.44*	.23**	0.03	.02
5. Personnel	0.28	.06	0.33	.06	4.33*	$-.22**$

*significant at .05
**significant at .01

shows some promise that might be fulfilled if the *ad hoc* procedure used here to define "high allocation" were refined to provide a more sensitive measure. Nevertheless, we must once again remind the reader against interpreting these findings too rigidly. High military allocations may have little relationship with conflict escalation and consequently the indicators with approximately zero correlations could be the most valid. Although we believe otherwise, a greater knowledge of allocation and conflict is necessary before a more definitive interpretation can be made.

Conclusions

At the outset of this study, we identified the major approaches in conflict research for measuring military allocations. Our goal was to test the validity of those indicators and make a series of generalizations regarding their use.

One conclusion is that one should proceed cautiously in choosing a military allocation indicator; that choice is likely to strongly affect the strength of the relationships discovered. Researchers might do well to test their hypotheses using more than one indicator of military allocations in order to determine whether the results are mere artifacts of the indicator's construction. Indeed, it might be desirable to use multiple indicators to form a composite score. Different indicators are not likely to be affected by the same measurement error, and in a composite score, the errors could cancel each other out (Manheim and Rich 1981). Furthermore, scholars must be sensitive to changes over time in the average allocation. What is high allocation in one period may be well below the norm in a later period as nations grow accustomed to increasing levels of military allocation.

Finally, one must be sensitive to the possibility that his or her allocation indicator is inappropriate for a particular historical epoch or set of countries. Even within our limited domain (major powers since 1860), we noted problems with using certain indicators for some time periods and different economic systems. We would expect these difficulties to be at least as prevalent when the spatial-temporal domain is expanded.

In the way of specific conclusions, we cannot give our unqualified endorsement to any of the indicators. Despite using the same spatial-temporal domain and, in many cases, the same data in indicator construction, the convergence among the indicators was rather poor. Nevertheless, two indicators appear to be superior to the others. The stratified epochs approach has strong face validity, scoring well on the criteria of data availability, ability to detect system change, and applicability over a wide spatial-temporal domain. It also yielded positive results when tested for discriminant and predictive validity, although the relationships in the latter are not terribly strong. Its drawbacks, however, were that it was virtually unrelated to its peers as indicated by the low correlations in the analysis of convergent validity. We believe that this approach might be best used in longitudinal studies of allocations by countries that collectively exhibit a variety of economic systems.

The GNP method consistently performed better than the other indicators in the convergent validity analyses and was better than average with respect to discriminant and predictive validity. Although on a relative basis this indicator did well, on an absolute scale, the case for its validity was not overly compelling. The GNP method appeared to have severe problems with the face validity criteria. Data availability and accuracy seem to be serious problems in the years before World War II, and at any point in time with respect to non-capitalist states. It appears the GNP method might be useful in a study that has a narrow spatial-temporal domain, encompassing only capitalist countries in the last forty years (for example, a study on burden sharing in NATO).

The remaining three indicators generally scored low on almost all the dimensions of validity. The system percentage method intuitively has some attractive attributes, but its empirical performance usually rated it poorly compared to the other indicators. The government budget indicator suffers from the same spatial-temporal limits as the GNP indicator and did not yield strong empirical results in any phase of the investigation. Finally, the military personnel method seems inappropriate for modern society. Its ignorance of the technological features of conflict is born out by its poor performance in the empirical analyses. It may be that this indicator has some value for the early nineteenth century and before, or for underdeveloped countries, but because of the limited domain of our venture we can only suggest this possibility.

Overall, we suggest that scholars be cautious in their choice of military allocation indicators, cognizant of the scope and theoretical approach of the study in that choice. We would, however, hope that researchers will not be content to utilize only the indicators outlined here. The need for a better measure of military allocations seems to outweigh the convenience associated with acceptance of current methods.

3
Systemic Attributes

The Measurement of System Structure

James Lee Ray

One of the distinctive features of the Correlates of War Project has been its emphasis on the importance of system structure in accounting for international war. Many researchers have looked to national attributes, dyadic relationships, and internation interactions as possible explanatory variables, but few have looked to the characteristics of the international system itself. My purpose in this essay is to put the idea of system structure into theoretical context, examine the diverse ways in which it may be understood, and then spell out some of the issues and strategies involved in measuring it. In doing so, I hope to provide colleagues working in the field of global politics with a more integrated overview of system structure as we see it and a clearer understanding of the relationship among some of the separate studies that have emerged from the Project or are now under way.

Before turning to a discussion of the theoretical usefulness and promise of the concept, a brief definitional aside would seem to be in order. We can think of few words that are so casually and imprecisely used as *system* and *structure;* this semantic permissiveness has even gone so far as to see them used interchangeably. Thus any pattern, order, or regularity—real or imagined—in the referent world may well be graced with the label "system" or "structure." We mean, of course, to use them rather more carefully here. By *system,* we mean an aggregation of social entities that share a common fate (Campbell 1958), or are sufficiently interdependent to have the actions of some consistently affect the behavior and fate of the rest. In addition, our definition of system is clearly distinct from those that focus on "systems of action" and thus fail to specify which social entities constitute the system (Singer 1971). By the *structure* of the system we mean the way in which relationships are arranged, but this definition leaves unclear the distinction between two kinds of relationships, that is, those based on *comparisons*

Reprinted from *Correlates of War II: Testing Some Realpolitik Models.* J. David Singer, Editor. Copyright © 1980 by The Free Press, a Division of Macmillan, Inc. (pp. 36–54). Reprinted by permission of the publisher.

between and among states or other entities and those based on *links* or *bonds* between them. For example, if we refer to the concentration of military-industrial capability in the international system, we are focusing on a structural attribute based on comparisons of the attributes of states. However, if we focus on the bipolarity of the system, we are then discussing a structural attribute that arises out of the links and bonds among states. It should also be pointed out that these two kinds of structural attributes are related in the sense that variation in one may produce variation in the other. For example, a concentration of military-industrial capability in the hands of two dominant states in the system may well lead to its bipolarization.

Use of Structural Concepts

It has long been the custom of scholars who analyze social systems to attach great importance to their structure. From Aristotle through Marx and beyond, social thinkers have assumed and/or theorized that the structure of social systems has an important impact on the behavior of constituent units, as well as on the fate of the system as a whole. For example, Marx argued that a focus on the structural links between those who own the means of production and those who engage in that production is crucial to the understanding of any society. Contemporary social scientists generally find this somewhat incomplete and suggest that structural patterns based on the distribution of power, prestige, income, education, religious beliefs, and ethnic group membership must also be taken into account (Barber 1968). Disagreement about the relative importance of various structural attributes has persisted, but most observers have agreed on the explanatory importance of social structure.

Coincident with, and perhaps as a consequence of, the system analysis focus that has emerged in the study of international politics, there has been an interest in system structure that borrows from the conceptual repertoire of sociologists. Whereas scholars of international politics have long been concerned with such concepts as polarity and the "balance of power," emphasis on such concepts as status inconsistency, structural isomorphism, and vertical mobility is, for the most part, a recent trend and one that we would like to encourage.

This is so, first, because we think that such variables will be crucial to a scientific understanding of war. For example, we believe that knowledge about the impact of structural variables should allow scholars to make theoretically interesting and data-based decisions about "cut points" that delineate time periods during which relationships and processes may differ. We have, for example, rather consistently found relationships that exist between variables in the nineteenth century but that disappear, or change direction, when we shift our focus to the twentieth century. This is interesting, but also disturbing. Until we can identify the factors that account for these intercentury differences, it will be difficult to predict how far into the future present relationships will persist. Structural variables seem to us to be prime candidates for a key role in the explanations of changes in relationships. Concentrating on such variables should help us to explain those changes that we discover empirically and to predict and discover other changes about which we are still ignorant.

Furthermore, we believe that system structural variables will be important as explanatory and/or control variables in system level models of conflict and war and that variation in a single nation's role or location within the system structure might have a significant impact on its war proneness. And even though we are particularly concerned with questions concerning international war, we should also point out that structural variables may have an important impact on other interesting phenomena in international politics. For example, the relationship between bipolarity and levels of, and rates of change in, defense budgets might be explored more fully; as might the effect of a nation's role in alliance structures on its rate of industrialization (Bueno de Mesquita 1973). One might also hypothesize that votes in the United Nations are affected by a state's place in the system structure or that levels of interaction between and among states will be a function of various structural factors (Galtung 1964 and 1966; Gleditsch 1967).

Types of Structural Attributes

In this section, we will categorize structural attributes of the international system, to permit the full range of these to be appreciated and also to facilitate discussion of the measurement problems as presented in the next section. We have already mentioned one distinction that we find useful, that is, the distinction between structural attributes based on comparisons among states and those based on linkages and bonds. Both kinds of structural variables order states (or, of course, other social entities) either vertically or horizontally.

To elaborate, comparison of the resources of states allows one to order them vertically, and these rank orders can be analyzed to determine the extent to which power, or military-industrial capability, is concentrated in the system. One might want to develop a composite index of capability in the manner of Singer, Bremer, and Stuckey (1972), or focus on the distribution of the various resources one at a time. Linkage-based variables, such as those based on the exchange of diplomatic missions (Alger and Brams 1967; Singer and Small 1966a; Small and Singer 1973), also order states vertically. By now it is a rather well-established procedure to treat the number of states that establish diplomatic missions in the measured state's capital city as an indicator of that state's diplomatic importance (Wallace 1973b; East 1972). Once these diplomatic importance scores have been assigned, their effect on individual states can be explored, and the impact of the distribution of diplomatic importance on the system can be analyzed (Ray 1974a, 1974b). States are also ordered vertically by the number of alliance bonds they form (Singer and Small 1966a; Small and Singer 1969) and by the number of intergovernmental organization (IGO) memberships they maintain (Wallace and Singer 1970). Both these variables also have their system level counterparts, of course, that focus on the number of alliance bonds in the system on the one hand (Singer and Small 1968), and the number of IGO memberships in the system, on the other.

As for structural variables that order states horizontally, one type is generated by comparing the distribution of states across categories of nominal variables. For example, one structural variable would focus on the percentages of states that fall into different categories of types of regime, such as personalist, centralist, and polyarchist (Wilkenfeld 1968). Linkages such as alliance bonds, diplomatic bonds, and common IGO memberships also order states horizontally into clusters. The form, number, and relationships between and among these clusters can be analyzed in turn to determine the extent to which the system is polarized, which opens the way to empirical analysis of the questions concerning the relative stability of multipolar versus bipolar patterns (Deutsch and Singer 1964; Rosecrance 1966; Waltz 1967).

In short, comparison-based and linkage-based interunit relationships order those units vertically and horizontally. Additional structural characteristics of the system arise as a result of differences among these relationships at one point in time or in their changes over time. For example, differences in the distribution of military-industrial capability and diplomatic importance lead to status inconsistency, both on the system and the national level. Comparisons of the clusters that emerge from trading ties, on the one hand, and the formation of alliances, on the other, can also yield interesting information about the system. If these clusters are isomorphic, then the structural order is clear, and it should be relatively predictable which states will be on whose side in the various conflicts that arise in the system. If, contrariwise, the clusters are quite different, one might reason that the system members are highly cross-pressured, that the structural order in the system is unclear, and that the alignments among states on different issues will be relatively unpredictable. Changes in interstate relationships over time, whether comparison-based or linkage-based, also have implications for the structural clarity of the system. Generally speaking, rapid changes in those structural variables that rank order states will indicate that those states are exhibiting rapid vertical mobility; they may be moving up or down the capability or the diplomatic importance dimensions, for example. Similarly, rapid changes in those structural variables that order states horizontally into categories or clusters would indicate substantial lateral mobility. States might be changing alliance partners with unusual frequency or breaking and forming diplomatic bonds in unusually large numbers, again making for reduced predictability.

A final important set of variables is based on comparisons of those concepts that order states vertically (i.e., stratify them) and those that order them horizontally into clusters. Galtung (1966) has tested the hypothesis, for a variety of post–World War II spatial-temporal domains, that a variety of interstate relationships will depend on the ranking of those involved. In an egalitarian system, states of various ranks would be equally likely to interact with, and establish bonds with, each other. In a feudal, or oligopolistic, system, however, top dogs would interact with each other more frequently than those with lower ranks, and those lower-ranked states would interact with each other less than they would with the top dogs. Galtung found that the system was more "feudal" than egalitarian for the time period he analyzed. This might well be expected, but it would be interesting to know, if the post–World War II system is more feudal than the prewar system, how much variation there is between the feudal and the egalitarian extremes and what effect this variation has on the stability or the war proneness of the system. The answers to all of these questions would begin with an analysis and comparison of the strata and the clusters of the international system.

Measuring Structural Attributes

Let us focus first on that class of structural variables that order states vertically into strata. The first of these that comes to mind would probably be "power," or military-industrial capability. Not much need be said here about the measurement problems involved with this variable, as we have already discussed it elsewhere (Ray and Singer 1973). Suffice it to say that the project has based its measure of military-industrial capability on six indicators: (1) total population, (2) urban population, (3) iron and steel production, (4) fuel consumption, (5) military personnel, and (6) military expenditures. We felt that these tap three important dimensions of the concept of "power," namely, the demographic, industrial, and military dimensions. We have experimented with giving more weight to some of these indicators and less to others, as well as with weighting some of them differently for different time periods, and this remains a continuing concern of the Correlates of War Project.

The measurement of the concept of "diplomatic importance" has involved the project in a process that has been enlightening to us as well as others but—we hope—that has now run its course. Here we will briefly describe this process to help foster an understanding of the measure as it now stands. Originally, it was proposed (Singer and Small 1966a) that the number of states that establish diplomatic missions in a given state's capital would serve as a good indicator of that state's diplomatic importance. Most governments, it is noted, do not establish diplomatic missions in the capital cities of every other state in the system. In fact, in the past 155 years, the capital city of the average state has been the site of missions from only 45 percent of the other states in the system. This less than universal exchange is an indication that states make recurrent choices among their peers in the system when they establish missions, depending, inter alia, upon the latters' diplomatic importance to the sending state. Therefore, one can reason that the more missions a state has in its capital, the larger the number of states that consider it to be sufficiently important to warrant the establishment of a diplomatic mission.

When this measure was originally presented, the number of missions received was weighted in various ways. For example, for each ambassador, minister, or chargé d'affaires accredited to a given capital, the host state received three, two, and one points, respectively. In short, a state was given more credit for receiving representatives of higher rank. However, this refinement was later discarded, not only because in recent years nearly all missions are headed by ambassadors, but also because the extra information had virtually no effect on the rankings of the states. Another refinement of the measurement in the first article that was abandoned in the second article reflected the importance of nations sending the particular missions. A state received an increment to its importance score based on the number of missions in the capital of the state that sent the mission. This procedure also failed to make an empirically important difference in the measure.

One more problem concerning the data on diplomatic missions deserves brief mention. When the data set was first compiled, about 10 percent of the diplomatic bonds were reported as asymmetrical. That is, the data sources indicated that, in some instances, state A had sent a mission to state B but that B had not reciprocated. Later, we concluded that it would be more accurate to assume that all diplomatic bonds were symmetrical, even if no official record of the second mission could be found. Most recently, however, the evidence convinces us that a few diplomatic bonds were indeed asymmetrical and that most of them have now been identified. Therefore, the data set now in use includes asymmetrical bonds, and the diplomatic scores reflect such asymmetries.

As suggested earlier, an actor experiences status inconsistency when its score on one dimension (such as military strength) is high and its status or rank on another (such as diplomatic importance) is low. These scores may rest on ordinal or interval scales, each with some possible dangers. For example, Wallace (1973b) shows that an indicator of status inconsistency that rests on two interval scales will be inflated if one of the distributions is positively skewed and the other is negatively skewed. Given this problem, plus the reasonable assumption that decision makers are often more attentive to mere differences in rank than to the interval distances between ranks, one may use the former alone to tap this phenomenon. Thus, he measures status inconsistency at the system level by adding the differences between each of the states' ranks on strength and importance, and then normalizes this sum by dividing it by $n^2 + n$, where n is the number of states in the system, to control for variation due to fluctuation in system size. Ray (1974a, 1974b) discusses a possible modification of this index on the assumption that differences between higher ranks are likely to be more important than differences between lower rank positions. For example, a state that ranks first on a military-industrial dimension and fifth on a diplomatic importance dimension is likely to perceive itself (and be perceived) as more status inconsistent than a state whose rank scores on those same dimensions are sixteen and twenty, respectively. Ray incorporates this idea into his index of status inconsistency by basing the index on the differences between the squares of reverse rank scores. (Assigning reverse rank scores involves giving the highest score to the state that scores highest on the ranking criterion. For example, if there are ten states in the system, and state A has the highest score, its normal rank score would be one, but its reverse rank score would be ten.)

A comparison of stratification patterns by different criteria does not necessarily confine us to the concept of status inconsistency. One might, for example, be interested in the more general concept of structural clarity as it pertains to the classical balance of power model. This implies that states must make rather fine judgments with regard to the relative power of all the states in the system, and, if these judgments are mistaken, the balance may be lost. One could reasonably hypothesize, therefore, that such judgments would be more difficult if states are ranked differently on the several dimensions of military-industrial capability. That is, if a state has the largest population, and the largest industrial capacity, and the largest military establishment in the system, there is not much doubt that this state is the most powerful in the system. On the other hand, if a state has the largest population, but only the fifth largest industrial capacity and the tenth largest military establishment, it might very well be difficult to calculate just how powerful this state is. If we carry this problem to the system level and imagine that most of the states in the system rank differently on the different power dimensions, it makes sense to argue that this lack of structural clarity might lead to confusion in the system and, hence, war. It would, of course, make equal sense to argue that such a situation would lead to uncertainty about the outcome of any war and, therefore, reluctance by decision makers to commit their states to war.

How would one measure this aspect of structural clarity? What is needed is a measure of rank order correlation that is applicable to more than two rank orders, of which Kendall's W (Hays 1963, 657) is a useful, if not widely known, example. One could rank order the states at, say, five-year intervals according to the various indicators of military-industrial capability, calculate

Kendall's W as an index of the similarity of these rank orderings, and then analyze the relationship between these scores and the war proneness of the system.

Clusters and Poles

The most prominent structural concepts that are used to order states horizontally are clustering and polarization. No measurement problem has evoked more disagreement and a wider variety of approaches among those associated with the Correlates of War Project than that involving the detection of clusters, and the degree of polarization in the international system. Although this indicates the difficulty of the task, the greater difficulty seems to be in choosing among the many possible approaches.

Two basic choices are to be made. First, one must decide what kinds of bonds—and what kinds of information about these bonds—will be analyzed to establish the strength of the relationships between pairs of nations. This information will typically be recorded in a nation-by-nation matrix, at which time one must decide which of the various matrix decomposition techniques will be used.

Composing the Matrix

With regard to the first of these choices, there are several ways in which the clustering of nations can be manifested. Nations might reveal commitments to one another, or at least agreement and cooperation on issues in the international political system, by their voting patterns in the League of Nations or the United Nations (Alker and Russett 1965) or by the number of common IGO memberships they maintain (Wallace and Singer 1970). The degree to which nations trade with each other might also be taken as an indication of the strength of bonds among them, as might the exchange of diplomatic missions or the signing of formal alliance agreements.

Which of these dimensions is most relevant to the measurement of the extent to which the nations in the international system are clustered or polarized? If one is particularly concerned with questions about the war proneness of the international system, Bueno de Mesquita (1975) argues that military alliances are the most relevant indicator. There is a serious problem with concentrating on this indicator alone, however, as many states—including many highly important ones—go along for years without belonging to any alliances. One solution to this problem might be to concentrate on bonds established by the exchange of diplomatic missions, as this indicator is sensitive enough to include interactions among all the states in the system. However, it can be argued that an exchange of diplomatic missions involves a commitment between states of such a minor nature that focusing on such exchanges alone will mask clustering patterns. Two groups of states might, for example, be quite antagonistic toward one another (and this might be revealed in the structure of alliance bonds) but still maintain a large number of diplomatic bonds between them. In short, the trouble with focusing on alliance bonds as an indicator of clustering in the system is that too many states are excluded from view. But the trouble with focusing on diplomatic bonds is that the presence of such bonds does not indicate any real commitment between states (and therefore may exist between nations that belong to different clusters), and the absence of such bonds may indicate either substantial antagonism (states usually withdraw recognition from each other only as a result of substantial disagreement) or simple lack of interest and contact between the states involved. These two cases, of course, have quite different implications for the clustering structure of the system.

Ideally, then, for the purpose of detecting clusters in the international system, one should be able to differentiate between the absence of a link (be it a diplomatic bond or an alliance bond) that (1) is the result of antagonism and (2) is the result of mere indifference or lack of contact. One could move in this direction in the manner of Savage and Deutsch (1960), who interpreted the relative strength of trading bonds by comparing the actual amount of trade between nations with that which might be expected given the assumptions of their null model. This would be easier and more fruitful for diplomatic bonds than alliances, because alliances are relatively rare. Any null model of the probability of the formation of an alliance bond between two states would predict the absence of such a bond in the vast majority of cases, and the development of the model would not provide sufficient differentiation among pairs of nations to be worthwhile. However, in the case of diplomatic bonds, a null model might help distinguish, at least in a general way, between the absence of a bond caused by antagonism and that caused by indifference.

One might, for example, reason that the probability of any given pair of nations exchanging diplomatic missions is a function, first, of the geographic distance between them. Bolivia and Paraguay, barring some political conflict between them, will probably exchange diplomatic missions; Bolivia and Afghanistan probably will not. Also, the probability that a given pair of states will exchange diplomatic missions is a function of their joint diplomatic importance in the system as a whole.

Perhaps other factors that might predict an exchange of diplomatic missions between a pair of states could be included in this null model. In any case, once such a model were fully developed, one could use, for example, discriminant analysis to specify whether or not a given dyad would be expected to exchange missions. This would, finally, allow one to distinguish between pairs of states that fail to exchange missions because of a lack of contact and those that, under "normal" conditions, would be expected to exchange missions.

This would be one way to deal with the general problem of what kind of information concerning the strength of internation bonds should be included in the nation-by-nation matrix to be analyzed. Another way to deal with the same problem focuses on available information regarding the different types of diplomatic bonds that states form. For example, states may exchange officials of such lowly status as "trade agents" or "vice-consuls," or they may exchange minister plenipotentiaries or full ambassadors. Similarly, alliance bonds may vary in strength, according to the strength of the commitments made by signatories, and differentiate among defense pacts, neutrality or nonaggression pacts, and ententes.

This may be the sort of information that should be included in any effort to detect clusters of states in the international system, because it would help to differentiate degrees of commitment between states, but again there are problems. As noted, states are much more likely to exchange ambassadors now (as opposed to officials of lower rank), meaning that the ranks of officials that head diplomatic missions are not comparable over time. Similarly, with regard to alliances, Wallace (1973a) argues that differences between defense pacts, neutrality pacts, and ententes are not consistent enough across time to allow one to rank them as to the degree of commitment they entail.

It may be possible to (1) satisfy the need for information about differing degrees of commitment among pairs of states and (2) meet the objections of those who insist that discriminating among types of alliance bonds and diplomatic bonds is unjustified. We could develop continuum of commitment between states that would rely only on the distinction between the presence and the absence of diplomatic and alliance bonds. Pairs of states would then fall into three categories: (1) those joined by both alliance and diplomatic bonds, (2) those joined by diplomatic bonds only, and (3) those joined by neither alliance nor diplomatic bonds. Another logically possible category would embrace states that belong to the same alliance while having no diplomatic missions in the others' capital, but this must be close to a null set. This procedure could be refined by relying on the null model referred to earlier. In effect, this would replace the third category above with two categories, of which both would contain states without alliance or diplomatic bonds. But our null model would allow us to differentiate between those pairs that do *not* have diplomatic bonds even though, given the geographic distance between them and their diplomatic importance, such bonds would be expected, and those pairs in which the absence of a bond *is* expected. The former pairs of states would be assumed to be farther apart in the clustering structure of the system than the latter pairs.

There are at least two ways to measure the strength of bonds between states that do not rely solely on the direct official links between them. First, it can be argued that the relationship between two states is reflected in the number of links necessary to establish contact between them. If states A and B are not directly linked to each other, but are both linked to state C, they have a second-order link between them. If A and B not only have no link to each other, but also no links to common third states, then they are separated by an even greater distance.

Second, the relationship between two states is reflected in the manner in which they relate to all other states in the system. The more alliance partners they share, for example, the stronger the bond between the two states may be. If one state in the pair has alliance partners not shared by the other, it is reasonable to assume that there is a corresponding weakening of the link between the two states. Here again, however, it is possible for reasonable men to disagree. Wallace (1973a) takes into account only those alliance partners shared by each of two states in determining the strength of bonds between them, but Bueno de Mesquita (1975) also takes into account that set of states that is allied to one, but not the other, of the measured pair of states, as well as those states with which neither of that pair is aligned. There are plausible reasons for ignoring this information, and they will be discussed in the following paragraphs.

Decomposing the Matrix

The choice of indicator, whether or not to discriminate among bonds of different strength, and what information to include concerning the relationship of the measured pair of states to others in the system are all decisions that must be made to compose the nation-by-nation matrix. Whatever choices are made, the matrix will contain coefficients pertaining to each pair of states and reflecting the strength of the bond between them. To that matrix can be applied a variety of cluster detection techniques, many of which have found at least one advocate among those involved with the Correlates of War Project. It is to these techniques that we now turn our attention.

There is little doubt that the simplest, most straightforward clustering technique available is McQuitty's typal analysis (1957). We will not describe the procedure here, except to say that it is simple enough that the analysis can be done easily and quickly by hand; no computer, or even a calculator, is necessary. In using this method as one step in his measure of polarization, Bueno de Mesquita defends it on the grounds that it is easy and inexpensive to compute and that it keeps between-cluster discriminations as large as possible.

The most damaging argument that can be made against typal analysis is that it is too simple. Why should we use it to maximize between-cluster discriminations if it does this by brute force and in a way that may possibly distort the data. In any event, McQuitty (1957), Smoker (1968), and Lankford (1974) have all found that typal analysis and factor analysis yield similar results, with the latter particularly interesting in this regard. Having used McQuitty's typal analysis, factor analysis, direct factor analysis, and multidimensional scaling to detect clusters in the same data matrix, Lankford concludes (1974, 303) that "the great similarity between factor analysis and McQuitty's method shows the latter is a good approximation of the most cohesive groups." He nevertheless concludes that factor analysis of the correlation matrix remains the most efficient method of cluster identification. Following that reasoning, Bremer (1972) uses factor analysis to detect clusters in formal alliance bonds from 1816 to 1965 "because of personal preference and experience and because of the potential analytical power of the method."

On the other hand, Wallace (1973a) explicitly rejects factor analysis as a method of cluster detection in his study of the relationship between polarization and international war. He has two basic reasons for doing this, the first of which is that factor analysis requires that the measure of the strength of internation bonds be at the ratio level. He does not believe that his measure, based on alliance bonds, meets this requirement. Second, he argues that factor analysis requires too many difficult decisions to be made before the final results are generated. "At several stages in its complex sequence of operations, a priori decisions must be made as to how the algorithm shall proceed. . . . The need to make such crucial theoretical decisions at the very outset weighs heavily against the procedure, given the underdeveloped state of our knowledge" (1973a, 585).

The first of these arguments, concerning the requirement of ratio level measures is, perhaps, overstated. Rummel (1970, 17) states that it is based on a misconception: "factor analysis can be meaningfully applied even to nominally scaled data of a yes-no, or presence-absence type, the lowest and least demanding rung of the measurement ladder." ("Direct" factor analysis would be particularly appropriate for the kind of matrix Rummel refers to here. See Wright and Evitts 1961; MacRae 1960.)

The second argument by Wallace against factor analysis is more important, and more damaging. Selection of the number of factors to be extracted and rotated is a complex matter, leaving the door open to arbitrary intervention by the investigator. Rummel (1970, 18) admits that the idea of arbitrariness in factor analysis has arisen largely from problems associated with rotating factors, that this sometimes involves "an intuitive or manual determination," and that therefore "rotations will then vary to a certain degree with the intuition of the investigator." As Wallace implies, our knowledge concerning matters of clustering in the international system is not well developed; this may be a good reason for avoiding factor analysis, assuming, of course, that a better alternative is available. His candidate is smallest space analysis (SSA), a multidimensional scaling procedure developed by Guttman (1968) and Lingoes (1965 and 1966). Wallace prefers this procedure because it only demands ordinal level measurement and because the solutions it generates depend on fewer intermediate assumptions and decisions than those provided by factor analysis. Finally, the SSA solutions are usually less complex, involving only two or three dimensions.

In criticism of SSA, we would make the following points. It is true that some intuitive, perhaps arbitrary, choices must be made in the course of factor analysis. However, SSA does not deliver us entirely from this problem. The selection of the "appropriate" number of dimensions to be generated, for example, is not automatic. Shepard (1972, 9–10), a pioneer in the development of "nonmetric," multidimensional scaling, suggests that the decision should be guided by whether or not the resulting representations generated by the algorithm are "interpretable and visualizeable." He further suggests that, with the appropriate number of dimensions, the departure from monotonicity should not be "too large." None of these are particularly operational or robust criteria.

Second, although SSA does allow one to plot states visually in *n*-dimensional space, it does not lead to clear differentiation of clusters. It is often difficult to decide, just by looking at the location of a state in space, which cluster it belongs to, and which other states belong in that same cluster. Typal analysis allows these decisions to be made easily, perhaps too easily. Mihalka (1974) uses Johnson's (1967) hierarchical clustering algorithm to approach this problem but admits that, even with this additional tool, the clusters are sometimes not very distinct.

It is also interesting to note that Lankford (1974, 303), comparing five different cluster detection techniques, found that the multidimensional scaling method did not do well, producing clusters dissimilar to those produced by the other four. However, he used the "classical" or "metric" approach to multidimensional scaling developed by Torgerson (1958) rather than the nonmetric variety of which SSA is an example (Shepard 1972).

Bueno de Mesquita criticizes Wallace's use of SSA on the grounds that this technique requires an indicator of distance between states; Wallace's index of distance is only sensitive to the number of common alliance partners that both states share, whereas the former utilizes a coefficient of similarity that also includes information about those states with which only one, or neither, of the measured pair of states is aligned. Wallace claims that the exclusion of this latter information is a virtue of his index, differentiating it from similarity measures, but they both seem to agree that SSA requires coefficients that can be interpreted as measures of distance, not similarity. If this were true, and if this meant that Wallace were forced by his choice of technique to ignore the information that Bueno de Mesquita is able to incorporate into his measure of polarity, then this would be an unfortunate handicap for Wallace. However, Lingoes (1972, 53) himself says of SSA that "any matrix of real numbers may be analyzed by this technique provided that the formal requirements are met . . . and the substantive requirement that the values make sense as measures of *similarity* or *dissimilarity*" (italics added). Therefore, it is probably unfortunate that Wallace does not include the information used by Bueno de Mesquita, but it does not appear that his choice of the SSA algorithm required this.

None of the clustering techniques used by those associated with the Correlates of War Project has established itself as clearly superior. It seems to us that this will not happen until there is substantial progress on three related, but distinguishable fronts. First, the different methods will have to be applied to the same referent world matrices, as opposed to matrices of different coefficients pertaining to the same states, and the intuitive plausibility of the different results then compared. Second, ideal, simplified matrices, with relatively clear structures, should be contrived and then subjected to the different clustering techniques to see which produces the most sensible interpretation of these clear structures. (The factor analytic technique has been investigated in this way by applying it to data concerning cups of coffee; see Cattell and Sullivan 1962.) Finally, the results of the different measures should be subjected to "criterion validation." "If an indicator of a variable proves to be related to measures of other variables in predicted ways, our confidence in its validity increases. The greater number of such 'tests' an indictor passes . . . , the greater its criterion validity" (Gurr 1972, 47). In short, the different measures of clustering and polarity must be incorporated into models addressed to international war to see which relates most consistently, in the hypothesized way, to the outcome variable.

Measuring Changes Over Time

All the variables we have discussed, of course, change over time, and all these changes can be monitored for direction and magnitude. Perhaps the most prominent of the variables that are generated in this fashion are vertical mobility and lateral mobility, both discussed earlier. Measurement of vertical mobility has been discussed carefully by Wallace (1973a). A system-level measure of vertical mobility, as well as a measure of changes in the concentration of military-industrial capability, are presented by Singer, Bremer, and Stuckey (1972), and the measurement problems associated with these concepts seem relatively simple.

Measurement of lateral mobility, however, may not be so simple. Generally speaking, we would want an index of lateral mobility to reflect the extent to which a state is changing its place in the structure of the system by making or breaking, for example, diplomatic bonds, alliance bonds, or bonds in the form of common IGO memberships. One way to do this is simply to count the number of such bonds that are made or broken. But this procedure is obviously less than ideal, because it ignores the fact that some bonds are much more important than others in their implications for the lateral mobility of a state. If State A forms an alliance bond with a state that is already aligned with most of State A's allies, this does not indicate much lateral mobility on the part of State A. But, if A forms an alliance with a state in an entirely different cluster, this does indicate substantial lateral mobility on the part of A, even though the simple number of bonds formed is the same as in the previous case. Obviously, what is needed here is some system of weighting the bonds that are made or broken according to some criterion that would reflect the relative importance of these bonds.

This, of course, is exactly what a clustering technique will provide. If SSA were used, states could be placed in two-dimensional space, and comparing each state's location in that space at two points in time would provide an indication of its lateral mobility. Thus, if a state forms an alliance bond with another that is already aligned with its allies, this will not greatly affect its location in space, and the lateral mobility index will be appropriately low. Conversely, if that same state forms a bond with another that is clearly in a different cluster, this will have an impact on its location in the SSA-defined space, and the lateral mobility index that is sensitive to this will be high.

However, it should be clear that a state could receive a high lateral mobility score without breaking or making bonds of any kind or having other states break or make bonds with it. This is because a state's location in space as defined by a technique such as SSA is a function of what the other states in the system do. If those states break and make a sufficient number of bonds with each other, even if none of these involve the state whose lateral mobility we are measuring, this may result in a substantial change in the location of that state in the SSA space and, therefore, a large lateral mobility index score. Do we want an individual state to receive such a score when it has not made or broken any interstate bonds itself? Perhaps it will be necessary to distinguish between active lateral mobility brought about by the actions of the state itself (or at least by actions in which it was directly involved) and passive lateral mobility brought about by the actions of other states in the system.

Conclusion

Scholars interested in the operation of social systems have long been convinced that the structure of those systems must play a key role in explanatory models. The field of international politics has recently been marked by an increased appreciation of this notion. In this essay we have defined several categories of variables that focus on structural characteristics of the international system, as well as the roles and the relationships of states and other entities within that system's structure. Our purpose was to clarify distinctions among these variables and to discuss briefly some of the research possibilities they present.

We have also discussed some of the measurement problems posed by research that relies on these variables. The Correlates of War Project has generated the data on which several measures of structural characteristics of the international system can be based, and researchers associated with the project have also devised and experimented with a number of indices of different structural variables. We have analyzed here the rationale behind some of the coding procedures used to generate various data sets, as well as the design of different indices. Although this discussion revealed that the Project's approach to these problems has not always been monolithic, we hope, nevertheless, that it provides a basis for a clearer understanding of the relationship among some of the separate studies that have emerged from the project.

If this discourse has been at least partially successful, its readers are now more aware of the structural attributes of the international system that may be important to an understanding of international politics. If it inspires an inclination to investigate the impact of these variables, so much the better. In any case, many of the measurement problems involving structural variables have only been touched on here, and none were resolved entirely. They will continue to be a major concern to those involved with the Correlates of War Project and, we hope, an expanding number of interested scholars.

Measuring the Concentration of Power in the International System

James Lee Ray and J. David Singer

While notions of equality and distributive justice are dear to the hearts of most social scientists, the hard fact of life is that almost nothing is equally distributed. Whether the valued object is something as tangible as income, land, or votes, or so elusive a thing as status or influence, some individuals usually have more than others. The same holds for groups, be they social classes, labor unions, political parties, or nations; in any social system, the chances are slim that each will possess the same fraction or share of valued objects. Nor is the problem restricted to the distribution of "goods." Such neutral distributions as age or hair color may be of concern, as might the distribution of such "bads" as the tax burden or the incidence of crime. This ubiquitous phenomenon is, furthermore, not merely a matter of idle curiosity or a simple question of social description. To the contrary, many theoretical arguments rest heavily on the predictive or explanatory power of a given set of distributions. From the primary group up through the international system, theoretical enlightenment often flows from an understanding of the pattern in which certain values or attributes are distributed among the component units.

Measuring such inequality in these varying contexts may seem, at first blush, to be a simple and straightforward matter. In a system having two component units, for example, we need merely measure the arithmetic difference or the ratio of their percentage shares in order to get an intuitively reasonable measure of the equality of a given distribution. A more difficult problem arises, however, when we try to quantify the inequality among more than two units. Even if the system at hand contains only three units, there are no longer such obvious ways to measure the inequality of a given distribution. Among three groups, for example, which of the following distribution patterns is most unequal: 70 percent, 20 percent, 10 percent; 70 percent, 30 percent, 0 percent; 70 percent, 15 percent, 15 percent? The answer is far from clear.

Reprinted from *Sociological Methods & Research* 1, no. 4 (May 1973); 403–37. © 1973 Sage Publications, Inc. Reprinted by permission of Sage Publications, Inc.

115

The purpose of this essay is to examine some earlier efforts to measure the inequality of distribution within several different substantive contexts, and to see how appropriate these different measures might be if they were applied to the distribution of "power potential" in the international system or any of its subsystems. In the course of our discussion, we will describe the fascinating, if sometimes laborious, journey we have taken through a maze of indices reflecting an impressive variety of related—but not identical—concepts. Our hope will be to share with readers some of the fascination, while saving them most of the labor involved in tracking these various indices back to their disparate origins. We shall conclude by describing an index we have found to be especially helpful if one is dealing with a system containing a relatively small, but variable number of units or categories.

There have been several illuminating discussions of measures of inequality, among which the one by Alker and Russett (1964) is perhaps most familiar to political scientists. Others of importance are Alker (1965), Hall and Tideman (1967), Nutter (1968), Horvath (1970), Silberman (1967), and Singer (1968a). But rather than summarize all of them here, we will introduce them in context as they become relevant to the issues at hand. We begin by briefly delineating some of the more important characteristics we expect to find in a useful measure of inequality or concentration.

We should admit, and indeed will even emphasize, that the criteria for selection of an index will vary as research purposes change. Generally speaking, however, we suggest that an index should have a range of zero to one; while not an essential requirement, such a range is readily accomplished in most cases, and it makes the measure easier to interpret, and index scores easier to compare. Second, its magnitude should *increase* if there is an upward redistribution of shares from any lower-ranked unit to any higher-ranked unit, and vice versa. Third, it should reflect the shares of *all* the units in the system and not be largely or entirely determined by the shares of only a few of the component members. Finally, it is critical that the measure react to changes in system size in a manner that is appropriate to one's theoretical concerns. Such "appropriateness" is a major preoccupation in this essay, and we focus first on that particular problem.

Sensitivity to System Size

Most of the indices we will discuss here satisfy the first three criteria mentioned above. However, several of them are inadequate (for our purposes) in their response to changes in system size, especially when N (referring to the number of component units, groups, or categories, regardless of how many subgroups or individuals are in each) is small. Some existing indices tend to increase in value when N increases, others decrease, and some are relatively insensitive to the size of the system, or, alternatively, to the number of categories used. Which of these relationships between an index of inequality and system size or category number is desirable? It turns out that there is no single answer to that question; rather, it depends very much on one's substantive concern. Consider the following examples.

If Nation *A* possesses 90 percent of the military aircraft within a three-nation subsystem, and the rest of the aircraft are distributed evenly between the other two, the inequality in the subsystem is certainly high. But if two or more nations entered the subsystem, and Nation *A* managed to increase production or imports enough to maintain its share at 90 percent, one might say the inequality within the subsystem is higher. That is, 90 percent of the hardware was originally "concentrated" in the hands of one-third of the actors (i.e., Nation *A*), while, later on, that 90 percent is concentrated in the hands of a mere 20 percent of the units. The percentage controlled by *A* has remained the same, as has the percentage controlled by the rest of the subsystem members. Despite this basic similarity, from one point of view it seems obvious that an increase in *N* has led to a greater inequality or concentration within the subsystem. If one accepts this point of view, then one would want an index of inequality that increases with *N*.

However, if one were interested in inequality of a different kind—e.g., industrial concentration—there are good reasons for wanting a different kind of index, even if one is dealing with exactly the same distributions. If an industry was formerly concentrated entirely in the hands of three firms, and two firms are added, the concentration of this industry has decreased, even if the largest firm manages to maintain its 90 percent share of the market, because the entire economic pie is now divided among five rather than three firms. This situation would suggest the need for an index that decreases when *N* increases.

Finally, there may be times when any kind of sensitivity to *N* will be inappropriate. Lieberson (1969), discussing a concept that is admittedly different from, but still related to, inequality—i.e., "religious diversity"—suggests such a case. Suppose we are comparing the diversity between two campus fraternities. Both fraternities have ten Jews and twenty Catholics, but the second fraternity also has one Protestant. Lieberson points out that a measure that increased with *N* (which in this case equals the number of categories) would give a significantly higher score to the second fraternity. This "radical difference" would be misleading, as would any significant difference that resulted from an index' sensitivity to the number of categories, Lieberson maintains, because the groups have nearly identical religious composition.

These examples make it clear that, depending on one's theoretical concerns and the particular concept at hand, one may want an inequality index that rises with N, falls when N rises, or that is not sensitive to changes in system size or category number. In a recent paper of ours (Singer, Bremer, and Stuckey 1972), one of the predictor variables in the model was the changing distribution of power potential among the major powers during the 1816–1965 period.[1] During that epoch, the size of the major power subset ranged between five and eight. In such a longitudinal analysis, where one of the goals was to ascertain the effect of changing concentration of power upon variations in the incidence of major power war, the concentration measure has to be comparable from one observation to the next, despite fluctuations in size. That led us into a literature search in pursuit of such a measure, and that pursuit—plus the difficulty we had in finding such a measure—led to the essay at hand.

Evaluating Some Previous Measures

While the idea of concentration or unequal distribution seems unambiguous, attempts to make it operational, verbally or mathematically, reflect a remarkably wide range of interpretations. On the other hand, the diversity is not nearly as great as the number of alternative indices might lead one to suspect. Many of the indices of inequality (as well as indices of a variety of related concepts) turn out, despite surface differences, to be functionally equivalent. One set of measures is based on the sum of squares, or ΣP_i^2 approach, and the other is based on deviations from a line of perfect equality. And in the conclusion we will show that even these two types of indices are translatable into equivalent terms.

Sum of Squares Indices

The first category contains measures known variously as indices of concentration, fractionalization, diversity, or heterogeneity. Perhaps the best known of these is the Herfindahl-Hirschman (HH) index of industrial concentration, which simply equals the sum of the squares of each unit's percentage share, or ΣP_i^2 (Herfindahl 1950). While this measure uses information about all the units in the system, its magnitude is heavily influenced by the scores of those with the largest shares of the market. That is, the squares of small percentages are very small indeed, and thus have a disproportionately modest impact on the final index score.

---

1. The power—or more accurately, power potential—index reflects three sets of dimensions, each of which taps two phenomena; military (personnel and expenditures); industrial (energy consumption and iron/steel production); and demographic (total population and urban population).

To illustrate, if the shares of the market (or other valued objects) are equally distributed in a five-unit system, HH = $(20\%)^2 + (20\%)^2 + (20\%)^2 + (20\%)^2 + (20\%)^2 = .20$. If ten new units are added to the system, and each controls 0.1 percent, leaving the original five with 19.8 percent each, that makes virtually no impression on HH, reducing it slightly to .196. This decrease in the index score occurs despite the fact that the addition of ten almost totally deprived units to the system—and the resulting predominant position of the original five units—has, at least from one point of view, substantially increased the inequality in the system.

However, we should remember that HH is a measure of a special kind of inequality (i.e., industrial concentration) and one can certainly argue, as we already have, that the addition of ten new firms is "deconcentrating" even if those firms only capture a very small share of the market. This kind of reasoning leads Hall and Tideman (1967) to argue that "a measure of concentration should be a decreasing function of N." The ten new firms in this example are "underprivileged" to a marked degree, but they still have succeeded in breaking into a market formerly dominated completely by five firms. The inequality added by the ten new firms exerts an upward pressure on HH, but that is more than offset by the increase in N—i.e., an increase in the number of firms that have managed to capture a share, no matter how small, of the market.

Such sensitivity to N may be appropriate when measuring industrial concentration, but its appropriateness is at least questionable when measuring the concentration of power potential in an international system. Consider these two simple systems:

I		II	
States	Percentage Shares	States	Percentage Shares
A	90	A	85
B	5	B	5
C	5	C	2.5
		D	2.5
		E	1
		F	1
		G	1
		H	1
		I	0.5
		J	0.5
HH = .82		HH = .73	

The HH index suggests that there is more inequality in system I than in system II. In some contexts, that judgment would be acceptable, but it should be noted that, in the first system, 90 percent of the power potential is in the hands of the upper third of the states, whereas in the second, 90 percent of the power potential is controlled by an even smaller minority—i.e., the upper fifth of the states.

The results in both examples are, of course, affected by the fact that HH does not have a range of zero to one. The lower limit of HH is $1/N$, which means that HH can approach zero only as N approaches infinity. When N is as small as three, or even ten, the lower limits of HH are .33 and .10, respectively. In the example immediately above, HH "starts out" from a higher level in system I than in II, and the final index score is higher in that case, even though (to repeat) 90 percent of the power potential in system II is concentrated in a smaller proportion of its component units.

A perusal of the literature reveals that there are several measures that are similar, or algebraically identical, to HH, even though some of them are not designed to measure industrial concentration, or even inequality, per se. The discussion that follows should make obvious the similarity of such concepts as inequality, concentration, fractionalization, ethnicity, diversity, and heterogeneity. Greenberg (1956), for example, presents a measure of linguistic diversity, which is basically the sum of the probabilities that two individuals randomly chosen from a population will belong to the same linguistic group.[2] If one group makes up 50 percent of the society, then the probability that any two individuals chosen from the total population will be chosen from that particular group is .50 × .50, or .25. If .25 is added to the probability of randomly choosing two individuals from each of the remaining groups (whose number and size are of consequence only when their probability value is being computed), the result is Greenberg's index.

But this index turns out to be identical to ΣP_i^2, where P_i in this case is the percentage share of the total population held by the ith group, rather than the percentage share of the market controlled by the ith firm. The linguistic diversity index is functionally and arithmetically equal to the Herfindahl-Hirschman index of industrial concentration.

Similar to both these measures is the Rae and Taylor (1970) index of fragmentation. Their formula is

$$1 - \frac{1}{N(N-1)} \Sigma f_i(f_i - 1),$$

---

2. Greenberg also presents a more complex measure that is modified to reflect the dissimilarity of the languages involved.

where f_i equals the number in the ith subgroup and N equals the number in the total group. A slight rearrangement of terms[3] reveals that this formula is equivalent to

$$1 - \sum \frac{(f_i)}{(N)} \frac{(f_i - 1)}{(N) - 1} .$$

It then becomes obvious that f_i/N is a term representing the proportion of the whole made up by the ith subgroup, and that $(f_i - 1)/(N - 1)$ is only a very slight modification of that term. In short, this measure is equivalent to—or, more precisely, the complement of—ΣP_i^2.

However, we should point out that, if one is measuring fragmentation of a comparatively small body, such as a committee or legislature, the second term in Rae and Taylor's equation will not be identical to the first term, and the index will deviate perceptibly from the simple ΣP_i^2. To illustrate, if there were 100 representatives in a legislative body, the contribution of a group of 25 to the fragmentation index score would be $25/100 \times 24/99$, or .0606, whereas if ΣP_i^2 were the index, that group's contribution to the score would be .0625. Such differences, when summed over several groups, can lead to a noticeable difference between the Rae and Taylor index and ΣP_i^2.

Furthermore, the small difference will make conceptual sense. If we reason that the measure should reflect the sum of probabilities that two individuals randomly chosen from the legislative body will belong to the same party, then the smallness of the body makes it strictly incorrect to calculate those probabilities by simply squaring f_i/N. Replacement of individuals drawn from a population, and/or an infinitely large population should not be assumed; therefore f_i/N should be multiplied by $(f_i - 1)/(N - 1)$ in order to obtain those probabilities.

Yet another index that is based on the ΣP_i^2 is the Michaely (1962) concentration index, which does not measure industrial concentration, but "tendencies toward geographic concentration in transactions" (Puchala 1970). It shows the extent to which an actor's transactions are widely distributed throughout the system (low score), focused on a small cluster of partners (high score), or shared with a single partner only (highest score). The index formula is

$$100 \ \sqrt{\Sigma (X_{sj}/X._j)^2} ,$$

where X_{sj} equals j's transactions with s, and $X._j$ equals the total transactions for j; $X_{sj}/X._j$ is a proportion, of course, and since it is squared, the similarity

---

3. Charles Taylor (1970) uses this formula to measure party concentration in legislatures.

of this measure to ΣP_i^2 is obvious. Taking the square root of the summed squares changes the range within which the index is most sensitive. We used this same technique in constructing the measure to be described below.

This list of measures based on ΣP_i^2 can be continued almost indefinitely. Another important one is Lieberson's (1969) index of population diversity, as are several that he discusses: the Bachi (1956) and Simpson (1949) indices of diversity, the Bell (1954) index of ecological segregation, and the Gibbs and Martin (1962) measure of diversification in an industry.

Finally we would like to mention a measure of industrial concentration that "owes its intellectual parentage to the Herfindahl Summary Index" (Horvath 1970), but which is sufficiently different to be worth considering if the ΣP_i^2 is not deemed satisfactory. Horvath's measure,

$$ CCI = x_i + \sum_{j=2}^{n} (x_j)^2[1 + (1 - x_j)], $$

where I equals 1, j equals 2, 3, 4, . . . ,n, n equals the number of firms in the industry, and x equals the decimal fraction of assets (or sales, employment, or profit) belonging to each individual firm. A detailed discussion of this measure would be out of place here, since for our purposes this measure shares the disadvantages of its intellectual parent, ΣP_i^2. Suffice it to say that this measure focuses upon—and therefore reflects—both *absolute* concentration (having to do with the smallness of the number of firms in the industry) and *relative* concentration (having to do with comparisons of the sizes of the firms in the industry, regardless of the number of firms that exist).[4]

Deviation from Equality Indices

Our second category contains perhaps the best known measures of inequality in economics and political science—the Gini index[5] and the Schutz coefficient. Both are based upon the deviation of a Lorenz curve from the "line of perfect equality." The rationale behind these measures is indeed intuitively appealing. If one constructs a graph (see fig. 1) indicating what percentage of

---

4. A good discussion of the measure can be found in Horvath's article. For those who want to compare "within subset" concentration to "between subset" concentration, see Hexter and Snow (1970). And for a discussion of the special problem of inferring the concentration of an industry from the observation of a few firms, see Silberman (1967) and Hart and Prais (1956).

5. Several indices similar to the Gini index have been used to measure "segregation." For example, see the "nonwhite section index" and the "nonwhite ghetto index" (Jahn et al. 1947), the Cowgills' (1951) index of segregation, and the "reproducibility index" (Jahn 1950). For a discussion of all these measures and their similarity to the Gini index and to each other, see Duncan and Duncan (1955) and Hornseth (1947).

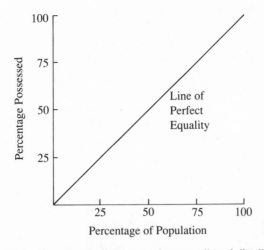

Fig. 1. Lorenz curve indicating perfect equality of distribution

a good is held by each percentage of a population, and if each 1 percent of the population possesses 1 percent of the good, the Lorenz curve will fall completely on the line of perfect equality, whose slope equals one. However, if the goods are not distributed evenly, the Lorenz curve will deviate from the line of perfect equality, as in examples in figures 2 and 3.

The Gini index and the Schutz coefficient measure these deviations in

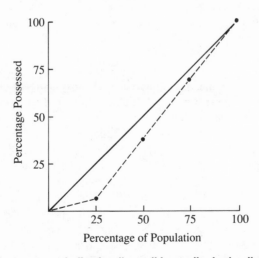

Fig. 2. Lorenz curve indicating "some" inequality in the distribution

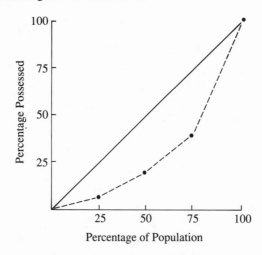

Fig. 3. Lorenz curve indicating "greater" inequality in the distribution

slightly different ways. According to Alker (1965), "the Gini index sums for each individual in the population, the difference between where he is on the Lorenz curve and where he would be expected to be in the case of democratic equality." The Schutz coefficient, on the other hand, sums "ratios of advantage" for each population percentile above *or* below the equal share point. It is based on the *slope* of the Lorenz curve, and in effect reflects how close the slope of the line below the equal share point is to zero, *or* how close the slope of the line *above* the equal share point is to infinity.

The Gini index appears to meet most of the basic requirements of a good measure of inequality. It utilizes the information available about all units, increases in response to exchanges of shares from lower- to higher-ranked units, and vice versa. However, if one is measuring the concentration of power potential in a rather small international subsystem, the Gini index has some properties that might not be desirable. Some of these are related to the fact that it has an upper limit of $1 - 1/N$, because it was originally designed for continuous, rather than discrete, distributions. Figure 4—in which A holds all and B holds none—illustrates this problem. Even though the inequality of this situation is complete, only half of the "area of inequality" (the triangle below and to the right of the line of perfect equality) lies between the line of perfect equality and the Lorenz curve. Therefore, the Gini index—reflecting the percentage of the total area of inequality falling between the Lorenz curve and the line of perfect equality—equals .50, the upper limit in the two-unit case. In the three-unit case, of course, the upper limit would be .67.

This fluctuation in the upper limit of the Gini index, much like that of the

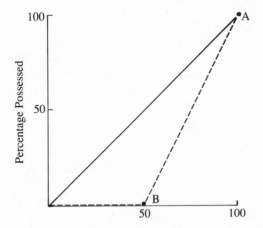

Gini index $= 2\Sigma(X_i - Y_i)\ \Delta X_i = 2[(.50 - 0).50] + (1.00 - 1.00).50 = .50$

Fig. 4. Lorenz curve with one unit (*A*) possessing all and the other unit (*B*) none

lower limit of HH, can have an undesirable effect on index scores. Consider, for example, an attempt to measure the concentration of power potential at two points in time in a small international subsystem.

t_0		t_1	
States	Percentage Shares	States	Percentage Shares
A	90	A	70
B	6	B	15
C	4	C	10
		D	3
		E	2
Gini = .57		Gini = .59	

If the Gini index—calculated according to Alker's (1965) formula for approximations in case of discrete distributions—is used as one's measure of concentration of power potential, the subsystem appears to be marked by greater concentration at the second point in time.

In fact, however, the Gini index is slightly higher in the second case, *not* because the subsystem more nearly approaches the condition of perfect concentration (with one state so "unequal" as to control 100 percent of the power potential) in the latter case, but because the upper limit of the index has been increased by the addition of two states to the subsystem at that point in time. Although Gini has probably not been used in exactly this way, it would not be obviously unreasonable to make such a use of it. Our point here is that if it is used for this (or similar) purposes, it will be very sensitive to differences in system size when N is small, and the user should be sure that this sensitivity is appropriate for his or her purposes.

Gini Versus HH

As we have seen above, Gini has an upper limit of $1 - 1/N$, while HH (and the various similar measures) has a lower limit of $1/N$. There is at least one other striking difference that should be mentioned here. Hall and Tideman (1967) claim that if "a [system] A has k times the number f units as [system] B, with $k > 1$, and the P_i's [percentage shares] in A are distributed such that corresponding to each P_i in B there are k units of size P_i/k, then the measure of concentration for A should be $1/k$ times the measure for B." The explanation is that "if each [unit] in a given [system] is divided into two [units] of equal size, the effect on a measure of concentration should be to reduce it by ½."

Although we agree that such a property may be desirable if industrial concentration is being measured, we are less certain that it is appropriate when measuring concentration of power potential, or other kinds of inequality. In any case, HH and the Gini index react very differently to situations such as that described above by Hall and Tideman. For example, consider the following two subsystems.

	I			II	
States	Percentage Shares		States		Percentage Shares
A	40		A		20
B	30		B		20
C	20		C		15
D	10		D		15
			E		10
			F		10
			G		5
			H		5
	HH = .30			HH = .15	
	Gini = .25			Gini = .25	

It is readily seen that HH for system II equals one-half the HH score for system I, which, according to Hall and Tideman, is expected and desirable. But the

Gini index remains unchanged, since in both system I and system II the upper 25 percent of the units control 40 percent of the goods, the next 25 percent control 30 percent of the goods, and so on. The "blindness" of the Gini index to the differences in these two cases is again attributable to the fact that it was not designed for discrete distributions. This difference between these indices cannot be resolved by "controlling for" N. If N is controlled for, HH = .20 in both cases, while Gini = .33 in the first case, and .29 in the second.

Another Gini "Blind Spot"
Kravis (1962) has pointed out that the Gini index assumes that "equal importance may be attached to equal absolute differences in income . . . even though one of the differences is taken between two low [value positions] and the other between two high ones." This means that very different distributions can and will generate Lorenz curves that deviate to the same extent from the line of perfect equality. The following very disparate distribution patterns, for example, both have a Gini value of .50.

I	II
70.0%	45%
7.5%	35%
7.5%	20%
7.5%	0%
7.5%	0%

If one is particularly interested in an inequality that tends toward monopoly (one unit controls 100 percent), then one would probably want system I to receive a higher score. On the other hand, if one's interest is in the extent to which the smaller units in a system are deprived, system II should receive a higher score. (Of course, no single measure can satisfy all theoretical needs, since one which would rank both of these cases "higher" is obviously not feasible.)[6]

The Schutz Coefficient
Shifting now to the Schutz coefficient, we find that it is similar to the Gini index in that its upper limit is also $1 - 1/N$. However, the reason for this may not be so intuitively clear. The Schutz coefficient sums "ratios of advantage,"

---

6. It should also be noted that this example does not involve a change in the number of units (since we could have given the lowest two units in the second case a percentage only slightly larger than zero to meet the objection that system 2 "really" only contains three units); this is another case in which Gini cannot be made more "reasonable" simply by correcting it with a denominator of $1 - 1/N$.

and these ratios are comparisons of the holdings of the advantaged (or the disadvantaged) to the *average* percentage of holdings of all the units in the system. (Formally, the Schutz coefficient is

$$\sum_{v_i \geq \bar{v}} \left(\frac{v_i}{\bar{v}} - 1 \right) \Delta X_i,$$

or

$$\sum_{v_i \leq \bar{v}} \left(1 - \frac{v_i}{\bar{v}} \right) \Delta X_i,$$

where $\bar{v}$ equals the average share of the units in the system; v_i equals the share of the ith unit; and $\Delta X_i = X_{i+1} - X_i$, when $X_i = i/N$.) These average holdings become smaller with every increase in N. Again, in the extreme case, if the system has only two units, the *average* holding is 50 percent no matter how unequally the holdings may be distributed, and when N increases to 4, 5, or 10, the average holding decreases to 25 percent, 20 percent, and 10 percent, respectively. The larger N is, the larger is the ratio of advantage of the one unit which controls 100 percent of the goods, and the larger is the upper limit of the Schutz coefficient.

Perhaps the most unattractive characteristic of this measure is that it does not make use of all available information. Alker (1965) points out that Schutz can be calculated either by summing the ratios of advantage for those above the mean or by summing the ratios of disadvantage for those below the mean. Of course, this means that the coefficient cannot be sensitive to variations within that part of the distribution which is *not* included in the calculations. Furthermore, because the coefficient *sums* the ratios of advantage, and since different combinations of ratios can give the same sum, the coefficient can also be insensitive to variations in the distribution in the group that *is* included in the calculations. For example, the Schutz coefficient equals .50 in all three of the cases below.

I	II	III
70%	70.0%	70%
20%	7.5%	15%
10%	7.5%	15%
0%	7.5%	0%
0%	7.5%	0%

Before turning to our own proposed index, we should briefly mention several other measures of inequality, some of which may be excellent for certain purposes. One widely used measure of industrial concentration, CR, equals the fraction of the market held by the L largest firms, where L usually equals 4, 8, or 20. Another measure of industrial concentration, introduced by Hall and Tideman, is TH, defined as $1/(2\Sigma iP_i) - 1$, where i equals the rank of the ith largest unit, and P_i equals the percentage share of that unit. Several other measures are discussed by Alker and Russett (1964), including the ratio of the percentage controlled by the largest unit to the percentage controlled by the smallest unit, the Pareto coefficient, and the skewness of a distribution. Though it is possible that one of the measures might be ideal for some specialized purpose, we agree with Alker and Russett that in most cases they are not as generally applicable as the other measures discussed above.

The Proposed Index of Concentration

Before describing the index that we decided to use for our own purposes, let us restate briefly the criteria we hope to satisfy. First, we want our measure to have a range of zero to one, even at the lower end of the size spectrum, because we seek to measure concentration in both the full international system, with an N as large as 135, and in its smaller regional and functional subsystems—with Ns as low as 5. Also its magnitude should increase if there is an upward redistribution of shares from any lower-ranked to any higher-ranked unit, and vice versa. Furthermore, it should reflect the shares of every unit in the system, and not merely of those that fall, for example, above or below the mean. Finally, it is critical that the measure react to changes in system size in a manner that is appropriate to our theoretical concern.

With the few exceptions that we have mentioned explicitly above, most measures satisfy the first three criteria, but meeting the fourth criterion proves to be more problematical. As we have implied in the discussion above, because the measures we looked at had different *ranges* for different Ns, they appeared to us to be overly sensitive to changes in N. This led us to prefer a *standardized* measure that has the same range regardless of system size. The basic formula for our index of concentration (or CON) is: standard deviation of the percentage shares divided by the maximum possible standard deviation in a system of size N. Fortunately, this simplifies to

$$CON = \sqrt{\frac{\Sigma P_i^2 - 1/N}{1 - 1/N}}$$

The maximum possible standard deviation of the percentage shares occurs when one unit controls 100 percent of the goods, while the rest of the units control none at all. And the minimum (zero) occurs when all the units control equal shares. Thus CON is equal to 1 whenever a single unit controls 100 percent of the goods, regardless of system size. It also has the virtue of taking into account information regarding all units, and it increases in value if there is a shift in shares from a lower-ranked to a higher-ranked unit, and vice versa.[7]

Now the fact that we opted for a standardized measure does not mean that we wanted or have a measure that is totally insensitive to system size. While the *range* of this measure is constant, and therefore insensitive, the *scores* on the index will rise and fall with system size, even when nothing else changes. For example, consider this subsystem at two points in time:

t_0		t_1	
States	Percentage Shares	States	Percentage Shares
A	90	A	90
B	6	B	6
C	4	C	4
		D	0
		E	0
CON=.85		CON=.88	

The only difference is that two units have been added at t_1; no shares have been shifted from some units to others. Yet CON is higher (because of the change in the standardizing denominator), as we believe it should be, since more power potential is concentrated in the hands of a smaller percentage of the subsystem's members. Had we wanted a measure that was insensitive to N (when nothing else changes), we could have used an unstandardized measure such as HH. In the case at hand, HH would equal .82 on both occasions; the *range* of HH is sensitive to changes in N in such cases, but the *scores* are not. The advantage, we believe, of a standardized measure such as CON is that scores are comparable, in the sense that a score of .33, for example, indicates that the system shows one-third as much concentration as is possible, no matter what the size of the system. Unstandardized measures such as HH or Gini will reflect changes in N only because their ranges will change (and therefore may appear to be too sensitive to such changes) but not necessarily because the degree of concentration has changed. And in examples like the one above, the *scores* may not change when N changes, but those scores will not be comparable.

Now the price of this comparability as we have defined it is an insen-

---

7. It was interesting to discover while preparing this essay that Janda (1971) has come up with exactly the same formula to cope with the problem of measuring "party articulation."

sitivity to changes in N at the extremes of the index. For example, if there are five units in a system and one unit controls 100 percent, CON = 1. If seven units are added to the system, but one unit still controls 100 percent, CON still equals 1. This is so even though all the goods are concentrated in the hands of 20 percent of the units in the first case, but in the hands of an even smaller minority of 12.5 percent of the units in the second case. Such changes in N (when nothing else changes) will be reflected in CON as long as no single unit controls 100 percent. If one is dealing with that rare empirical domain in which such extreme cases occur, and one wants an index that will be sensitive to changes in N, then CON should not be used. In our case, these extreme distributions are not possible, and it seemed worthwhile to forego sensitivity to N in such cases for the sake of comparability across the much more common cases where there is some, but not absolute, inequality.

Perhaps the best way to illustrate the characteristics of the CON measure is to show how it varies vis-à-vis several alternative indices in a few simple examples. Assume that we are measuring the concentration of power potential among states in two different international subsystems containing three and five states, respectively.

	I			II
	Percentage			Percentage
States	Shares	States		Shares
A	90	A		70
B	6	B		15
C	4	C		10
		D		3
		E		2
.57		Gini	.59	
.82		HH	.52	
.85		CON	.64	

While HH and CON produce the intuitively reasonable higher index score for case 1, the Gini scores are just the opposite, albeit not by much. This latter result is largely a function of N, since the upper limit of the Gini index is only .67 in case 1, but .80 in case 2. If we correct Gini for N (by dividing it by $1 - 1/N$), it rises to .85 in case 1 and only to .74 in case 2, making it more consonant with the HH and CON results. However, when Gini is corrected in this fashion, it has less discriminating power in this example (i.e., the sensitivity of the index as reflected in the difference between the scores in the two cases is diminished), a characteristic which also showed up when we used this modified Gini on our own historical data. One can enhance the discriminating power of some indices by taking the square root of the raw scores. But when we used that technique on our data with the Gini index, its discriminating power decreased, as it does in this example (that is, the square root values of the Gini corrected for N are .92 and .86).

As we noted, the HH and CON scores seem to be in the "correct" order, but the HH pattern is largely a function of its lower limits, which are .33 and .20, respectively. And while such sensitivity to N happens to produce the appropriate scores in the cases at hand, it often will not. Consider the following pair of subsystems.

	I				II
States	Percentage Shares	States			Percentage Shares
A	33.3	A			32
B	33.3	B			32
C	33.3	C			32
		D			2
		E			2
.333		HH			.31
.00		CON			.37

HH indicates that the concentration of power potential in case 1 is slightly higher, even though its equality of distribution is perfect. CON, on the other hand, reacts more appropriately in this empirical and theoretical context, since its upper and lower limits do not vary with the size of the system.

Let us consider one more example.

	I				II
States	Percentage Shares	States			Percentage Shares
A	40	A			20
B	30	B			20
C	20	C			15
D	10	D			15
		E			10
		F			10
		G			5
		H			5
.25		Gini			.25
.30		HH			.15
.26		CON			.17

While the HH results are appropriate according to the Hall and Tideman criterion, with its value in case I twice that produced for case II, the Gini index scores are identical. For our purposes, the face validity of both of these results leaves something to be desired. Conversely, the CON scores of .26 and .17 seem to us to reflect most appropriately the differences in the inequality of the distribution of power potential in the two systems. In any case, these illustrations demonstrate that—at least when one is measuring concentration or inequality among a rather small, but changing number of units—there are differences among such measures as HH, the Gini index, the Schutz coefficient, and CON which should be taken into account by any potential user.

Similarity to Other Measures

Over fifteen years ago, in the conclusion of an article analyzing indices of segregation, Duncan and Duncan (1955) lamented that

> on∿ lesson to be learned from the relatively unproductive experience with segregation indexes to date is that similar problems are often dealt with under different headings. Most of the issues which have come up in the literature on segregation indexes . . . had already been encountered in the methodological work on measures of inequality, spatial distribution, and localization in geography and economics.

We have learned a similar lesson from our experience with indexes of inequality. The major problem we have discussed here—i.e., comparability in the face of a small but changing N—has been dealt with under different headings and solved in essentially the same manner. For example, Amemiya (1963) has developed an index of economic differentiation (IED) that equals

$$\sum_{i=1}^{n} \frac{n}{n-1}\left(\frac{P_i - 1}{n}\right)^2 ,$$

where n equals the number of classifications of industry, and P_i is defined as the proportion of workers in the ith industry. If we say that $n = N =$ the number of units in the system, and that P_i is the percentage controlled by the ith unit, we can see that IED is essentially the same as CON. That is,

$$\text{IED} = \sum_{i=1}^{N} N/N - 1(P_i - 1/N)^2 = N/N - 1\Sigma(P_i - 1/N)^2$$

$$= N/N - 1\Sigma(P_i^2 - 2P_i/N + 1/N^2) = N/N - 1\Sigma P_i^2$$
$$-2/N\Sigma P_i + N(1/N)^2 = N/N - 1\Sigma P_i^2 - 2/N(1) + 1/N$$
$$= N/N - 1\Sigma P_i^2 - 1/N = \frac{\Sigma P_i^2 - 1/N}{N - 1/N} = \frac{\Sigma P_i^2 - 1/N}{1 - 1/N}$$

Thus, CON is equivalent to the square root of IED.

Similarly, Labovitz and Gibbs (1964) present a measure of the degree of division of labor (D) that equals

$$1 - \frac{(\Sigma X^2 / [\Sigma X]^2)}{1 - 1/N},$$

where N equals the number of occupations, and X is the number of individuals in each occupational category. This is also essentially equal to CON. The term $\Sigma X^2/(\Sigma X)^2 = \Sigma P_i^2$, which means that $D = 1 - \Sigma P_i^2 / 1 - 1/N$. Therefore,

$$\sqrt{1 - \frac{1 - \Sigma P_i^2}{1 - 1/N}} = CON.$$

In short, $\sqrt{1 - D} = CON$. It can further be shown that the index of qualitative variation (IQV), presented by Mueller et al. (1970), which equals

$$\frac{\Sigma n_i n_j}{\dfrac{k(k - 1)}{2} (n/k)^2}$$

(where n_i equals the number in the ith category, i does not equal j, and k equals the number of categories) is related to CON in the same way. That is, $\sqrt{1 - IQV} = CON$.

Aside from the fact that we use the index as a measure of concentration, rather than of economic differentiation, division of labor, qualitative diversity, and so one, the only substantial difference between CON and these other measures is that we use the square root of the same basic formula. We do this for several reasons. First, this procedure increases the discrimination of CON within the range of inequality in the small N systems that are of concern to us here. Second, we find the conceptual definition of CON as the standard deviation of the percentage shares divided by the maximum possible standard deviation in a system of size N an intuitively appealing one; this means that by definition, we should use the square root. Finally, one critic has already pointed out that, despite the fact that we criticize HH on the grounds that the squares of small percentages are very small, and that therefore they have a disproportionately small impact on the final index score, we turn around and use the squares of small percentages in our own index. But, by using the square root of the difference between these small squared percentages and $1/N$, and even more importantly, by standardizing the measure the way we do, CON avoids this insensitivity to small percentages that HH displays, even though the squares of small percentages are used in both indices.

Convergence of Measures

In examining the important differences among the available measures of concentration, we noted that they nevertheless fall into two basic classes. While retaining the distinction (sum of squares versus deviation from equality) for the sake of clarity, we now follow up the earlier suggestion that even this distinction if far from fundamental.

The mathematical convergence among these diverse measures begins to become evident when we note that all of them can be expressed in the same basic terms: P_i, i, and N, where P_i equals the percentage share of the ith unit, i equals the rank of the ith largest unit, and N equals the number of units in the system. This equivalence is further reflected by the fact that—with the exception of the Schutz coefficient—all the major measures are a function of either: (*a*) the sum of squared percentage shares, or (*b*) the sum of rank share products.

The most obvious similarity, already discussed above, is that between CON and HH, both of which are originally expressed in terms of P_i and N. If

$$\text{CON} = \sqrt{\frac{\Sigma P_i^2 - 1/N}{1 - 1/N}},$$

and $\text{HH} = \Sigma P_i^2$, we can also express CON as

$$\sqrt{\frac{\text{HH} - 1/N}{1 - 1/N}}.$$

Hence, it is clear that CON^2—and therefore CON itself—is a perfectly predictable function of HH, as long as we know the value of N. What is true of the relationship between CON and HH is also true, of course, of the relationship between CON and all those other measures discussed that are based on the sum of squared percentage shares, or some slight mutation thereof.

The Gini index can also be expressed in terms of P_i, i, and N, as may be seen by referring to figure 5. What the Gini formula does, in effect, is to sum the area of the rectangles in the figure, and subtract that sum from one, the total "area of inequality" that lies above and below the line of perfect equality. The resulting difference is the proportion of the *total* area that lies between the Lorenz curve and the line of perfect equality; that proportion *is* the Gini index score. By referring to figure 5, one can see that there are $2i - 1$ rectangles associated with each group. For example, group *A*, which is the *fourth* largest group, has $(2 \times 4) - 1$, or 7 rectangles associated with it. The area of each of the rectangles in the figure equals the product of $1/N$ (i.e., the proportion of the whole that each group constitutes, which is represented

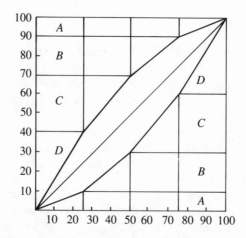

Fig. 5. Lorenz curves encompassing proportion of total area equal to the Gini index. Percentage of shares is as follows: A = 10%, B = 20%, C= 30%, D = 40%.

by the length of each rectangle as measured along the horizontal axis), and P_i (the proportion of the whole that each group controls, which is represented by the width of each rectangle as measured along the vertical axis), or P_i/N. Therefore, the area of the rectangles associated with group A is .25 × .10, or ·10/4, which equals .025. There are 7 such rectangles, so group A's contribution is 7 × .025, or .1750. The contribution of all the other groups can be calculated in the same way. The Gini index is thus equal to $1 - \Sigma[2i-1 (P_i/N)]$. But this can be simplified to

$$1 - \frac{\Sigma(2i - 1)(P_i)}{N} = 1 - 1/N\Sigma(2i - 1)(P_i)$$
$$= 1 - 1/N\Sigma(2iP_i - P_i) = 1 - 1/N\Sigma 2iP_i - 1/N\Sigma P_i.$$

Since ΣP_i equals 1, and the constant 2 can be brought outside the summation sign, this further simplifies to $1 - (2/N\Sigma iP_i) - 1/N$. Thus, it can be seen that the Gini index is a function of the rank share products, or ΣiP_i, as is TH, which, as we recall, equals $1/(2\Sigma iP_i) - 1$.

Turning to the Schutz coefficient, we find that it, too, can be expressed in terms of P_i and N. Recall that the original formula is

$$\sum_{v_i \geq \bar{v}} (v_i/\bar{v} - 1)\Delta X_i.$$

However, v_i is equivalent to P_i, and both v and ΔX_i equal $1/N$, as long as each unit represents an equal percentage of the total number of units. Thus the formula can be rewritten as:

$$\sum_{P_i \geqq 1/N} \frac{P_i}{1/N - 1} \frac{1}{N},$$

and this in turn simplifies to

$$\sum_{P_i \geqq 1/N} (P_i - 1/N).$$

Similarly, the alternative formula for the Schutz coefficient simplifies to

$$\sum_{P_i \leqq 1/N} (1/N - P_i).$$

Summary

The measurement of inequality and related concepts is a pervasive problem in several social sciences. We have discussed various attempts to solve this problem and have found that the measures often differ in their reaction to changes in system size. In that discussion, we pointed out that some measures might not be appropriate if one were measuring the concentration of power potential in the international system or its subsystems. We have presented a measure that seems appropriate for such a purpose, and then examined its similarity to other measures that have been used for quite different purposes. Finally, we concluded, by focusing on the essential similarity of most of the measures we discussed, that they are all a function of P_i, N, and/or i, where P_i equals the percentage share of the ith unit, N equals the number of units in the system, and i equals the rank of the ith largest unit.

We trust that this effort represents a modest accretion to our methodological armamentarium. In addition to offering a small improvement on some existing indicators of concentration, it should help to put the problem into fuller context, offering as it does a synthesis and a codification of those that have gone before. At the least, its circulation among political scientists should serve as a reminder that crossing disciplinary boundaries may often be a salutary, sobering experience.

Measuring Polarity in the International System

Frank Whelon Wayman and T. Clifton Morgan

Science often advances as an iterative process in which a theory is first formulated, then tested, and then reformulated on the basis of the test results. The reformulation can be subject to further tests, which lead to more accurate reformulations, and so on. Ideally, this process results in a theoretical model that is a better explanatory and predictive tool than its predecessors. This cycle of theorizing and testing often breaks down, however, and frequently because of measurement problems. Such problems, which must be of particular concern to social scientists, are especially severe when there exist numerous purported indicators of what began as a single concept, and when the use of these indicators in empirical tests produces different results. Theory alone is not sufficient to untangle these difficulties, unless one takes the position that most of the previously published empirical research findings were not worth publishing, that they should be ignored, and that current theorists, oblivious to the empirical findings, can leapfrog the iterative process and produce improved theories that render the earlier work irrelevant. When no such utopian theoretical breakthroughs have appeared in print, it is appropriate to sort out the conflicting empirical results to see how they converge and differ. It is entirely possible that extant theory is sufficient to explain the phenomenon in question and that seemingly contradictory empirical results can be reconciled. This would be particularly true if the competing indicators are tapping the various dimensions of a multidimensional concept. Thus, one important avenue of inquiry is to evaluate the similarities and dissimilarities among the various indicators and to determine what aspects of the concept each indicator is tapping.

One area in which such work is needed is in the field of peace research, where much time and energy have been spent in efforts to relate the characteristics of the international system to the occurrence of conflict among nations.[1] Many of these efforts have been attempts by social scientists to account

1. We would like to thank Professors Aldrich, Bueno de Mesquita, Ostrom, Thompson, and Wallace, who were very gracious in pointing out the proper interpretations of their definitions

for war by using some indicator of the polarity of the international system. Little progress has been made in this area in that very little of the variance in the war indicators has been accounted for by polarity,[2] and, perhaps more importantly, different studies have reached conflicting conclusions. It is almost certainly the case that many of the differences in the findings of these studies can be attributed to the use of different operational indicators of the independent variable. In our opinion, the fact that a variety of indicators of polarity exist and that these have led to divergent conclusions regarding the association between the polarity of the system and war is a product of an inadequate conceptualization of "polarity." We do not believe, however, that any one of the indicators is "correct" and the others wrong; rather, it is more likely that "polarity" is a multidimensional concept and that each indicator is capturing some aspect of the variable.

In this essay we will examine a variety of measures of polarity and polarization, developed for use in the publications by Singer and Small (1968); Singer, Bremer, and Stuckey (1972); Bueno de Mesquita (1975b); Li and Thompson (1977); Thompson, Rasler, and Li (1980); Stoll (1984a); and Wayman (1984). The purpose is to determine objectively, without judging the relative quality of the works in question, the degree to which the various measures of systemic polarity and polarization are convergent. Given the number and variety of indicators that have been constructed, it would be somewhat surprising to find a high level of intercorrelation among all the measures. We hope to show that the measures can be meaningfully grouped in a manner that demonstrates the indicators are tapping several related features of the international system. Ideally, this will serve as a useful guide toward refining the conceptualizations of polarity and polarization, which, in turn, will lead to valid indicators of these system characteristics. Ultimately, such refinements will allow us to determine the true nature of the relationship between the structure of the system and war.

There is no official professional archive that receives data on all of the measures of polarity and polarization. The analysis performed here focuses on the major indicators for which data were available in publications or social science archives. This selection procedure is biased toward authors who report their raw data in an article or accompanying appendix. While other lists of indicators might have altered the study, and while the present selection is not completely exhaustive, there are enough indicators included to provide some

---

and operationalizations. We are also grateful to David Singer and Mike Champion. We alone are responsible for remaining errors.

2. It is beyond the scope of this essay to present these war indicators in detail. Generally, these indicators deal with the occurrence of war, the severity of war, and the magnitude of war. For a complete description of the various indicators, the reader should refer to the articles reviewed here.

important new insights into the bulk of the writings on systemic power concentration (polarity), systemic alliance configuration (polarization), and war.[3]

Theoretical Underpinnings

The quantitative studies under review had their theoretical basis in the mid-1960s debate concerning the relative war proneness of bipolar international systems and multipolar international systems. Waltz (1964) argued that bipolar systems are more peaceful. The absence of peripheries, the intensity of duopolistic competition, and the recurrence of crises force and enable the two powers to maintain a stable relationship with each other while their preponderant power allows them to adapt to changes in the system brought about by the actions of other states. His position is that the certainty brought about by knowledge of the reactions with which unacceptable behavior would be met fosters sufficiently cautious behavior on the part of each power to keep the system at peace.

Deutsch and Singer (1964), on the other hand, argued that multipolar systems are more peaceful. They argued that for two powers to engage in war requires that each must pay some minimum level of attention to the other. In multipolar systems each state must show some concern for every other state so the level of attention any state can pay to any other is reduced below this minimum threshold. Furthermore, any potential aggressor must consider the possibility of being faced with the overwhelming power of a coalition of other powers. The uncertainty regarding the actions of the other powers serves to deter aggression, making the system more peaceful.

The desire to resolve this debate empirically has generated a great deal of quantitative research. While the early protagonists were able to take for granted that their readers would understand the meaning of "polarity," those performing the empirical work that followed were constrained by measurement issues, which forced them to define the concept more specifically. By examining some of the conceptual definitions upon which some of the measurements were based, we can begin to distinguish a number of dimensions of the concept of systemic polarity.

In one of the early empirical studies, Haas (1970, 99 and 121) defined a

---

3. A number of other measures of polarity are not strictly comparable to those included here. Levy (1985) and Haas (1974), for example, characterize the system as being unipolar, bipolar, or multipolar. These indicators are rigorously defined and constructed, and they may ultimately be determined to be more valid and useful than more sophisticated measures, but they are basically ordinal level variables while those examined here are constructed on an interval scale. Others (Hart 1974; Caporaso 1976; Rapkin et. al. 1979) have gathered data for only a short period of time. Obviously, a comparison of indicators would be most difficult with such a limited number of data points.

pole as "a militarily significant cluster of units within an international arena." Within this definition, "significant military power centers" are considered to be either unaligned major powers or rival alliances. This definition seems to capture the general concept as envisioned by Deutsch and Singer and it brings forth the distinctions later scholars were to draw between the dimensions of "polarity." The most common such distinction has been to distinguish between "polarity" and "polarization."[4] The former term refers to the distribution of power in the international system. If power is highly concentrated in the hands of two states the system is bipolar while the system is multipolar when power is more diffused throughout several states. In his later work, Waltz (1979) is fairly clear that this is the sense in which he uses the term *polarity*. "Polarization" refers to the pattern of alliance bonds within the system. When states are tightly bonded into two discrete groupings, the system is highly polarized. The system is less polarized to the extent that alliance bonds are absent or are characterized by cross-cutting ties among the members of various groups. It should be clear that the two concepts are analytically distinct: it is possible, for example, for a multipolar system to be highly polarized or to be relatively unpolarized.

The other distinction to be made is whether or not the focus should be exclusively on the great powers. Some scholars (e.g., Haas 1970; Bueno de Mesquita 1975b) include all system members in their analyses. The general argument in favor of this approach is that it is conceivable that a well-coordinated coalition of minor powers could exercise as much influence as a major power. To take a hypothetical example, if the members of the Group of 77 were able to bond tightly and coordinate their economic, political, and military policies, they would certainly constitute a major force in international politics. Given that such an eventuality is conceivable, so the argument goes, it is essential to include minor powers at least in our measures of polarization.

The alternative approach is to focus entirely on the great powers (Ostrom and Aldrich 1979; Levy 1984 and 1985). One aspect of the argument in favor of this approach is empirical—to date, no clustering of states that did not include a great power has been able to become a dominant international actor. Therefore, any indicator based on historical data that includes minor powers would be either unnecessarily complex (if the inclusion of minor powers made no difference) or invalid (if the value of the indicator were altered because of the minor powers).

---

4. A thorough discussion of the distinction between polarity and polarization can be found in Rapkin et al. (1979). Trade and other economic relations are potentially of high value as measures of polarization (Wall 1972; Goldman 1974), but these data are not available over the broad time span of 1815–1965, and so studies of them have been largely limited to the post-war world, and as such fall outside the purview of this review.

A more important aspect of this argument is based on theoretical grounds. Any grouping of minor powers able to constitute a major power center would require participation of a large number of states. Even under the best of circumstances, such an alliance would be a fragile thing. We have no reason to expect a large number of states to put aside their differences and coordinate policies to such an extent. Thus, it is likely that only a major power, or a coalition including a major power, could exert the kind of influence necessary to constitute a "pole" over a period of time. Furthermore, the majority of theoretical works that have been concerned with polarity as an important variable have focused upon the great powers. The impetus for the early debate was in the balance of power theoretical tradition which focused almost entirely on the great powers, and most arguments linking the polarity of the system to the stability of the system are, at least implicitly, concerned with the distribution of power and alliance configuration of the great powers. The reason for this focus is simply that the great powers are believed to be actors who determine the structure of the system as well as its stability. Thus, according to this argument, any research linking the structure of the international system to its war-proneness should focus only on great power behavior.

These arguments have, of necessity, been presented too briefly to capture fully their theoretical intricacies. We can, nevertheless, distinguish conceptual variations that could be expected to lead to differences in operational indicators. On the one hand, we would expect the indicators to fall into groups according to whether they are designed to capture the polarity or the polarization of the system. On the other hand, the indicators may also be grouped according to whether they reflect an exclusively great powers focus. On the basis of this, we can expect our attempt in the remainder of this essay to uncover meaningful groupings of the indicators to show that they can be arranged into as many as four categories. It is probably more reasonable, however, to expect there to be three groups since any measure of polarity is likely to be restricted to a great power focus. In the following section we will briefly identify the indicators incorporated into this study. If these indicators are, in fact, capturing different dimensions of the concept, we may then be able to associate these differences with the divergent findings among the studies.

Quantitative Indicators of Polarity and Polarization

The first of all these empirical efforts was that of Singer and Small (1968). Their study was performed from the theoretical orientation that the relationship between polarity and war is a product of the number of interaction opportunities available to system members. Anything that reduces the number of available interaction opportunities (e.g., alliances) reduces the ability of states to freely pursue their interests and increases the likelihood of war (Singer and Small 1968). Their indicator, therefore, is a measure of the proportion of interaction opportunities not exhausted by alliances. The denominator of the index is the total number of possible interaction opportunities among major powers. The numerator is the number of interaction opportunities not exhausted by alliances. An opportunity is exhausted by a dyad when the states align together or when one is the target of an alliance to which the other belongs.

Because of ambiguities about what country is the target of an alliance, Singer and Small actually created two polarization indices. One index included questionable targets, while an alternative index was constructed omitting questionable targets. Singer and Small also provided several measures of alliance aggregation: the percentage of nations in any alliance, the percentage of nations in a defense pact, the percentage of major powers in any alliance, the percentage of major powers in a defense pact, and the percentage of major powers aligned with a minor power.

Following the Singer and Small effort were a number of studies in which the authors attempted to construct more sophisticated measures of polarization. Wallace (1973b) conceptualized polarization as "the number of independent power centers in the system and the tightness with which nations are bound to them" (Wallace 1973a, 577). He proposes three indices of polarization which "take into account the multidimensional character of alignment patterns" by examining IGO and diplomatic bonds as well as military alliance bonds between nations. He also focuses on the "configuration," or distances among clusters, of alliance patterns.

Bueno de Mesquita (1975b) asserts that there are three aspects of polarity that are of concern: the number of poles, or clusters, in the system; the "tightness" of the clusters, or how similar the foreign policies of cluster members are; and, the "discreetness" of clusters, or how dissimilar the foreign policies of nations in different clusters are.

To determine the clustering of nations in any given year, Bueno de Mesquita focuses on military alliance commitments. Using the Singer and Small (1966b) classification for alliance, he creates a matrix for each dyad in the system. In matrix 1, Nation C has been placed to indicate that it has a neutrality pact with A and a defense pact with B. Bueno de Mesquita assumes that all states have a defense pact with themselves (i.e., A has a defense pact with A, B has a defense pact with B). In the illustrative matrix, A and B have been placed under the assumption that they have no alliance with each other. Such a matrix is compiled for each dyad. Tau-beta scores are calculated for each matrix to determine the similarity of alliance commitments for each pair of nations. A square matrix is then created with the tau-beta scores in the cells and typal analysis is used to identify clusters of nations. The clustering is

	Nation A			
	Defense Pact	Neutrality Pact	Entente	No Alliance
Nation B				
Defense Pact		C, D		B
Neutrality Pact			E	
Entente				F
No Alliance	A			G, H, I

Matrix 1

performed using only states involved in at least one alliance in a given year. The polarity of the system is taken to be the number of clusters present.

In a later paper, Ostrom and Aldrich (1978) altered Bueno de Mesquita's index to correspond more closely with their conceptualization of polarity. They argue that the power dimension of polarity is not taken into account by Bueno de Mesquita's indicator and that a pole should be defined as a non-aligned major power or a cluster containing at least one major power. They rely on Bueno de Mesquita's clustering of nations, but the polarity of the system for each year is measured as the number of clusters containing at least one major power plus the number of nonaligned major powers.

Bueno de Mesquita also uses the tau-beta scores to measure the tightness and discreetness of clusters in the system. The tightness of a cluster is measured by the fraction,

$$\frac{\text{sum of tau-betas for within cluster dyads}}{\text{number of possible within cluster dyads}}$$

Systemic tightness is measured by the fraction,

$$\frac{\Sigma\ (\text{sum of tau-betas for within cluster dyads})}{\Sigma\ (\text{number of possible within cluster dyads})}$$

Finally, discreteness is measured by

$$\frac{(-1)\ (\text{sum of tau-betas for between cluster dyads})}{\text{total \# of dyads} - \text{number of within cluster dyads}}$$

Li and Thompson (1977), like Ostrom and Aldrich, argue that all states are not equally important in determining the system's structure; Li and Thompson go further than Ostrom and Aldrich, and assert that determining the system's polarity requires that we focus solely upon the alignment patterns of the major powers. Additionally, they focus solely on defense pacts to determine the clustering of the major powers. This is justified on the grounds that, due to their direct military implications, defense pacts are most important in binding nations and in restricting their freedom of choice (Li and Thompson 1977, 14).

Li and Thompson provide two measures; one indicates the proportion of interaction opportunities lost, the other indicates the number of poles in the system. The first, the network density index, is simply the number of major power dyads characterized by defense pacts divided by the number of possible major power dyads. The latter is the number of discrete clusters (no interalliance connections) of major powers with single, nonaligned major powers counting as one cluster.

Wayman (1984) studied the clustering of the major powers by defining a cluster as a subset of the majors in which each nation was allied with each other nation. For example, in 1950, Britain, France, and the United States were all members of NATO, and therefore constituted a cluster. Wayman then constructs a polarization index in which the denominator is the number of major powers, and the numerator is the sum of the clusters and of the nonclustered major powers. In 1950, with five majors and two clusters (NATO and Sino-Soviet), the index would be 0.40, for instance.

While measures of alliance polarization are thus numerous and complicated, measures of polarity (i.e., power concentration) are fewer and more straightforward. Singer, Bremer, and Stuckey (1972) contributed a measure of the concentration of power among the major powers. Their indicator, "CON," rests on the three-fold Correlates of War measures of the military, industrial, and demographic material capabilities of nations. Each of these three facets of capability is made up of two components: military expenditures and military personnel for the military facet, energy consumption and iron and steel production for the industrial facet, and urban population and total population for the demographic facet. Each nation's percentage share of total major power capabilities is computed for each of these six capabilities. The six resulting percentages are averaged to get the nation's overall share. CON is then computed by calculating the standard deviation of the overall shares of the major powers, and dividing that number by the maximum possible standard deviation for that number of nations:

$$\text{CON} = \sqrt{\frac{\sum_{i=1}^{n} (S_i)^2 - \frac{1}{n}}{1 - \frac{1}{n}}}$$

where n = number of nations in the system, and S_i = nation i's share (from 0.00 to 1.00) of the system's capabilities.

Wayman (1984), modifying Singer, Bremer and Stuckey, computed a measure of bipolar power concentration, "TWOCON," by adding up the S_is for the two largest nations in the system. In effect, TWOCON emphasizes the importance of the gap between the two largest powers and everyone else, whereas CON treats the gaps between any of the major powers as equally important.

Finally, Stoll (1984a) capped all this work by developing a single indicator that contains elements of polarity (concentration of power) and polarization (number of poles and tightness of poles). Stoll's index of bloc concentration (BLOCCON) is constructed in four steps, using building materials we have already reviewed:

1. Obtaining a measure of each major power's capability in each year.
2. Placing each major power in an alliance-based cluster in each half-year.
3. Combining these two measures, so that each major power alliance cluster is weighted by the amount of capability and the degree of commitment of its members.
4. Calculating the concentration of capability across the weighted major power alliance clusters. (Stoll 1984, 35)

In step one, Stoll uses the COW capabilities indicators to compute each nation's percentage share of major power capabilities, in the same manner as Singer, Bremer, and Stuckey (1972), but with some minor variations in the dating of certain nations' entry into major power status. In step two, Bueno de Mesquita's (1975b) clustering technique is applied, except only major powers are included, wartime as well as peacetime alliances are included, and any nonaligned major power is put in a cluster by itself. In step three, "the capability weight for each cluster [is] . . . derived by summing the percentage capability scores of each cluster's major power members and discounting this sum by the tightness of the cluster," using Bueno de Mesquita's formula for tightness (Stoll 1984a, 37). Fourth, the BLOCCON score is computed using the CON algorithm (Singer, Bremer, and Stuckey 1972).

This discussion has hardly exhausted the list of measures of polarity and polarization. It has gone far enough to give some feel for the variety of the definitions. Variety at the conceptual level, however, may not be reflected in the measurement level. For example, some measures of polarization are based on the number of clusters, while others are based on the number of clusters divided by the number of states. These two concepts seem very different, but a glance at the analyses below indicates that they, at least in the case of the major powers, produce very similar results and often load on the same factor. This can occur because the denominator in the second measure—the number of major powers—varies little compared to the numerator, so that the variations of the fraction are highly correlated with the variations of the number of clusters. For such reasons, we should now turn our attention to the actual correlations between these measures of polarity and polarization.

Dimensions of Polarity and Polarization

To measure the association between indicators, a dozen of the above indices were examined at five-year intervals, 1820–1965. The correlations between those variables over this time span were then observed. Observations at Correlates of War five-year intervals (1820, 1825, 1830, . . . , 1965) were recorded for the following variables:

V1. Wayman's measure of alliance bipolarization among major powers;
V2. Singer and Small's measure of alliance bipolarization among major powers, leaving out debatable targets;
V3. Singer and Small's measure of alliance bipolarization among major powers, including debatable targets;
V4. Singer and Small's measure of alliance aggregation among all nations;
V5. Li and Thompson's measure of the number of discrete clusters of major powers;
V6. Li and Thompson's measure of major power dyads with defense pacts as a proportion of the possible;
V7. Bueno de Mesquita's measure of the number of poles among all nations;
V8. Bueno de Mesquita's measure of the tightness of those poles;
V9. Bueno de Mesquita's measure of the discreteness of those poles;
V10. Singer, Bremer, and Stuckey's measure of the concentration of major power capabilities (CON);
V11. Wayman's measure of the bipolar concentration of major power capabilities (TWOCON); and
V12. Stoll's measure of major power bloc capability concentration (BLOCCON).

The correlations among these measures are presented in table 1, which, based on the deletion of a year in which data are missing for any variable, is limited to 1820–1939 ($N=24$).[5] As may be seen in table 1, the degree of convergence among indicators of polarity and polarization is not encouraging. To begin with, there are a number of weak and even negative correlations. Serious doubts concerning the validity of the measures are raised in that a number of explanations could account for the low correlations: (1) perhaps one indicator is valid and the rest should be discarded, but, since no indicator has performed much better than the others in predicting war (which is what they are all designed to do), it is not clear which is the best; (2) perhaps all are imperfect measures of the same phenomenon, none inherently better than the rest; or (3) perhaps the phenomena being measured are actually multidimensional in nature; the respective measures could be capturing various, related aspects of these concepts, and thus would not necessarily be "competing." If the measures under examination could be meaningfully grouped, support for this third interpretation would be provided; although we shall shortly see that there is some evidence in favor of this third position, at first glance (table 1) no such neat and tidy solution is revealed. Instead, whether because describing the system is inherently complicated, or because of idiosyncrasies of the researchers, the reader is left with a complex array of associations. To organize the presentation, we will focus successively on the measures of major powers' alliance polarization, major powers' capability concentration, all-states' alliance polarization, and finally the one hybrid measure, Stoll's BLOCCON. The measures of major powers' alliance polarization (V1–3 and V5–6) are, in nine out of ten instances, strongly and significantly correlated with each other. The two measures of major powers' capability concentration (V10–11) are also strongly intercorrelated. The measures of all-states' alliance polarization are not as simple to describe; only half of the correlations among these variables are statistically significant. Turning from within the three groups to comparisons across the groups, one finds, as expected, weaker relationships. Only four out of ten of the correlations between major power polarization and major power capability concentration are statistically significant. None of the correlations between major power capability concentration and all-states' alliance polarization are statistically significant. Finally, only three out of twenty of the correlations between major alliance polarization and all-states' alliance polarization are significant.

---

5. Some of the correlations in table 1, especially those involving power concentration, are different than the values reported in Wayman (1984) because of different Ns. In table 1, with so many variables included and consequently so much opportunity for missing data, the $N=24$. In Wayman (1984, 32–34), the $N=28$ or 29, depending on the pair of variables being analyzed. The instability of the results, with large shifts in r because of the exclusion of a few time points, should give the reader further pause in considering the possible validity of studies of polarity and polarization.

TABLE 1. Correlations between Selected Indicators of Polarity and Polarization, 1825–1938

Variable	States Included	Concept	V1	V2	V3	V4	V5	V6	V7	V8	V9	V10	V11	V12
V1. Wayman Bipolarization	Majors	Clusters as a proportion of potential clusters	1.0											
V2. Singer-Small Bipolarization (alternate)	Majors	Alignments as proportion of potential alignments (omits debatable targets)	0.66	1.0										
V3. Singer-Small Bipolarization (initial)	Majors	Alignments as proportion of potential alignments (includes all targets)	0.62	0.75	1.0									
V4. Singer-Small Alliance Aggregation	All	Alignments as proportion of possible alignments	−0.06	0.04	0.22	1.0								
V5. Li and Thompson Cluster	Majors	Number of discrete clusters	0.42	0.50	0.64	0.71	1.0							
V6. Li and Thompson Alliance	Majors	Dyads with defense pacts as proportion of possible	0.35	0.48	0.48	0.70	0.89	1.0						

V7.	Bueno de Mesquita Poles	All	Number of poles	−0.30	−0.15	−0.24	0.61	0.06	0.30	1.0				
V8.	Bueno de Mesquita Tightness	All	Tightness of Poles	−0.01	−0.14	0.21	0.58	0.46	0.19	0.08	1.0			
V9.	Bueno de Mesquita Discreteness	All	Discreteness of Poles	0.13	−0.09	0.12	−0.24	−0.04	−0.15	−0.47	0.34	1.0		
V10.	Singer, Bremer, and Stuckey Concentration	Majors	Standard Deviation of capability shares	0.37	0.68	0.39	0.08	0.41	0.42	0.02	0.03	0.08	1.0	
V11.		Majors	Combined capabilities of two largest powers as percentage of total capabilities											
V12.	Wayman Bipolar Concentration	Majors	Standard Deviation of capability shares of major power clusters, adjusted for tightness	0.24	0.50	0.06	−0.13	0.03	0.23	0.29	−0.33	−0.14	0.77	1.0
	Stoll Bloc Concentration	Majors	tightness	0.33	0.41	0.26	0.08	0.18	0.28	0.17	−0.15	−0.24	0.38	0.37

(Underlined correlations, statistically significant at the .05 level: 0.61; 0.58, 0.46; −0.47; 0.68, 0.41, 0.42; 0.50; 0.77; 0.41. Final diagonal value for the Stoll Bloc Concentration row = 1.0.)

Source: Correlates of War Project archives.

Note: Pearson product-moment correlation coefficients based on measurements at five-year intervals. Underlined correlations are statistically significant at the .05 level. N = 24. Listwise deletion of missing cases. Valid years (no missing data) 1825–1938.

Unlike the other eleven measures, Stoll's BLOCCON does not focus on one aspect of polarity, but rather tries to capture many key facets. BLOCCON is designed to incorporate alliance clustering, the tightness of those clusters, and the concentration of power among them, for the major power subsystem. Perhaps this diversity accounts for the BLOCCON correlations, which are at least weakly positive with all the other measures of major power polarity, but which are statistically significant in only one instance (with the Singer and Small alternate bipolarization measure).

The variable that comes closest to capturing the common thread of polarity and polarization is the Li and Thompson measure of discrete clusters. It is significantly related to seven of the ten other measures, including all the other measures of major power alliance polarization, two of the four measures of all-states' alliance polarization, and one of the two measures of major powers' capability concentration. Next closest to being the common thread is the alternate Singer and Small major power alliance polarization measure. Best among the all-states' measures in matching the common thread is the Singer and Small alliance aggregation measure. Lastly, the Singer, Bremer and Stuckey power concentration measure is more strongly associated with the alliance polarization measures than is the Wayman power concentration measure.

There is enough variety in these correlation patterns to boggle the mind. Factor analysis is a useful technique for imposing order on such chaos. In this essay, we used a principal components factor analysis to identify the number of underlying dimensions in the polarity and polarization indicators, and then used an orthogonal varimax rotation to match groups of indicators with the axes of the n-dimensional space.

A series of factor analyses were performed, altering slightly the number of variables included. In all the analyses, four factors emerged from the analysis. This was established by two different criteria: the number of dimensions should equal the number of factors with eigenvalues greater than one, and the plot of the amount of variance accounted for by the factors should show a kink, with a sharp increase in the total "explained" variance until all relevant factors have been included, and then a leveling off, with only small and uniform increases thereafter. These two criteria were in agreement, both indicating a four-dimensional solution.

The purpose of the varimax rotation is to transform the four-dimensional space so that, if those variables measuring the same thing (e.g., great power polarization) form a set of vectors projecting like a sheaf of arrows in the same direction from the origin of the space, then the axes of the space will each run as close to the center of each sheaf as possible within the constraint that the axes be at right angles to each other. The consequence is a set of dimensions that are substantively meaningful because each is associated with a set of variables that have a great deal of shared variance with the dimension—i.e., that have high factor loadings on that dimension. The emergence of such a solution depends on the existence of distinct clusters of variables.

In general, such clusters existed and meaningful dimensions emerged. The results are displayed in table 2, in which the cell entries are the factor loadings of each variable on each factor. Four factors (with eigenvalues greater than one) emerged from the analysis: alliance polarization—all states; alliance polarization—majors; capability concentration—majors; and discreteness—all states. The first dimension is most clearly associated with the Singer and Small alliance aggregation measure for all states, and from this fact the dimension takes its name. The second dimension is dominated by the Wayman and Singer and Small major power alliance polarization measures. There is a bridge between the first two dimensions, in that the Li and Thompson measures are associated with each. The third dimension is clearly the domain of the two measures of major power capability concentration. There is a small bridge between the second and third dimensions in that the Singer, Bremer, and Stuckey capability concentration measure loads to some degree on both. Finally, we have an odd fourth dimension, dominated by Bueno de Mesquita's measure of discreteness of poles for all states. Tightness has a sizeable secondary loading on this dimension, and the Bueno de Mesquita measure of the number of poles loads, with the opposite sign, on the same dimension. To some extent, the number of poles is varying inversely with their discreteness and tightness, so the fourth dimension is dominated by Bueno de Mesquita measures. The fourth factor also is home to the Stoll measure of bloc concentration, which had conceptual roots in more than one dimension. This eclecticism is mirrored in the loadings of Stoll's measure, which shares variance with so many of the other variables, and which loads moderately on three dimensions, with its primary loading on the discreteness dimension.

The four factors together explain 83 percent of the variance in the dozen variables, with the two polarization dimensions accounting for most of the explanatory power. The three dimensions that we predicted did, as expected, emerge as the first three factors. The fourth factor, discreteness, was not predicted, and seems due to the idiosyncratic nature of Bueno de Mesquita's indicators.

Conclusions

Although factor analysis does indicate that some smaller number of dimensions underlies the measures of polarity and polarization, it should nonetheless be clear to the reader that the empirical studies under review have

TABLE 2. Factor Analysis (Varimax Rotation) of Polarity and Polarization, 1820–1939

Indicators			Factors			
			1	2	3	4
Author	Variable Name	Powers	Alliance Polarization, All States	Alliance Polarization, Major Powers	Capability Concentration, Major Powers	Discreteness of Poles, All States
Singer and Small	Alliance Aggregation	All	.973	−.056	.058	−.151
Li and Thompson	Alliance	Majors	.746	.406	−.243	−.202
Li and Thompson	Cluster	Majors	.789	.545	−.083	.025
Bueno de Mesquita	Tightness	All	.683	−.046	.166	.557
Bueno de Mesquita	Poles	All	.524	−.516	−.267	−.488
Singer and Small	Initial Alliance Polarization	Majors	.288	.863	−.061	.081
Singer and Small Wayman	Alliance Polarization	Majors	−.009	.830	−.169	.029
Singer and Small Wayman	Alternate Alliance Polarization	Majors	.078	.773	−.479	−.146
	Bipolar Capability Concentration	Majors	−.094	.041	−.949	−.186
Singer, Bremer, and Stuckey	Capability Concentration	Majors	.166	.332	−.873	.118
Bueno de Mesquita	Discreteness of Poles	All	−.114	.093	−.038	.900
Stoll	Bloc Concentration	Majors	−.048	−.339	.384	.450
% of Variance Explained			25%	25%	19%	14%

produced a far more varied set of indicators than one would have anticipated from a cursory or even careful reading of the classic articles of Kaplan (1957), Waltz (1964), and Deutsch and Singer (1964).

It may be that the weak relationships we have discovered are the "fault" of some of the scholarship. Perhaps some of the measures of polarity and polarization are better than others, and the weak correlations are a consequence of the flawed measures. In this view, one might argue that Singer and Small and Li and Thompson have come closest to measuring the core element of what drives the system, and therefore their measures of major power polarization are highly correlated with a host of other measures of polarity and polarization. From this perspective, the goal would be for future scholars to move further in the direction of developing improved indicators, based on an application of the mistakes of the past, refining the work of Singer and Small and Li and Thompson.

But an alternate view is that there is more multidimensionality in table 1 than would be attributable to measurement error and other scholarly foibles. Instead, there really do seem to be differences between polarity and polarization, between trends in the major power subsystem and in the system as a whole, and between such aspects of polarization as the tightness of the clusters and the number of interaction opportunities across clusters. In this perspective, it is going to be hard to find a clear pattern relating polarity/polarization to war, because polarity/polarization is such a complex concept.

To see the difficulties that arise, assume for the moment that high scores on (each dimension of) bipolarity and bipolarization all lead to war. Then, *if* a system that had a high concentration of power in the hands of the two superpowers (a bipolar system) were also necessarily a system in which all major powers were concentrated in two camps, and in which all minor powers were bipolarized as well, and in which the two blocs were tight and discrete, that system would be faced with war. And any indicator of polarity, when correlated with war frequency over time, would show a strong positive association between such periods of polarization and the outbreak of war. But in practice, during periods when the major power subsystem has been bipolar, such as the 1950s, there have been countervailing tendencies in the global system, such as the development of the nonaligned movement. With some forces pushing in the direction of peace and others pushing the other way, the force vectors would tend to cancel each other out, reducing systemic forces to an apparently more humble role. Then, an effort to correlate war frequency with an indicator of just one dimension of polarization would be doomed to give weak results.

From this second perspective the idiosyncratic indicators such as those of Bueno de Mesquita are an asset to the profession, because they force us to attend to the complexity of the real world and how multidimensionality can affect war and peace. This second perspective is a little discouraging, however, to those who want a clear answer about the relation of polarity and polarization to war. With only the 1815–1976 period available for detailed scrutiny, and with polarity and polarization patterns changing so slowly, there may not be enough time points to allow a multivariate test of the relation of system structure to war, if the structure is so multidimensional. One way around this difficulty is to adopt a long-term historical perspective in our research, as has been done by Haas (1974) and Levy (1983 and 1985).

Alternatively the best strategy may be to focus future investigations of these questions more at the dyadic and national levels of analysis. While some work has been done in this way on the issue of power distribution (Organski and Kugler 1980; Doran 1983), much less has been done on the role of alliances and alignments (Ward 1982). Perhaps this would be a productive direction for future research; indeed, when we know more about the relationship of alliances to war at the dyadic level, we should be able to return more cogently to an examination of the relationship between systemic alliance polarization and war.

4
Inter-nation Relationships

Formal Alliances, 1816–1965: An Extension of the Basic Data

Melvin Small and J. David Singer

In an earlier article, we published our findings on the distribution of formal alliances among the members of the interstate system during the period between the Napoleonic Wars and World War II. Our purpose there was to present a systematic and quantitative description of all formal alliances, their membership, duration, and type, as well as the procedures we used in generating those data (Singer and Small 1966b). While our major motivation was to provide the empirical basis for a number of inquiries into the correlates of war during that 125 years, it also seemed likely that these data might be of use to others in the scholarly community.[1]

Since completing the original paper, however, we have been under some compulsion to extend our data beyond World War II and up to the quite recent past, so that the period on which we concentrate is now the 150 years from January 1, 1816, to December 31, 1965. Some of the pressure has been self-induced and some has come via encouragement from the increasing number of scholars who are now engaged in data-based, quantitative research in international politics.[2] At the outset, we had planned to restrict the entire project to the 1816–1945 period, but for a variety of scientific as well as policy reasons we later decided to extend it up through the mid-1960s. Given this set of considerations, it now seems appropriate to update the earlier study and make our findings available to others whose work embraces the two decades following Hiroshima and Nagasaki.[3]

Reprinted from *Journal of Peace Research* 3 (1969): 257–82. Reprinted with permission.

1. In addition to several masters' and doctoral dissertations that have utilized those materials, and some employment for teaching and simulation purposes, there are several other papers based on these data; see, for example, Zinnes (1967) and Haas (1968). We have ourselves published two studies based on them; see Singer and Small (1967 and 1968).

2. Much of this work will be found in such journals as the present one, the *Journal of Conflict Resolution*, and Peace Research Society *Papers*, and a representative sampling is available in *Quantitative International Politics* (Singer 1968c).

3. The data may be had at nominal cost from the authors.

While much of the theoretical and methodological discussion found in the earlier paper need not be repeated here, some of the latter problems are sufficiently different to merit brief attention; this is particularly true of our data sources and their reliability, to which we will address ourselves at the outset. Following that, we will identify and justify the composition of the post-1945 interstate system and its major power subsystem, describe the three classes of alliance with which we are concerned, outline the coding and measuring procedures, and then present our results in a variety of forms. Throughout, we will compare our procedures and results with those of the original study and note any deviations therefrom; those who utilize these data are urged to note such deviations, especially as summarized in the appendix.

The Sources of Information

For a great deal of diplomatic information, one may readily turn to the diplomatic archives of many national governments and to the published volumes which subsequently embrace and codify a large portion of those archives. But this only holds true for materials that are at least two (and often, more) decades in the past; few, if any, governments make such documents available until twenty or more years after the fact. For the earlier study, then, we had the documentary evidence to make us quite confident that all relevant alliances had indeed been identified. But for the more recent years, it looked as if we might be in somewhat the same situation as the Wilhelmstrasse in 1910; it was known for example, that some sort of undertaking existed between France and Britain, but the German Foreign Office could not be at all certain what the specific commitments were. Similarly today, Western scholars know that the USSR and North Vietnam enjoy some sort of fraternal relationship, for instance, but cannot ascertain whether a formal alliance was contracted, no less ascertain the nature of the obligations involved. And even if we know that a formal alliance does exist, and have identified it, we still may wonder whether there are secret provisions which significantly alter the publicly stated arrangements, and which may not become known until the archives are eventually opened.

The picture is not, however, quite as bleak as it might appear. First of all, in the period since World War I, and even more since World War II, the League of Nations and the United Nations have maintained a registry wherein all treaties, conventions, and agreements may be recorded by the signatory governments. While registration is not compulsory, the consensus is that a very large percentage of all post-1945 agreements have been deposited with the Secretariat.[4] This gives us, at the least, a single and comprehensive source

---

4. On the basis of his UN Treaty Series project, however, Rohn (1968; 177) concludes "no government had ever checked whether all their treaties actually appeared in the UNTS," and that

with which to begin. Second, with the many changes in the culture of diplomacy, its increasing visibility, and the heightened role of ideological appeals and propaganda moves, governments are less and less prone to undertake secret commitments. Third, and closely related, the initiators of most of the alliances of the past two decades have been eager to present them—both for domestic and foreign consumption—as strictly defensive moves, undertaken reluctantly in the face of potential aggression. Fourth, in light of the consequences of America's failure to make explicit its commitments to South Korea before June, 1950, there has since been a strong desire to reduce the ambiguities and uncertainties; secrecy would not be useful in such a context. Finally, as the material that follows will make abundantly clear, it is nearly impossible to think of any alliances that have not already been consummated—and publicized. In every part of the world, just about any alliance that one could reasonably expect to be made since 1945 *has* been made.

Thus, despite the unavailability of the standard archival sources, we are persuaded that the present compilation includes virtually every single alliance that satisfies the criteria which are described below. In addition to the United Nations *Treaty Series* and the League of Nations *Treaty Series,* we have turned to the governmental and secondary sources cited in table 3 and in the references for the texts of the sixty-two qualifying alliances extant during the post–World War II period.[5]

Membership in the System

It may be recalled that in the earlier paper we differentiated between the total interstate system and its more restricted subsystems: that comprising most of the European and a few of the most important non-European states (which we called the central system), and that comprising the major powers only. Those states that did not qualify for inclusion in the central system were assigned to the peripheral system. The central-peripheral distinction might have been quite justified during the period 1816–1919, but by the end of World War I, most of the independent nations of the world were sufficiently interdependent, and the primacy of Europe was sufficiently ambiguous to permit the termination of that distinction as of 1920.[6] In this paper, therefore, the only two types

---

no hard evidence as to its completeness yet exists. In one such inquiry he found a 23 percent gap between "Canada's own published treaty records and Canada's treaties in the UNTS" (1966, 116).

 5. We have not had a chance to consult *Treaties and Alliances of the World* (1969), a new volume that may prove to be useful.

 6. A small terminological change was also made. In order to differentiate between independent national entities that had all the earmarks of sovereignty and thus qualified for inclusion, and those that lacked one or more critical attributes of statehood, we now include both sets of nations in the *international* system, but only include the former in the more restricted *interstate* system.

of nations are those that qualify for the interstate system, and those five that comprise the major power subsystem after 1945.

The justification and a detailed description of our coding procedures will be found in Singer and Small (1966a) and Russett, Singer, and Small (1968), but they may be summarized here. Essentially any putatively sovereign state with a population of at least 500,000 was included, provided that it enjoyed the de facto diplomatic recognition of the two "legitimizers," France and Britain. This latter requirement was only used up through 1919, and since then the basic criterion has been either: (a) membership in the League or the United Nations, or (b) a population of 500,000 or more and recognition by any two major powers.[7] Because the 1816–1945 period was marked by the consolidation and redistribution of empires and by many major wars, the composition of the interstate system underwent frequent shifts. The post-1945 system, on the other hand, shows greater stability. While we do see an appreciable upsurge in system size due to the "liquidation of colonialism," the only other change is the disappearance of two members. One case is that of Syria, which "federated" with Egypt to become a part of the United Arab Republic from 1958 to 1961, and the other is Zanzibar, which achieved independence in 1963 but which joined with Tanganyika to form Tanzania in 1964.

As to the major powers—whom we must identify in order to treat their alliance patterns separately later on in the paper—the problem is more complicated in the recent past than it was earlier. There would seem to be two sets of criteria here, regardless of time period; one is the judgment and consensus of the historians who specialize in the diplomacy of the period, and who, in turn, largely reflect the consensus of the practitioners. The other might be more objective criteria, such as military power, industrial capability, or diplomatic status.

Fortunately enough, both sets of criteria produce essentially the same set of nations. Thus, for most of the nineteenth and that part of the twentieth century embraced in the Correlates of War Project, we find that those states that score at or very near the top in military-industrial capability and diplomatic status are the same ones assigned to the major power category by those whose research focuses on the several epochs and regions involved.[8] Out of this consensus comes the following. Going back to the pre–World War I decades, we included: England, France, Germany, Austria-Hungary, Italy,

---

7. There are a few minor exceptions: India, despite League membership, was not included until 1947, and Byelorussia and the Ukraine have never been included despite UN membership. The alternative rule is necessary because several important states are not UN members: Switzerland and the two Germanies, Koreas, and Vietnams.

8. For diplomatic status data and rankings, see Singer and Small (1966a) and Singer, Handley, and Small (1969).

Russia, Japan, and the United States. When the debris and chaos of that war were cleared away (by the mid-1920s) the Hapsburgs were gone, but the other seven remained in (or had returned to) the ranks of the major powers. In the wake of World War II, the ranks were further reduced, leaving in 1946 only the USSR and the United States plus England and France; and with the consolidation of the Communist revolution and their creditable showing in the Korean War, China entered this oligarchy for the first time. By 1950, then, the major powers were exactly those nations that had been assigned special status (via the veto power) in the United Nations Security Council, and that would soon also become the five nuclear powers.

Having summarized our criteria and line of reasoning, we can now turn to the system membership compilations that emerged. In table 1, then, we list those states that comprised the total interstate system during all or part of the period 1946–65. They are listed by regional location with their standardized code numbers to the left and their date of entry into the system shown to the right; if their qualification for membership preceded 1946, no date is shown, and if they did not remain in the system for the entire twenty years (Syria and Zanzibar) the dates of departure and/or return are shown as well.[9]

Coding the Alliances

With the spatial-temporal domain identified, we can now turn to the alliances entered into by the members of the defined system during the twenty years under study, or carried over from prior years. It may be recalled that we defined three different classes of alliance in the original study: defense pacts, neutrality and nonaggression pacts, and ententes, with the following distinguishing characteristics. In the defense pact (class 1), the signatories obligated themselves to intervene militarily on behalf of one another if either were attacked. In the neutrality pact (class 2), the commitment was to remain militarily neutral if the partner were attacked. And in the entente (class 3), the only obligation was to consult with, or cooperate, in such a military contingency. Treaties of friendship, etc. (which we do not include) merely involve a more general promise of mutual cordiality.[10]

---

9. The nation code numbers, which have been adopted by a number of projects other than those at Yale and Michigan, and by the Inter-University Consortium for Political Research, are presented in Russett, Singer, and Small (1968).

10. The designations class 1, 2, and 3 suggest a hierarchy based upon levels of political commitment, with the defense pact a more serious commitment than the neutrality pact, and the neutrality pact a more serious commitment than the entente. While a class 1 alliance obviously is more serious than a class 2 or a class 3, a class 3 *may* be more serious than a class 2. In the nineteenth century, a neutrality pact was generally a more serious commitment than an entente. In the twentieth century, however, the entente seems to be a more serious commitment than the nonaggression pact.

TABLE 1. Membership in the Interstate System, 1946–65

Western Hemisphere (002–199)	Europe (200–399)
002 United States	350 Greece
020 Canada	352 Cyprus 1960
040 Cuba	355 Bulgaria
041 Haiti	360 Rumania
042 Dominican Republic	365 Russia
051 Jamaica 1962	375 Finland
052 Trinidad and Tobago 1962	380 Sweden
070 Mexico	385 Norway
090 Guatemala	390 Denmark
091 Honduras	395 Iceland
092 El Salvador	
093 Nicaragua	**Africa (400–599)**
094 Costa Rica	
095 Panama	
100 Colombia	420 Gambia 1965
101 Venezuela	432 Mali 1960
130 Ecuador	433 Senegal 1960
135 Peru	434 Dahomey 1960
140 Brazil	435 Mauritania 1960
145 Bolivia	436 Niger 1960
150 Paraguay	437 Ivory Coast 1960
155 Chile	438 Guinea 1958
160 Argentina	439 Upper Volta 1960
165 Uruguay	450 Liberia
	451 Sierra Leone 1961
Europe (200–399)	452 Ghana 1957
	461 Togo 1960
200 England	471 Cameroon 1960
205 Ireland	475 Nigeria 1960
210 Netherlands	481 Gabon 1960
211 Belgium	482 Central African Republic 1960
212 Luxemburg	483 Chad 1960
220 France	484 Congo (Brazzaville) 1960
225 Switzerland	490 Congo (Kinshasa) 1960
230 Spain	500 Uganda 1962
235 Portugal	501 Kenya 1963
255 German Federal Repulic 1955	510 Tanzania 1961
265 German Democratic Republic 1954	511 Zanzibar 1963–64
290 Poland	516 Burundi 1962
305 Austria 1955	517 Rwanda 1962
310 Hungary	520 Somalia 1960
315 Czechoslovakia	530 Ethiopia
325 Italy	551 Zambia 1964
338 Malta 1964	553 Malawi 1964
339 Albania	560 South Africa
345 Yugoslavia	580 Malagasy 1960

TABLE 1—*Continued*

Middle East (600–699)	Asia (700–999)

Middle East (600–699)	Asia (700–999)
600 Morocco	713 Taiwan 1949
615 Algeria 1962	731 People's Democratic Republic of Korea
616 Tunisia 1956	1948
620 Libya 1952	732 Republic of Korea 1949
625 Sudan 1956	740 Japan 1952
630 Iran	750 India 1947
640 Turkey	770 Pakistan 1947
645 Iraq	775 Burma 1948
650 United Arab Republic (Egypt)	780 Ceylon 1948
652 Syria 1946–58, 1962	781 Maldive Islands 1965
660 Lebanon 1946	790 Nepal
663 Jordan 1946	800 Thailand
666 Israel 1948	811 Cambodia 1953
670 Saudi Arabia	812 Laos 1954
678 Yemen	816 Democratic Republic of Vietnam 1954
690 Kuwait 1961	817 Republic of Vietnam 1954
	820 Malaysia 1947
Asia (700–999)	830 Singapore 1945
	840 Philippines 1946
700 Afghanistan	850 Indonesia 1949
710 China	900 Australia
712 Mongolia	920 New Zealand

The treaty obligations were ascertained by a literal reading of the texts, supplemented (if there were any verbal ambiguities) by the interpretations of the diplomatic historians. In other words, the classification is not sensitive to the political relations of the governments involved, nor to interpretations made by other governments. Second, no indirect alliance obligations were inferred via overlapping memberships. That is, even if Nation B was allied with both A and C via separate treaties, A and C were not treated as allies unless they were both also signatories to the same treaty of alliance. Third, a variety of more general commitments were not classified as alliances. Among those excluded were: (*a*) charters of global or quasi-global international organizations, such as the League, the United Nations, or their specialized agencies; (*b*) treaties of guarantee to which all relevant parties registered their assent, such as the 1960 Greek-Turkish guarantee of Cyprus; (*c*) conventions or agreements setting out general rules of state behavior, such as the Geneva Conventions; (*d*) "mutual security" arrangements that involve bases, financial aid, and training programs exclusively, such as the Spanish-American Treaty; (*e*) unilateral and asymmetric guarantees, such as the 1951 Japanese-American security treaty, in which only one signatory is committed to defend the other. On the latter rule, we must reiterate that we are concerned exclusively with the commitments and resultant cross-pressures that bind two or more states to concert their policies in time of crisis. An alliance, in other words, must contain at least two member states. Without this distinction, any pronouncement that declared that one nation would protect the territory of another nation would have to be considered as an alliance. For example, in 1951, Egypt denounced her 1936 alliance with England, but England refused to accept this unfriendly gesture and maintained that the alliance was still in force. Obviously, after 1951, the 1936 alliance became a unilateral (and unwanted) guarantee of the territory of Egypt by England, signifying something quite different from reciprocal obligation and cooperation.

Let us shift now from the *nature* of the alliance commitments which concern us here to the problem of identifying the *span of time* during which they are in force. In this connection, a preliminary point is in order, clarifying the connection between the data presented here and those shown in the original paper. Our major purpose in gathering alliance data is to ascertain the extent to which the resulting clusters and configurations correlate with the onset of war in the years following each set of observations of such alliance distributions. We have, therefore—and those who use our data for other purposes should take careful note—not included any alliances that were consummated by nations while participating in war or within three months prior to such participation, unless those alliances emerged from the war intact. Likewise, no alliances consummated during either of the World Wars were included unless they, too, continued in force during the postwar period.[11] One effect of this particular coding rule is to make it unnecessary for us to cover the 1914–18 and 1939–45 periods, and this is what accounts for the gap between the dates in the original paper and those used here.

Turning, then, to the effective dates of any alliance, the beginning date was a relatively simple matter. Even though some months may pass between the necessary signatures and ratification, the former date is always used; if, however, the treaty failed of ratification (such as EDC), it is of course not included at all. As to termination dates, the problem—especially in more recent years—is more complex. That is, with the decreasing incidence of formal (or even informal) abrogations or denunciations of alliances, the termination of a treaty whose text does not specify an expiration date can become difficult to pinpoint. Thus, we have in several cases had to make a political judgment as to the year in which the obligations were no longer effectively binding on one, several, or all of the signatories. A good example might be Yugoslavia's leaving the Cominform in 1948. Even though not all of the states

---

11. While we are not immediately concerned with such alliances, we are planning to gather data on them in the near future. Aside from alliances contracted during the two wars, this will most likely involve fewer than 10 alliances.

that had joined in the Soviet bloc's alliance system (via the several bilateral treaties of 1945 and 1946) formally abrogated their commitments, it seems evident that neither the Yugoslav nor the other governments considered themselves bound after the Tito regime's expulsion. So that the user will know the basic reason for the termination dates assigned to those twelve of the sixty-nine qualifying alliances that did become, in our judgment, ineffective during the 1946–65 period, we indicate them briefly in table 2.

Another problem of a chronological nature is that of new alliance agreements that are undertaken between and among governments which were already allied. The question here is one of determining which commitment takes precedence, since we are concerned not merely with *whether* or not certain states are allied, but ascertaining the nature or class of that commitment. We begin with the assumption that—in terms of the obligations undertaken—a defense pact imposes greater commitments than a neutrality or nonaggression pact, and that each of these imposes a greater commitment than an entente. Therefore, whenever any two or more signatories to a treaty with lower level obligations subsequently join in one with greater obligations—and this says nothing about the probability of such obligations being fulfilled—the latter takes precedence and the former is no longer included for computational purposes. Conversely, if an entente were consummated between or among states that were already members of a defense pact, for example, the entente would not be included in our compilations, even though it followed the defense pact in the chronological sense.

A final question arises from cases in which a number of bilateral treaties of a given class and national membership are followed (or preceded) by a

TABLE 2. Alliances that Terminated during 1946–65

Signatories and Effective Date	Termination Date	Justification
England-Iraq 1930	1956	English invasion of Suez
England-Egypt 1936	1951	Unilateral abrogation by Egypt
England-Russia 1942	1947	Onset of cold war
France-Russia 1944	1947	Onset of cold war
China-Russia 1945	1947	Russian support of Communist insurgents
England-Jordan 1946	1957	Unilateral abrogation by Jordan
Yugoslavia–Soviet Bloc 1945–47	1948	Yugoslavia leaves Cominform
Cuba-Organization of American States 1947	1960	American-Cuban hostility followed by expulsion from OAS
China-Russia 1950	1961	Sino-Soviet split
Iraq-Central Treaty Organization 1954	1958	Change in Iraqi government
Albania–Warsaw Pact 1955	1961	Sino-Soviet split

multilateral one of the same class and membership. In such cases, the multilateral alliance takes priority and the bilateral ones are dropped from our computations. Typical of these would be the post–World War II bilateral arrangements that were superseded by the Warsaw and NATO pacts. It should be stressed here that these coding rules are not meant to imply that the superseded alliance is considered to be terminated and no longer in effect. They serve only to make our indicators of alliance aggregation and alliance commitment, as discussed below, more consonant with the empirical realities which they are meant to measure, and hence more valid.

The results of these coding procedures and classification criteria are shown in table 3. In addition to the names of the signatory states, we show the dates of inception and termination, the alliance class (defense, neutrality, or entente) and the place in which its text may most conveniently be found.

Before turning to the conversion procedures by which these raw data are made more useful for research purposes, it might be helpful to present some simple summaries. The most general summary, found in table 4, shows the frequency distribution of those alliances which were in force, according to our criteria, among the states which constituted the system during all or part of the twenty years that concern us here. It should be noted that the total number of alliances shown here (eighty) comes to more than the (sixty-nine) alliances actually in effect, since several of the multilateral ones link not only major powers with nonmajors (minors), but majors with majors, and minors with minors, thus falling into more than one of the rows.

If we may be permitted one interpretive comment here, it is worth noting how few neutrality and/or nonaggression pacts are found during these two recent decades. While there were only four such arrangements during the 1816–99 period, accounting for 11 percent of the nineteenth-century alliances, that number rose sharply to thirty-seven (or 48 percent) during the 1900–39 period. But the number dropped sharply for the post–World War II period, with the seven neutrality pacts accounting for only 9 percent of all the alliances in force at any time during those twenty years. The nonaggression pact, which is one variation of the traditional neutrality pact, was clearly an invention of the 1920s and 1930s, and if the amount of war that followed is any indication, they were not particularly effective. Given that experience, it is little wonder that only four such alliances were consummated after World War II and all of these involved China; the other three were signed during the heyday of the "nonaggression era" between the two world wars.

It might also be noted that the percentage of ententes—a modest consultative obligation—remained constant after the ceremonies in Tokyo Bay. Ententes accounted for 23 percent of the nineteenth-century alliances and 22 percent and 23 percent, respectively, for both twentieth-century periods; the latter figures somewhat overstate their importance, since all but a few of those since 1945 were consummated among the minor non-Western states. Be that

TABLE 3. Interstate Alliances in Force, 1946–65

Signatory States	Date of Inception	Last Year in Force	Alliance Class	Information Source[a]
England Portugal	10/99	1949*	1	BD, 93
Afghanistan Russia	8/26		2	L 157, 371
England Iraq	1932	1956	1	BFS 132, 280
Mongolia Russia	3/36		1	U 48, 177
England Egypt	10/36	1951	1	BFS 140, 179
Brazil Bolivia Chile Colombia Costa Rica Cuba Dominican Republic Ecuador El Salvador Guatemala Haiti Honduras Mexico Nicaragua Panama Paraguay Peru United States Uruguay Venezuela Argentina	12/26	1947* (1942)	3	Gantenbein, 772
Afghanistan Iraq Iran Turkey	9/37		2	L 190, 21
Portugal Spain	3/39		2	BFS 142, 673
Canada United States	8/40	1949*	3	DSB 3, 154; DSB 16, 361

(continued)

Note: Classes of Alliance are: 1–Defense Pact; 2–Neutrality or Nonagression Pact; 3–Entente. Asterisk (*) following termination date indicates that the alliance was superseded by another arrangement. Parentheses around a year indicate that it applies only to the state alongside which it appears.
[a]Full references are listed in Appendix B.

TABLE 3—Continued

Signatory States	Date of Inception	Last Year in Force	Alliance Class	Information Source
England Russia	5/42	1947	1	BFS 144, 1038
Czechoslovakia Russia	12/43	1955*	1	Benes, 255
Australia New Zealand	1/44	1951*	3	U 18, 357
France Russia	12/44	1947	1	DSB 12, 39
Egypt Iraq Lebanon Saudi Arabia Syria Transjordan Yemen	3/45	1950*	3	U 70, 237
Russia Yugoslavia	4/45	1948	1	DSB 12, 774
Poland Russia	4/45	1955*	1	U 12, 391
China Russia	8/45	1947	1	U 10, 300
Poland Yugoslavia	3/46	1948	1	U 1, 153
England Jordan	3/46	1957	1	U 6, 143
Czechoslovakia Yugoslavia	5/46	1948	1	U 1, 67
Albania Yugoslavia	7/46	1948	1	U 1, 81
Czechoslovakia Poland	3/47	1955*	1	U 25, 231
England France	4/47	1949*	1	U 9, 187
England Argentina Bolivia Brazil Chile Colombia	8/47		1	U 21, 77

TABLE 3—*Continued*

Signatory States	Date of Inception	Last Year in Force	Alliance Class	Information Source
Costa Rica				
Cuba		(1960)		
Dominican Republic				
Ecuador				
El Salvador				
Guatemala				
Haiti				
Honduras				
Mexico				
Nicaragua				
Panama				
Paraguay				
Peru				
United States				
Uruguay				
Venezuela				
Bulgaria	11/47	1948	1	SDD 4, 241
Yugoslavia				
Hungary	12/47	1948	1	SDD 4, 243
Yugoslavia				
Albania	12/47	1955*	1	SDD 4, 243
Bulgaria				
Rumania	12/47	1948	1	U 116, 89
Yugoslavia				
Hungary	1/48	1955*	1	U 477, 155
Rumania				
Bulgaria	1/48	1955*	1	SDD 4, 245
Rumania				
Hungary	2/48	1955*	1	U 48, 163
Russia				
Rumania	2/48	1955*	1	U 48, 189
Russia				
Belgium	3/48	1949*	1	U 19, 51
England				
France				
Luxemburg				
Netherlands				
Bulgaria	3/48	1955*	1	U 48, 135
Russia				
Finland	4/48		1	U 48, 149
Russia				

(*continued*)

TABLE 3—Continued

Signatory States	Date of Inception	Last Year in Force	Alliance Class	Information Source
Bulgaria Czechoslovakia	4/48	1955*	1	SDD 4, 248
Bulgaria Poland	5/48	1955*	1	U 26, 213
Hungary Poland	6/48	1955*	1	U 25, 319
Bulgaria Hungary	7/48	1955*	1	U 477, 169
Czechoslovakia Rumania	7/48	1955*	1	SDD 12–13, 633
Poland Rumania	1/49	1955*	1	U 85, 21
Czechoslovakia Hungary	4/49	1955*	1	U 477, 183
Belgium Canada Denmark England France Iceland Italy Luxemburg Netherlands Portugal United States Greece Turkey German Fd. Repub.	4/49 (1951) (1951) (1955)		1	U 34, 243
China Russia	2/50	1961	1	U 266, 3
Egypt Iraq Jordan Lebanon Saudi Arabia Yemen Syria Libya Sudan Tunisia Morocco Kuwait Algeria	4/50 (1950–58, 1961) (1953) (1956) (1956) (1958) (1961) (1962)		1	Lawson, 235

TABLE 3—*Continued*

Signatory States	Date of Inception	Last Year in Force	Alliance Class	Information Source
Philippines United States	8/51		3	U 177, 133
Australia New Zealand United States	9/51		3	U 131, 83
Greece Turkey Yugoslavia	2/53	1954*	3	U 167, 21
England Libya	7/53		1	U 186, 185
Republic of Korea United States	10/53		3	U 238, 199
Pakistan Turkey	8/54	1954*	3	U 211, 263
Greece Turkey Yugoslavia	8/54		1	U 211, 237
Australia England France New Zealand Pakistan Philippines Thailand United States	9/54		3	U 209, 28
Taiwan United States	12/54		3	U 248, 226
Turkey Iraq England Pakistan Iran	2/55 (4/55) (9/55) (11/55)	(1958)	3	U 233, 199
Bulgaria Czechoslovakia German Democratic Republic Hungary Rumania Russia Albania Poland	5/55	(1961)	1	U 219, 3

(*continued*)

TABLE 3—*Continued*

Signatory States	Date of Inception	Last Year in Force	Alliance Class	Information Source
England Malaysia	10/57		1	U 285, 59
Ghana Guinea	5/59	1961*	3	Legum, 178
Burma China	1/60		2	DIA 1960, 499
Afghanistan China	8/60		2	DIA 1960, 502
China Guinea	9/60		2	DIA 1960, 337
Ghana Guinea Mali	4/61	1963	1	Legum, 178
North Korea Russia	6/61		1	DIA 1961, 256
China North Korea	7/61		1	DIA 1961, 258
China Ghana	8/61		2	DIA 1961, 646
Cameroon Central African Republic Chad Congo (B) Dahomey Gabon Ivory Coast Malagasy Mauritania Niger Senegal Upper Volta Rwanda Togo	9/61 (3/63) (7/63)	1964	1	DIA 1961, 678
Algeria Burundi Cameroon Central African Republic Chad	5/63		3	Legum, 281

TABLE 3—*Continued*

Signatory States	Date of Inception	Last Year in Force	Alliance Class	Information Source
Congo (B)				
Congo (K)				
Dahomey				
Ethiopia				
Gabon				
Ghana				
Guinea				
Ivory Coast				
Liberia				
Libya				
Malagasy				
Mali				
Mauritania				
Morocco				
Niger				
Nigeria				
Rwanda				
Senegal				
Sierra Leone				
Somalia				
Sudan				
Tanzania				
Togo				
Tunisia				
Uganda				
United Arab Republic				
Upper Volta				
Malawi	(1964)			
Zambia	(1964)			
Gambia	(1965)			
Ethiopia	11/63		1	K, 19, 809
Kenya				
Gambia	(1965)		1	Rice, 387
Senegal				

TABLE 4. Distribution of Alliances by Class and Signatories, 1946–65

	1	2	3
Majors with Majors	7	0	1
Majors with Minors	21	5	7
Minors with Minors	27	2	10
Total	55	7	18

as it may, given the very low frequency of the class 2 (nonaggression) alliances, we have, for the aggregate computational purposes outlined in the next section, combined them with those of class 3.

An alternate way of summarizing the data is to shift from the number of alliances (and alliance bonds) to the number of national alliance commitments, counting each individual nation-to-nation commitment. Applying the formula $n(n-1)$ to the twenty-one-nation Rio Pact, for example, we get 420 national commitments. The frequencies resulting from this set of computations are found in table 5.

Annual Alliance Indicators

Returning once more to the presentation of our data, there is the problem to which we alluded earlier: How can the raw alliance figures be converted into a form that is useful for correlational analysis over time? That is, if our concern is to ascertain the extent to which alliance patterns predict to, and correlate with, fluctuations in the incidence of war, or any other types of event, the raw data must be converted into a variety of annual indicators.

As in the original paper, we suggest two different measures of this particular structural attribute of the interstate system. One, called Alliance Aggregation, reflects the percentage of states of a given type that belong to one or more alliances of any given class in each successive year. The other, called Alliance Commitment, is a bit more complex, and reflects the number of nation-to-nation commitments per system member for each year.[12]

TABLE 5. Distribution of Nation-to-Nation Alliance Commitments by Class and Signatories, 1946–65

	1	2	3
Majors with Majors	22	0	6
Majors with Minors	166	10	88
Minors with Minors	924	14	1,620
Total	1,112	24	1,714

---

12. In the original study, we used the concept of Alliance Involvement, measuring dyadic bonds via the equation $n(n-1)/2$. We believe that a more valid measure is the total number of nation-to-nation alliance commitments existing at any given time; thus, all such commitments, not only the dominant ones, are counted, and for any given alliance the number of commitments is $n(n-1)$.

In addition to the computation procedures, there are two specific coding rules worth reiterating. First, any pair of states may have more than one alliance commitment in force at any given time. But, second, we only count the strongest or most dominant bond which any state has vis-à-vis any other. Defense pacts take precedence over neutrality pacts, and these take precedence over ententes, and if A is in both a defense pact and an entente with B, the latter bond is not included in the computation. To illustrate, then, if the Alliance Commitment Indicator (ACI) for a given year is 7.12 (as in 1946 for all classes of commitments among all states in the system), there was an average of 7.12 alliance commitments per state; a figure of 1.00 indicates an average of one such commitment per state, but tells us of course nothing about the concentration or dispersion of such commitments.[13] One virtue of both sets of indicators is that they are normalized for system size, thus permitting comparisons across time.

Table 6, then, is divided into two parts, with the Alliance Aggregation scores on the left and the Alliance Commitment scores on the right. After showing, for each of the twenty years, the number of states in the system and the number in the major power subsystem, we present four separate indicators of Alliance Aggregation: the percentage of the system's members who are in one or more alliances of *any* class; the percentage in *defense* pacts only; the percentage of *major* powers in any alliance; and the percentage of majors in defense pacts only. On the right hand side, under Alliance Commitment, we show the following ratios between the number of national commitments and the system or subsystem size: the number of commitments of *any* class per member of the total system; number of *defense* pact commitments of any class by *major* powers (regardless of partner's status) per major; and number of major power defense pact commitments per major.

Having computed these ten indicators for each of the twenty years, we and others may next wonder as to their utility for analytical purposes. As independent, intervening, or dependent variables, we may find one or more of these several measures useful, depending on the systemic focus and theoretical inquiry at hand. But for more general purposes, it might be useful to have either a single combined index, or to select one of the indices as generally representative. The first could be generated by a variety of techniques, among which the "construct mapping" version of factor analysis (Jones 1966)

---

13. Such concentration might be computed by use of the Gini index, for example, which reflects what fraction of the system's members account for what fraction of the commitments in force. It should also be noted that whereas the decimal point was omitted from tables 5 and 6 of the original paper, we decided that the Alliance Commitment score would be more meaningful if we did include it here. The other difference, as indicated earlier, is that we have not computed either the Alliance Aggregation or Alliance Commitment Indicators for neutrality and entente agreements separately, since there were so few of either in this post-1945 period.

TABLE 6. Annual Alliance Indicators, 1946–65

Year	System Size	Number of Majors	Alliance Aggregation				Alliance Commitment			
			Percentage in any Class	Percentage in Defense Pacts	Percentage Majors in any Class	Percentage Majors in Defense Pacts	ACI in any Class	ACI in Defense Pacts	ACI of Majors in any Class	ACI of Majors in Defense Pacts
1946	66	4	67	20	100	75	7.12	0.42	8.5	3.25
1947	68	4	71	54	100	100	13.26	6.76	14.0	8.75
1948	72	4	71	56	100	100	7.75	6.81	11.0	10.50
1949	75	5	71	57	80	80	8.77	7.95	14.2	13.80
1950	75	5	72	64	100	100	8.75	8.21	12.6	12.40
1951	75	5	75	67	100	100	9.17	8.53	14.6	13.80
1952	77	5	73	65	100	100	8.88	8.57	14.2	13.40
1953	78	5	76	65	100	100	9.00	8.62	14.6	13.80
1954	82	5	76	63	100	100	9.34	8.27	18.8	13.80
1955	84	5	76	64	100	100	10.33	9.11	21.6	15.60
1956	87	5	76	64	100	100	10.00	8.83	20.6	14.80
1957	89	5	75	64	100	100	9.78	8.63	20.6	14.80
1958	90	5	76	64	100	100	9.87	8.73	20.4	14.60
1959	89	5	78	64	100	100	9.69	8.61	20.2	14.60
1960	107	5	65	53	100	100	8.11	7.16	20.8	14.60
1961	111	5	77	67	100	100	9.21	8.20	21.4	14.80
1962	117	5	73	63	100	100	8.79	7.85	20.8	14.20
1963	119	5	81	66	100	100	17.41	8.15	20.8	14.20
1964	122	5	80	61	100	100	18.00	7.90	20.8	14.20
1965	124	5	81	51	100	100	16.81	6.32	20.8	14.20

would seem particularly appropriate. We do not offer such combined measures here, but do suggest a basis for the second strategy. That is, if we find that the scores of all or most of the separate measures show a high correlation vis-à-vis one another, one may then be justified in using any one of them for certain purposes. Whereas the picture for much of the 1816–1939 period was a rather confusing and erratic one, the post–World War II pattern is remarkably clear. Even a cursory visual inspection of table 6 reveals that any rank-order correlation would be extremely high; whether one compares across alliance classes, nation types, or alternative indices, the years would fall into essentially the same ranking. Likewise, if we treated our data in interval-scale fashion, any of the appropriate correlation coefficients would turn out to be remarkably high. Thus we do not include here any of the correlation matrices which were quite necessary in the earlier paper.

Summary and Speculation

In this final section we want to compare the period under review here with that embraced in the original inquiry, but before doing so, it might be useful to summarize (verbally and statistically) the alliance patterns of this more recent period by itself. The post–World War II scene divides rather naturally into three subperiods. The first of these, extending up through 1951, saw not only the liquidation of the most severe war in human history and the establishment of a collective security system that might prevent another such holocaust, but the creation of an unprecedented number of alliances. While such "collective defense" treaties were explicitly permitted by the United Nations Charter, the speed with which they were formed could only cast doubt on the expressions of confidence that accompanied the birth of the world organization. By 1947, 71 percent of the nations in the interstate system were in one or more alliances of one class or another, and 54 percent of them were in the more concrete defense pacts; moreover, by the next year, 100 percent of the major powers were already committed to defense pacts, and when this flurry of alliance making came to an end in 1951, three-quarters of all the system's members were allied, as were all of the major powers.

The second period, extending from 1951 through 1959, was exceptionally stable in terms of alliance aggregation and alliance commitment scores, with no appreciable movement into, out of, or between, alliance blocs, even though the size of the system rose from 75 to 89. This is not to say, however, that no new treaties of alliance were consummated. That decade saw the establishment of the Central Treaty Organization (CENTO), the Southeast Asia Treaty Organization (SEATO), and the Warsaw Pact, and these certainly helped to further institutionalize the cold war cleavage. On the other hand, most of the alliance bonds represented in these three defense pacts had already been established, albeit sometimes at the entente level, via prior bilateral treaties. Hence—and this is precisely why our measures do not suffice for all theoretical purposes—there was no appreciable increase in the several indices during the 1950s.

A third period, from 1960 to the close of our study in 1965, was characterized by a momentary decline in both alliance aggregation and alliance commitment scores (largely as a result of the influx of new states) followed by a rapid rise in these indicators to new heights. By 1965, the year we close our study, 81 percent of the states in the system were allied, and the Alliance Commitment Indicator showed an average of 16.8 alliances for every member in the system. During the seven years from 1959 to 1965 the system increased in size from 89 to 124, leading to a much larger denominator in our ratio, but the several new alliances (largely African) led to a comparable increase in the numerator.

Turning from the sheer magnitude of our ten different indices of aggregation and commitment, another striking element is the relatively "natural" as well as stable pattern that developed. That is, since the cold war confrontation became apparent, all but five of the European members of the system,[14] and a good many in the other regions, had cast their lots with either the American or the Soviet bloc. In Asia, two relatively established states—Thailand and the Philippines—joined with two newly independent ones–Pakistan and Malaysia–to link up with SEATO. On top of this, Japan, Taiwan, and South Korea had bilateral commitments with the United States, which was the major architect of SEATO. On the opposing side, for much of these two decades, the Asian states of China, North Korea, and Mongolia were linked formally to the Soviet Union, while North Vietnam was an informal member of this anti-Western configuration. Equally interesting in this regard is the fact that, aside from two nonaggression pacts, none of the system members that began the cold war as announced neutrals defected from that position to join the major power blocs. At one point (the Bandung conference of 1955) there was some discussion of an alliance of the nonaligned nations to formalize that state of affairs, but it was not considered necessary enough to justify the costs and obligations that might be involved.[15]

In Latin America, Africa, and the Middle East, likewise, the picture

---

14. These were the three traditionally nonaligned states (Sweden, Switzerland, and Ireland), Spain, whose exclusion from NATO was largely in deference to antifascist views in some of the Western nations, and Yugoslavia, which left the Soviet bloc in 1948.

15. A provocative hypothesis regarding the costs and gains of alliance membership, and the coalition-building strategies that might be expected to result, is in Riker (1962). That hypothesis, based largely on domestic political systems, is now being tested for the international system; see Singer and Bueno de Mesquita (1969). A more general model of the factors that go into alliance formation is in Russett (1968a).

showed little change over these two decades. The first region's members revived their prewar regional bloc affiliated with the United States in the form of the Organization of American States, and only Cuba failed to remain in it during the entire period. In Africa, despite the pro-Soviet inclination of the "Casablanca group," the Organization of African Unity institutionalized the neutrality (in the cold war context at least) of almost every state in the region. In the north, the Arab League embraced all of the Moslem nations of North Africa and the Middle East. Thus, from the Dardanelles to the Cape, every system member was in one alliance or another, except for Israel and South Africa.[16]

The above patterns, while they held for most of the period under review, do not tell the entire story. As we urged in the earlier paper and elsewhere in this one, formal written alliances offer only one index of the system's basic configurations. A more complete picture of the system at any point in time must certainly take account of political alignments and predispositions that stem from strategic, geographic, economic, and ideological factors. And while all of these factors do exercise some impact on the decisions which lead to formal alliance, they do not all necessarily produce the same alliance configurations.

As a matter of fact, one of the working—but not yet tested—assumptions of this project is that the peacefulness of the system depends very much on the existence of strong cross-pressures among states, varying as to which sectors of activity and concern are involved. In other words, we posit that high alliance aggregation and commitment scores need not necessarily make the system more war-prone by and of themselves. But if such conditions are accompanied by configurations in which many of the states in the system divide up into two opposing blocs whose composition is constant across a wide range of issues, then we would expect the salutary effects of the "invisible hand" to be seriously inhibited. With the pluralistic, cross-cutting bonds thus weakened, we hypothesize that war becomes much more probable.[17]

This consideration leads, then, to our concluding comments. We found that high alliance aggregation scores in the nineteenth century did not precede, or predict to, increases in the incidence of war. On the contrary, the most peaceful periods in the 1816–99 period were largely those that were preceded

---

16. Another might be Rhodesia, but its failure to achieve any substantial diplomatic recognition after the unilateral declaration of independence in 1965, leaves it outside of our interstate system.

17. The reasoning behind this classical balance of power argument is summarized and partially operationalized in Deutsch and Singer (1964) and partially supported in Singer and Small (1968). For a critical reanalysis of our data, see Zinnes (1967); other discussions of the issue are Gulick (1955), Liska (1962), Waltz (1964) and Rothstein (1968). A suggestive alternative model is in Galtung (1964).

by the highest levels of alliance aggregation and commitment. In the twentieth century, however, quite the reverse obtained, with high alliance levels predicting all too regularly to sharp increases in the frequency, magnitude, and severity of war (Singer and Small 1968).

One plausible explanation might be that nineteenth century alliances were largely "affairs of convenience" rather than "marriages of passion," to reverse the conventional idiom. That is, only as the tradition of quiet diplomacy among culturally similar elites gave way to the welfare state, rising public and partisan involvement in foreign policy, and extensive use of psychological mobilization techniques did alliance bonds become increasingly inflexible and dysfunctional. Under such conditions, movement into and out of alliances became increasingly inhibited, and what had formerly been thought of as rational diplomacy and realpolitik became a matter of perfidy and condemnation. The question, then, is whether—assuming that this model is an accurate reflection of reality—the slight movement toward a loosening of the cold war alliance bonds in the 1960s will help make ours a more stable system. After all, the only other times in which the alliance indices stood at levels even approximately as high were 1912–14 and 1937–39, and the consequences then were disastrous.

Appendix A. Substantive Modifications of Original Data

In any enterprise of this kind, the researcher is bound to discover new or conflicting facts as the project unfolds and as comments come in from others in the field. This has certainly been our experience in the Correlates of War Project and, as a consequence, the following substantive modifications in our data have become desirable. First, these dates of qualification for system membership have been changed: Cuba, from 1934 to 1902; Hungary, from 1920 to 1919; Czechoslovakia, from 1919 to 1918; Estonia, Latvia, and Lithuania, from 1920 to 1918, and Yemen, from 1934 to 1926. Second, we are now persuaded that the Anglo-Portuguese defense pact of 1899 should be coded as surviving World War I, and terminating only with the NATO treaty (which supersedes it) rather than in 1914, as originally coded. Third, new evidence suggests that the 1933 treaty between Finland and eight Latin American states did not satisfy our criteria and should not be classified as an alliance in the sense used here; it is therefore excluded from our revised compilation. And last, we had originally ignored a treaty partner, and also overrated the classification of the Saudi Arabian–Yemeni alliance of 1937. It should now be coded as an Iraqi-Saudi entente of 4/36, to which Yemen adhered in 4/37. Those who utilize our data decks will find these modifications already made, but those who are working from the article itself should note the changes.

As a further aid to readers who are interested in alliance patterns since 1816, we offer again our basic listing (with the above modifications) from the original article (table 7). Sources and the distinctions between central and total system members have been eliminated for the sake of simplicity.

TABLE 7. Internation Alliances with Commitment Class and Dates, 1816–1945

Members	Inception	Termination	Class	Members	Inception	Termination	Class
Austria	6/1815–1848,	1866	1	England	4/1834–	1846	1
Baden	1850			France	1840,1841		
Bavaria				Portugal			
Hesse-Electoral				Spain			
Hesse-Grand Ducal							
Prussia				Austria	7/1840	1840	1
Saxony				England			
Württemberg				Prussia			
Hanover	1838			Russia			
Mecklenburg-Schwerin	1843			Turkey			
Austria	11/1815	1823	1	England	6/1844	1846	3
England				Russia		(1853?)	
Prussia							
Russia				Austria	12/1847	1859	1
France	11/1818			Modena			
England	7/1827	1830	3	Austria	1851	1859	1
France				Parma			
Russia							
				France	1/1859	1859	1
Russia	7/1833	1840	1	Sardinia			
Turkey							
				Modena	?/1859	1860	1
Austria	10/1833–	1854	3	Parma			
Prussia	1848,1850			Tuscany			
Russia							

(continued)

TABLE 7—*Continued*

Members	Inception	Termination	Class
Ecuador Peru	1/1860	1861(?)	1
England France Spain	10/1861	1862	3
Prussia Russia	2/1863	1864	1
Colombia Ecuador	1/1864	1865(?)	1
Baden Prussia	8/1866	1870	1
Prussia Württemberg	8/1866	1870	1
Bavaria Prussia	8/1866	1870	1
Austria Germany Russia	10/1873	1878	3
Bolivia Peru	2/1873	1883	1

Members	Inception	Termination	Class
Austria Italy Spain	5/1887	1895	2
France Russia	8/1891 1894	1894* 1914*	3 1
China Russia	5/1896	1902(?)	1
Japan Russia	6/1896	1903	3
Austria Russia	5/1897	1908	3
England Portugal	10/1899	1949*	1
France Italy	12/1900 7/1902	1902* 1915*	3 2
England Japan	1/1902	1921	1
England France	4/1904	1914*	3

Powers		Date		No.	Powers		Date		No.
Austria	Russia	1/1877	1878	2	France	Spain	10/1904	1918	3
England	Turkey	6/1878	1880	1	England	Spain	5/1907	1918	3
Austria	Germany	10/1879	1918	1	France	Japan	6/1907	1914*	3
	Italy	5/1882	(1914)		Japan	Russia	7/1907	1914*	3
Austria	Germany	6/1881	1887	2	England	Russia	8/1907	1914*	3
	Russia								
Austria	Serbia	6/1881	1889*	2	Japan	U.S.A.	10/1908	1909	3
		1889	1895	1					
Austria	Germany	10/1883	1914	1	Italy	Russia	10/1909	1915*	3
	Rumania								
	Italy	5/1888			Bulgaria	Serbia	3/1912	1913	1
Germany	Russia	6/1887	1890	2	Bulgaria	Greece	5/1912	1913	1
Austria	England	2/1887	1895	3	Greece	Serbia	6/1913	1918	1
	Italy		(1897?)						

(continued)

TABLE 7—Continued

Members	Inception	Termination	Class	Members	Inception	Termination	Class
Czechoslovakia Yugoslavia	8/1920	1933*		Afghanistan Russia	8/1926		2
Czechoslovakia Rumania	4/1921	1933*	1	Lithuania Russia	9/1926	1940	2
Rumania Yugoslavia	6/1921	1933*	1	Italy Rumania	9/1926	1930	3
Czechoslovakia Rumania Yugoslavia	2/1933	(1939) 1941	1	Albania Italy	11/1926 1927	1927* 1939	3 1
Belgium France	9/1920	1936	1	France Yugoslavia	1/1927	1940	2
France Poland	2/1921	1939	1	Hungary Italy	4/1927	1943	2
Poland Rumania	3/1921	1939	1	Persia Russia	10/1927	1945	2
Afghanistan Turkey	3/1921	1939(?)	1	Greece Rumania	3/1928	1934*	2
Persia Turkey	4/1926	1937*	2	Greece Turkey	10/1930	1934*	2

Countries				Countries			
Afghanistan Persia	11/1927	1937*	2	Rumania Turkey	10/1933	1934*	2
Afghanistan Iraq Persia Turkey	9/1937		2	Turkey Yugoslavia	11/1933	1934*	2
Austria Czechoslovakia	12/1921	1927	2	Greece Rumania Turkey Yugoslavia	2/1934	1941	1
Estonia Latvia	11/1923	1940	1	Italy Turkey	5/1928	1938	2
Czechoslovakia France	1/1924 1925	1924* 1939	3 1	Greece Italy	2/1928	1938	2
Italy Yugoslavia	1/1924	1927	2	Hungary Turkey	1/1929	1945	2
Czechoslovakia Italy	7/1924	1930	3	Bulgaria Turkey	3/1929	1938*	2
Russia Turkey	12/1925	1939(?)	2	Bulgaria Greece Rumania Turkey Yugoslavia	7/1938	1941	2
Germany Russia	4/1926	1936	2	France Turkey	2/1930	1940	2
France Rumania	6/1926	1940	2				

(continued)

TABLE 7—Continued

Members	Inception	Termination	Class	Members	Inception	Termination	Class
England	1932	1956	1	Bolivia	12/1936	1947	3
Iraq				Argentina		(1942)	
				Brazil			
Finland	1/1932	1939	2	Chile			
Russia				Colombia			
				Costa Rica			
Latvia	2/1932	1940	2	Cuba	12/1936	1947	3
Russia				Dominican Republic			
				Ecuador			
Estonia	5/1932	1940	2	El Salvador			
Russia				Guatemala			
				Haiti			
Poland	7/1932	1939	2	Honduras			
Russia				Mexico			
				Nicaragua			
France	11/1932	1935*	2	Panama			
Russia	1935	1939	1	Paraguay			
				Peru			
England	6/1933	1936(?)	3	U.S.A.			
France				Uruguay			
Germany				Venezuela			
Italy							
Italy	9/1933	1941	2	Italy	3/1937	1939	2
Russia				Yugoslavia			

Germany Poland	1/1934	1939	2	Arabia Iraq Yemen	4/1936 4/1937	1945*	3
Austria Hungary Italy	3/1934	1938	3	China Russia	8/1937	1945*	2
Estonia Latvia Lithuania	8/1934	1940	3	France Germany	12/1938	1939	3
France Italy	4/1935	1938	3	Portugal Spain	3/1939		2
Czechoslovakia Russia	5/1935	1939	1	Germany Italy	5/1939	1943	1
Mongolia Russia	3/1936			Denmark Germany	5/1939	1940	2
Egypt England	10/1936	1951	1	Estonia Germany	6/1939	1940	2
Germany Japan Italy	11/1936 11/1937	1945 (1943)	3	Germany Latvia	6/1939	1940	2

*We are indebted to a number of scholars who are using, and have commented upon, the earlier study of which this is a continuation. In addition to those identified in the footnotes we would like to particularly thank Bruce Russett, who has helped considerably in our data acquisition, and has gone over this manuscript in detail in the course of our collaboration on the role of alliances in the international system. Since his theoretical concerns are somewhat different from ours, there will be appreciable disparities between our data and those which he will be reporting; see Russett (1968a).

Appendix B. References to Table 3

BD   British Documents. 1927. *British Documents on the Origin of the War.*
             Vol. 1. London.
Benes   Benes, E. 1954. *Memoirs.* London: Allen and Unwin.
BFS   *British Foreign and State Papers.*
DIA   *Documents on International Affairs.*
DSB   United States State Department. *Bulletin.*
Gantenbein   Gantenbein, J., ed. 1950. *The Evolution of Our Latin American Policy.*
             New York: Columbia University Press.
K   Keesing's Contemporary Archive.
L   League of Nations. *Treaty Series.*
Lawson   Lawson, R. 1962. *International Regional Organizations.* New York:
             Praeger.
Legum   Legum, C. 1965. *Pan Africanism.* New York: Praeger.
Rice   Rice, B. 1967. *Enter Gambia.* Boston: Houghton-Mifflin.
SDD   United States State Department. *Documents and State Papers.*
U   United Nations. *Treaty Series.*

5
Inter-nation Interactions

Militarized Interstate Disputes, 1816–1976

Charles S. Gochman and Zeev Maoz

International conflict is a pervasive property of an interstate system lacking supreme political authority of generally accepted laws and behavioral norms. Yet despite the salience and centrality of conflict in world politics, speculation on its causes, courses, and consequences far exceeds our empirically based knowledge. It is, for example, commonplace to hear that international politics today is dramatically different than in the past because the advent of nuclear weapons has altered the utility of military force as an instrument of foreign policy. Exactly how these weapons have altered the calculus of decision makers is unclear. Some analysts claim that the threat of nuclear war has stabilized world politics in that nations in the nuclear era have been more restrained in their threats and uses of military force. Others contend that, despite the imminent threat of nuclear war or perhaps because of it, the resort to limited military force has become considerably more common. Yet, to the best of our knowledge, there exist few systematic attempts to compare the frequency and severity of international conflicts in the nuclear era with those in earlier historical epochs.[1]

The paucity of our empirically based knowledge on international conflict is due not only to a lack of empirical investigations but also to conceptual and methodological disagreements among researchers. Lack of consensus on conceptual and operational definitions, selection criteria, and assumptions about the nature of international conflict and the forces that produce it has led to noncomparable theses and noncumulative findings. In addition, historical

Reprinted from *Journal of Conflict Resolution*, 28, no. 4 (December 1984); 585–615. © 1984 Sage Publications, Inc. Reprinted by permission of Sage Publications, Inc.

1. Several recent publications have added significantly to our systematic knowledge on this subject. Small and Singer (1979) and Siverson and Tennefoss (1982) have presented initial descriptive analyses of major power conflict behavior since 1815. In addition, the March, 1982, issue of *International Interactions* contains four articles that utilize an extended version of the militarized interstate dispute data set employed by Small and Singer. Particularly germane for the present investigation is Cusack and Eberwein (1982). Our own investigation is based upon a further extension of that data base.

parochialism—that is, assumptions about the uniqueness of historical periods, international structures, geographic regions, or state actors—has often precluded the pursuit of comparative research.[2]

Our purpose in this article is to generate a degree of existential and correlational knowledge[3] about international conflict so as to provide an overview and some direction for dealing with the conflict puzzle. Below we provide a quantitative description of militarized interstate disputes that delineates some of the more important attributes of the phenomenon over time and across space. This description is based upon a newly completed data set compiled by the Correlates of War Project over the past eight years. Increasingly detailed descriptions and analyses of these data will appear in subsequent publications; here we utilize broad brush strokes to portray the major patterns of interstate disputes since the Congress of Vienna.

The Militarized Interstate Dispute Data Set

Definitions and Selection Criteria

The objects of our investigation are those interstate disputes that are serious enough to become militarized. More precisely, we define a "militarized interstate dispute" as a set of interactions between or among states involving threats to use military force, displays of military force, or actual uses of military force. To be included, these acts must be explicit, overt, nonaccidental, and government sanctioned.

This definition incorporates several criteria. First, participation in these disputes is limited to national political entities that qualify as members of the interstate system.[4] Second, the threshold for the disputes is conceived in terms of military force. We recognize that disputes among states often involve the use of other means of bargaining, but believe that the threat, display, or use of military force demarcates a particularly acute stage in a relationship among states. And, because we are interested in the processes by which peaceful relations among states evolve into wars, the notion of military force

---

2. Most available data sets on international conflict cover temporal domains limited to the post–World War I era at best and, more commonly, to the post–World War II era. See, for example, Holsti (1966, 1983), Butterworth (1976), Hazelwood and Hayes (1976), Eckhart and Azar (1978), and Brecher and Wilkenfeld (1982).

3. Existential knowledge refers to the "description of empirical regularities or patterns," and correlational knowledge refers to the "*covariation* between two or more sets of observations" (Singer 1972).

4. The criteria for interstate system membership, as well as a list of state members, appear in Small and Singer (1982).

is central to our endeavor. Third, these threats, displays, or uses of military force must be explicit. That is, a threatened action must clearly involve the use of military force and the target of a threat or an act must be clearly identifiable. Thus such acts as vague warnings of "serious consequences" or routine military maneuvers are not included within the data compilation. Finally, since our primary concern is with the evolution of conflict as a product or consequence of government decision making, we require that actions taken or threatened be attributable to responsible state authorities. Placing these restrictions on the phenomenon to be investigated obviously narrows the scope of our endeavor, but it also permits us to deal with a manageable, well-defined, and important subset of interstate interactions. Using explicit coding criteria and focusing on relatively visible acts enhance the probability that the data that have been generated are both valid and reliable.

Fourteen types of military acts, clustered into three broad categories, are included in the Correlates of War militarized interstate dispute data set. These acts and associated categories are as follows:[5]

Threat of Force

— *threat to use force:* threat by one state to use its regular armed forces to fire upon the armed forces or territory of another state
— *threat to blockade:* threat by one state to use ships or troops to seal off the territory of another state so as to prevent either entry or exit
— *threat to occupy territory:* threat by one state to use military force to occupy the whole or part of another state's territory
— *threat to declare war:* threat by one state to issue an official declaration of war against another state

Display of Force

— *alert:* a reported increase in the military readiness of a state's regular armed forces, directed at another state
— *mobilization:* the activation by a state of previously inactive armed forces
— *show of force:* a public demonstration by a state of its military capabilities, not involving combat operations, directed at another state

---

5. The typology of military acts outlined here is consistent with the coding scheme for events data used in Leng and Singer (1977). The grouping of military acts into the categories of threat, display, and use of force was suggested by Stoll (1977).

Use of Force

— *blockade:* use of ships or troops by one state to seal off the territory of another state so as to prevent entry or exit
— *occupation of territory:* use of military force by one state to occupy the whole or part of another state's territory for a period of at least 24 hours
— *other use of military force:* use of regular armed forces of a state to fire upon the armed forces, population, or territory of another state or to enter the territory of another state for a period of less than 24 hours
— *seizure:* the seizure by one state of material or personnel from another state for a period of at least 24 hours
— *clash:* military hostilities between the regular armed forces of two or more states that last for less than 24 hours and in which the initiator of the hostilities cannot be identified clearly
— *declaration of war:* an official statement by one state that it is in a state of war with another state[6]
— *war:* sustained military hostilities between the regular armed forces of two or more states, resulting in 1,000 or more battle fatalities; a minimum of 100 battle fatalities or 1,000 troops in active combat is required before a state is considered to be a participant in a war.

For the purpose of grouping individual acts (incidents) into temporally bounded disputes, three rules were employed. First, the incidents had to involve the same or an overlapping set of state actors. Second, the incidents had to involve the same issue or set of issues. Third, the elapsed time between consecutive incidents could not exceed six months.[7] The highest level of hostility and violence that a dispute could reach is what Small and Singer (1982) classify as a "war." A dispute was considered to have ended either when there were no codable incidents for a period of six months or when a war terminated.

---

6. Though the declaration of war may be seen more as a threat than as a use of force, several scaling efforts and intuitive expert judgments suggest that this action is second only to war in terms of the level of its dispute severity (see Maoz 1982).

7. The issue criterion was assumed to be superior to the time criterion. If the elapsed time between two incidents involving the same protagonists was less than six months but the issues involved in the two incidents were different, then the incidents were considered to be parts of separate disputes. Conversely, there were a few occasions when the elapsed time between codable incidents was greater than six months (although less than a year) but the issues involved were the same, and diplomatic historians considered the incidents part of a single dispute. On these occasions, we permitted the issue criterion to override the rule concerning elapsed time.

Data Sources and Data-Generation Procedures

The object of the data-generation process was to identify all occurrences of militarized interstate disputes from the end of the Napoleonic Wars through 1976, and efforts are now under way to extend the data base through the most recent calendar year. A wide variety of data sources were employed to identify militarized interstate disputes, including general diplomatic histories, historical monographs on interstate system members, case studies of individual disputes, existing data sets of international conflicts, and regional and global chronologies of events. The diversity of sources permitted dispute cases to be cross-checked and ambiguities to be clarified.[8]

Coders for the data-generation project were graduate students in political science and history at the University of Michigan. Special emphasis was placed on proficiency in foreign languages so that non-English, as well as English-language, sources could be utilized. Coders were given special training and supplied with coders' manuals and coding sheets. Intercoder reliability tests were employed to check and enhance the quality of data generation.

Following several years of data generation, we turn in this article to a quantitative description of patterns that emerge from the data, as well as some of the theoretical implications they suggest.

Patterns of Interstate Disputes

Historical Trends

The years 1816 through 1976 witnessed the occurrence of 960 militarized disputes involving two or more members of the interstate system. As is

---

8. Despite the diversity and extensiveness of source material used to identify militarized interstate disputes, some dispute cases undoubtedly have eluded the research net. The completeness of information concerning interstate behavior varies along several dimensions. Three appear to be particularly relevant to the dispute data set. First, as one moves further back in time, the extensiveness of global information networks diminishes, and one is forced to rely increasingly upon events reported by governments or recorded by historians. Second, there generally are more sources of information on the activities of major powers than on those of minor powers, and this increases the probability that overt interstate activities of major powers will be more completely reported. Third, events at high levels of violence tend to more salient (and, therefore, leave more visible traces) than less violent events. Thus, for example, uses of military force are more likely to be recorded than threats to use force. These three factors interact with one another, and it is difficult to know how many or precisely which cases might have escaped detection. For example, major powers constituted a larger proportion of interstate system membership in the early parts of the temporal domain, and this may offset the more limited scope of information networks. Keeping in mind the preceding caveats, we nevertheless believe that the concerted effort to identify the universe of militarized interstate disputes has produced the most complete data set of its kind to date.

evident from figure 1—in which moving averages have been employed to smooth the data—militarized disputes have not been distributed evenly across time. There has been a clear upward trend in the numbers of disputes begun (β = .08, $p < .001$, R^2 = .52), and under way (β = .12, $p < .001$, R^2 = .55), and nearly three-quarters of all militarized disputes since the Napoleonic Wars have erupted during the twentieth century.

The growth in the number of disputes has not been uniform, however. The peaks and valleys evident in figure 1 suggest a division of the temporal domain into several historical periods. These periods generally conform with those employed by diplomatic historians and are consistent with notions of traditional theorists regarding changes in the international system over time (Gottschalk and Lach, 1954; Rosecrance, 1963; Blum et al., 1970). The first period, corresponding with the Concert of Europe from 1816 through 1848, was the least dispute prone. It was followed by a period of heightened dispute activity that is often referred to as the period of "European national unification," running from the years of revolution to the rise of Bismarckian Germany as the central power in Europe. The third period is the Bismarckian era. The slight decline in the frequency of disputes begun and under way in this period and the flatness of the curves reflect the relative orderliness of the time. The fourth period, from the decline of Bismarck to the end of World War I, was an age of imperialism and witnessed a substantial increase in the numbers of militarized disputes begun and under way. The fifth period, containing the interwar and World War II years, saw dramatic changes in the annual frequency of disputes

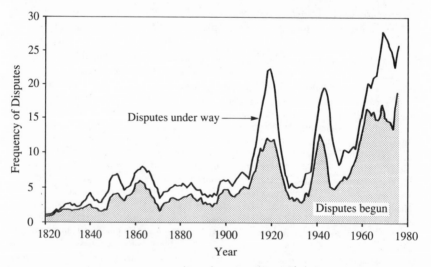

Fig. 1. Distribution of militarized interstate disputes, 1816–1976; five-year moving average of disputes begun and under way (unnormalized)

and was even more dispute prone than the preceding period. Yet by far the most disputatious period in terms of the numbers of disputes begun and under way has been the nuclear era, as is evident in table 1.

The absolute frequency of disputes over time, however interesting, does not reflect changes in the size of the international system. If it is assumed that the greater the number of states, the greater the number of conflict opportunities, then controlling for the number of states in the system allows for a more meaningful comparison of the conflictfulness of the interstate system during the various periods of the temporal domain. Figure 2 presents data on the number of disputes begun and under way each year, normalized by the number of states in the interstate system during that year.[9]

In comparing the patterns found in figure 1 with those in figure 2, we note the following: First, the general upward trend of the distributions that was evident in figure 1 is greatly reduced in figure 2 (for both disputes begun and under way: $\beta = .001$, $p < .001$, $R^2 = .12$), indicating that there is no substantial increase in the frequency of disputes, once one controls for the number of states in the system. Second, the same peaks and valleys that demarcated historical periods in figure 1 are present in figure 2. In four of the six periods, the normalized average numbers of disputes begun and under way each year were approximately equal ($N_{begun} = .10$, $N_{under\ way} = .16$; the Concert period was slightly more quiescent than the norm ($N_{begun} = .06$, $N_{under\ way} = .09$) and the age of imperialism was more dispute ridden (N_{begun}

TABLE 1. Distribution of Militarized Disputes across Historical Periods

Period		Average Number of Disputes Begun per Year	Average Number of Disputes under Way per Year	Percentage of Total (Begun)
Concert of Europe	(1816–48)	1.7	2.6	5.8
European national unification	(1849–70)	4.2	6.2	9.6
Bismarckian era	(1871–90)	3.4	4.9	7.0
Age of imperialism	(1891–1918)	6.1	9.4	17.9
Interwar and World War II era	(1919–45)	6.7	11.0	18.8
Nuclear era	(1946–76)	12.7	18.2	40.9
Entire period	(1816–1976)	6.0	9.0	100.0

9. Controlling for the number of states understates the number of conflictual interaction opportunities available in a system and thereby overstates the relative frequency of disputes. The degree to which the relative frequency is overestimated is greatest in those years when system membership is largest.

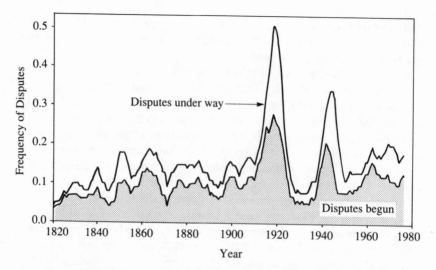

Fig. 2. Distribution of militarized interstate disputes, 1816–1976; five-year moving average of disputes begun and under way (normalized by the number of states in the system)

$= .14$, $N_{\text{under way}} = .22$). Once controls for the size of the interstate system are introduced, the nuclear era appears to be no more dispute prone than preceding historical periods.

The evidence in figures 1 and 2 suggests that the apparent increase in the disputatiousness of interstate relations over the past century and a half is, at least in part, a function of the growth in the size of the interstate system.[10] The frequency of disputes appears to be an early indicator of system transformation, wherein peaks in interstate dispute activity (particularly in the number of disputes under way) precede by several years traditionally recognized historical transformations. The rise in the number of disputes seems to indicate a decline in the degree of consensus on the "rules" of the international order. This heightened dissension (often culminating in large-scale wars) is followed by a restructuring or reimposition of order and an increase in consensus or acceptance of that order, indicated by a decline in interstate dispute activity. After a period of time, subsequent increases in dispute activity mark a return of dissension and set the stage for further system transformation. Although in terms of absolute numbers each subsequent historical period tends to be more dispute ridden than the preceding one, the dis-

---

10. For example, dividing the temporal domain of the study into sixteen decades, the product-moment correlation between the mean number of states per decade and the average number of disputes per decade is $r = .92$, $p < .001$.

putatiousness of historical periods—including the nuclear era—is relatively similar once the number of potential disputants is taken into account.

Dispute Participation

While the preceding subsection offers a broad overview of interstate dispute activity, it does not delineate which or how many states participated in these disputes, nor does it describe the ways in which these disputes expanded. To address these concerns, we employ the simple yet widely utilized distinction between major and minor powers. Almost all literature on state behavior in international politics assumes or asserts the validity of this distinction and reminds the reader that major powers are not minor powers writ large (see Bull 1977; Small 1978; Handel 1981). The behavior of states, the impact of the behavior on other states, and the acceptability and expectations concerning behavior differ for major powers and minor powers. It is therefore instructive to examine this behavior with respect to interstate dispute activity.

We adopt Small and Singer's (1982) widely used categorization of major and minor powers[11] and develop a fourfold typology:

1. *major-major* disputes are those that involve at least one major power on each side of the dispute.
2. *major-minor* disputes are those that involve at least one major power on the initiator's side but include only minor power participants on the target's side.[12]
3. *minor-major* disputes are those that involve only minor power participants on the initiator's side but include at least one major power on the target's side.
4. *minor-minor* disputes are those that involve minor power participants only.

Using this typology, we address two questions. First, are major powers more frequently involved in disputes than minor powers? Second, are they more

---

11. The major powers, along with the years for which they qualified for this status, are as follows: United Kingdom (1816–present), France (1816–1940, 1945–present), Prussia/Germany (1816–1918, 1925–45), Austria-Hungary (1816–1918), Russia/Soviet Union (1816–1917), 1922–present), Italy (1860–1943), Japan (1895–1945), United States (1899–present), and China (1950–present). While West Germany and Japan might be considered major economic actors by the early 1960s, they have not been restored to the status of major powers during the nuclear era due to constitutional restrictions on their military capabilities that prevent them from exercising a global military presence.

12. No evaluative connotation is attributed to the terms "initiator" and "target." The initiator of a dispute is defined as the state that takes the first codable action of a militarized interstate dispute; the target is the state that is the direct object of that action.

likely than minor powers to be initiators, rather than targets, in disputes? Intuitively, we would expect the answer to both of these questions to be yes, given that major powers have traditionally played the role of custodians of the international order and have possessed the capabilities to interact with states far beyond their national borders.

Table 2 confirms these expectations. For the entire 1816–1976 period, major powers have been involved in over half of all militarized disputes. Prior to 1946, the proportion of disputes in which they participated ranged between one-half and three-fourths. In the nuclear era, however, this proportion has dropped to only one-third of the militarized disputes—a substantial decline, but nonetheless a large proportion considering that major powers constituted, on average, only 5 percent of the interstate system membership during 1946–76. Indeed, if one compares the proportion of total disputes in which major powers have been involved with the proportion of total system membership they have made up, one finds that major powers have been involved in a relatively greater proportion of interstate disputes during the nuclear era than in any historical epoch since the Napoleonic Wars.[13] It also is interesting to note in table 2 that in every period except the nuclear one, major powers involved in interstate disputes have in a greater proportion of cases been on the initiator's side than on the target's. Because of the way dispute types are coded, table 2 does not necessarily imply that the converse is true for minor

TABLE 2.   Types of Militarized Disputes, by Historical Periods

	Dispute Type								Total Disputes	
	Major-Major		Major-Minor		Minor-Major		Minor-Minor			
Period	N	%	N	%	N	%	N	%	N	%
1816–48	9	16.1	24	42.9	7	12.5	16	28.6	56	5.8
1849–70	15	16.3	28	30.4	10	10.9	39	42.4	92	9.6
1871–90	6	9.0	18	26.9	7	10.4	36	53.7	67	7.0
1891–1918	30	17.4	68	39.5	15	8.7	59	34.3	172	17.9
1919–45	31	17.2	66	36.7	33	18.3	50	27.8	180	18.8
1946–76	28	7.1	47	12.0	60	15.3	258	65.6	393	40.9
1816–1976	119	12.4	251	26.1	132	13.8	458	47.7	960	100.0

13. As might be expected, much (59 percent) of the major power dispute activity during the years 1946–76 involved one or both of the superpowers. During these years, the United States participated in 42 percent (57 of 135) of the disputes in which major powers engaged; the Soviet Union participated in 27 percent (37 of 135). However, only infrequently (in 10 percent or 14 of 135 disputes) did the superpowers directly confront one another. These latter occurrences were, of course, extremely dangerous and constituted half (14 of 28) of all major-major disputes.

powers (i.e., that minor powers are more often on the target's side). We can, however, get a more complete view of these relationships by distinguishing between two-party (dyadic) and multiparty disputes.

Two-party disputes have constituted nearly 72 percent ($N = 690$) of interstate disputes since 1816. Of these dyadic disputes, 41 percent have involved major power participants on one or both sides. In 6 percent, major powers initiated disputes against other major powers; in 25 percent, they initiated disputes against minor powers; and in 10 percent of the cases, they were actually the targets of minor power initiators. The remaining 59 percent of the dyadic cases were instances of minor-minor disputes. Of the 270 multiparty disputes, 60 percent involved major power participants on one or both sides. In 19 percent of the cases, major powers initiated conflicts against other major powers; in 28 percent, major powers initiated conflicts against minor powers; and in 13 percent, minor powers initiated conflicts against major powers. The remaining 40 percent of the cases were initiated by minor powers against other minor powers. Three points are evident from these figures: (1) The large majority of militarized disputes has remained dyadic, (2) major powers have been much more likely to initiate disputes against minor powers than the converse, and (3) disputes involving major powers—particularly those pitting major powers against one another—have been much more likely to expand into multiparty conflicts than have disputes between minor powers.

This third point, in turn, raises the issue of dispute expansion. While the figures tell us that disputes that involved major powers (on one or both sides) in their initial phase have been significantly more likely to widen into multiparty conflicts, they do not tell us what types of states, on which side, or how many states were likely to join these conflicts.

Table 3 allows us to examine the first two of these matters by delineating patterns of dispute expansion, including the extent to which major and minor powers participated. The top half of the table reveals that most expanded disputes remained the same dispute type from beginning to end. The bottom half shows, first, that major powers and minor powers joined ongoing disputes with equal frequency; second, that rarely were both sides to a conflict joined by active third-party participants (i.e., states that entered ongoing disputes tended to coalesce around either the initiator or the target); and third, that joiners—whether major or minor powers—tended to enter on the side of the initial major power participant if there was one or, if there was none, on the side of the target. That is, if the initial disputants were both major powers, third-party joiners were about evenly split between initiator and target sides; if the initial dispute was between a major and a minor power, joiners tended to side with the major power participant, whether that participant was the initiator or the target; and, if the dispute began between two minor powers, joiners tended to side with the target.

TABLE 3. Patterns of Dispute Expansion, 1816–1976

Types of Expansion

Dispute Evolved into	Dispute Began as									Total	
	Major-Major		Major-Minor		Minor-Major		Minor-Minor				
	N	%	N	%	N	%	N	%	N	%	N	%
Major-Major	51	100.0	19	25.3	4	11.1	6	5.6	80	29.6
Major-Minor	0		56	74.7	0		19	17.6	75	27.8
Minor-Major	0		0		32	88.9	30	27.8	62	23.0
Minor-Minor	0		0		0		53	49.1	53	19.6
Total (%)	51	(18.9)	75	(27.8)	36	(13.3)	108	(40.0)	270	(100.0)

Patterns of Intervention in Ongoing Disputes

Major Power Joined

Dispute Began as	Initiator		Target		Both		Total
	N	%	N	%	N	%	
Major-Major	15	46.9	14	43.8	3	9.4	32
Major-Minor	41	68.3	16	26.7	3	5.0	60
Minor-Major	3	12.5	20	83.3	1	4.2	24
Minor-Minor	20	36.4	29	52.7	6	10.9	55
Total	79	46.2	79	46.2	13	7.6	171

Minor Power Joined

Dispute Began as	Initiator		Target		Both		Total
	N	%	N	%	N	%	
Major-Major	15	38.5	19	48.7	5	12.8	39
Major-Minor	24	68.6	11	31.4	0		35
Minor-Major	9	40.9	11	50.0	2	9.1	22
Minor-Minor	21	28.4	49	66.2	4	5.4	74
Total	69	40.6	90	52.9	11	6.5	170

Thus there are relatively clear patterns of dispute expansion in terms of who joined interstate disputes and on which side. But what about the magnitude of dispute expansion, that is, the number of states likely to participate in a given interstate dispute? As already pointed out, nearly 72 percent of all militarized disputes since 1816 have been two-party disputes and, consequently, the average number of participants per dispute has been small (mean = 2.6). Indeed, there is an inverse relationship between the number of participants in disputes and the frequency of such disputes. There have been some differences across dispute types. Consistent with our previous findings, major-major disputes have had, on average, the largest number of participants (mean = 3.7) and minor-minor disputes have had the smallest (mean = 2.2), but the average number of participants per dispute has remained virtually constant across time. Neither the increasing destructiveness of modern weapons systems nor the advances in technology that have made it possible for ever larger numbers of states to engage in long-distance intervention seem to have altered the willingness of states to enter ongoing conflicts.

Duration

Just as the normalized frequency of disputes and the patterns of participation have been relatively stable over time, so too has been the length of militarized disputes. The duration of disputes has ranged from a modal length of one day (22 percent of the disputes) to 10.8 years, in the case of the Vietnam War. The mean duration has been 211 days, but given the great variance in dispute duration, it is perhaps more meaningful to focus on the median as a measure of central tendency.

Militarized disputes have been, in general, relatively brief. Of those since the Napoleonic Wars, 82 percent have lasted less than a year, and the median length has been only 70 days, with little variation across historical epochs. There have been, however, noticeable differences in duration for the various dispute types, with those involving major powers tending to persist longer than those in which major powers have not been involved. The median duration for disputes involving major powers has been 102 days; that for minor-minor disputes only 43 days. The difference is statistically significant ($\chi^2 = 10.48; p < 0.001$)[14] and suggests not only that major powers have been disproportionately more involved in militarized disputes but that their involvement has made it more difficult to end such conflicts. It also should be noted that multiparty disputes tend to last significantly longer than two-party ones (medians of 173 days and 46 days, respectively) and, indeed, the median

---

14. For all tests of differences between medians, we computed the chi-square test for the cases in each category falling above or below the population median (Siegel 1956).

duration of interstate disputes has increased as the number of participants has risen.

Severity and Escalation

An examination of dispute severity offers additional insights into the nature of interstate dispute activity. We can categorize each dispute in our data set according to the highest level of hostility that it reached: threat of force, display of force, limited use of force, and large-scale use of force (i.e., war). Table 4 presents this distribution of disputes across historical periods.[15] When the data are broken down in this manner, no particular trend in the severity of disputes emerges (D_{yx} = .07).

However, if we regroup the data in table 4 into two categories—(a) threats and displays, and (b) limited and large-scale use of force—we find an interesting trend. The proportion of disputes involving *some* use of force (i.e., category b) decreased noticeably (from 71.4 percent to 53.8 percent across the first three historical periods, while in the succeeding three periods that proportion rose steadily (to 83.0 percent). This pattern of decline and resurgence closely parallels the decline and growth in the number of sovereign states during the same time span.[16] That is, the number of sovereign states dimin-

TABLE 4. Severity of Militarized Disputes Across Historical Periods

Historical Period	Threat of Force N	Threat of Force %	Display of Force N	Display of Force %	Use of Force N	Use of Force %	War N	War %	Total N	Total %
1816–48	2	3.6	14	25.0	35	62.5	5	8.9	56	5.8
1849–70	7	7.6	25	27.2	44	47.8	16	17.4	92	9.6
1871–90	8	11.9	23	34.3	32	47.8	4	6.0	67	7.0
1891–1918	14	8.1	44	25.6	96	55.8	18	10.5	172	17.9
1919–45	6	3.3	32	17.8	114	63.3	28	15.6	180	18.8
1946–76	21	5.3	46	11.7	306	77.9	20	5.1	393	40.9
1816–1976	58	6.0	184	19.2	627	65.3	91	9.5	960	100.0

Highest Level of Hostility Reached

15. As table 4 indicates, 91 militarized interstate disputes evolved into wars. This number exceeds the total number of interstate wars for 1816–1976 reported by Small and Singer (1982) because some multiparty wars (e.g., World Wars I and II) evolved from, or encompassed, more than one militarized interstate dispute.

16. Dividing the temporal domain into sixteen decades, the product-moment correlation between the mean number of states in the system per decade and the average level of dispute severity per decade is r = .53; the rank order correlation between these two variables is rho = .93.

ished during the 1860s and early 1870s with the unification of the Italian and German states and then slowly increased until, by the close of World War I, the number of states in the system had returned to the 1860 figure. Following World War I, and again after World War II, the number of sovereign states grew substantially as the tides of nationalism and decolonization swept the international system. Most of these new states were minor powers, limited with regard to the types of bargaining leverage they could bring to bear upon other states. As a result, the resort to military force was a particularly important tool in their bargaining repertoire. Thus it can be suggested that the trend in the use of force in interstate disputes reflects not so much a change in the behavior of states as a change in the composition of interstate system membership. Increased numbers of minor powers led to increased reliance on military force.

A comparison of conflict behavior in major-major disputes as opposed to minor-minor disputes casts some light upon this line of argument. As is evident from table 5, two-thirds of major-major disputes have involved some use of military force, while the comparable figure for minor-minor disputes exceeds 80 percent, a significantly larger proportion ($Z = 3.18; p < .01$). Thus minor powers have been more prone than major powers to use force to resolve their conflicts.[17]

Several other patterns are notable in table 5. Disputes among major powers have been unlikely to cease with the threat of force. Apparently displays of force have been necessary before a sense of prudence has set in. And if the actual use of force has been relatively less common in major-major

TABLE 5. Severity of Militarized Disputes, by Dispute Type, 1816–1976

Highest Level of Hostility Reached	Dispute Type								Total	
	Major-Major		Major-Minor		Minor-Major		Minor-Minor			
	N	%	N	%	N	%	N	%	N	%
Threat of force	1	0.8	24	9.6	6	4.5	27	5.9	58	6.0
Display of force	38	31.9	66	26.3	18	13.6	62	13.5	184	19.2
Use of force	54	45.4	139	55.4	96	72.7	338	73.8	627	65.3
War	26	21.8	22	8.8	12	9.1	31	6.8	91	9.5
Total (%)	119	(12.4)	251	(26.1)	132	(13.8)	458	(47.7)	960	(100.0)

17. There is always a possibility that threats and displays of force in minor-minor disputes are underrepresented in the data, since their traces may be less visible than threats and displays in major-major disputes. Conceptually, however, the distribution of cases in table 5 is consistent with the theoretical notion concerning "bargaining leverage" noted above and developed more fully by Gochman (1979).

disputes, the likelihood that the use of force would escalate to war has been much higher. The distribution of cases for major-minor disputes suggests that threats to use force in this type of dispute have been much more successful in achieving objectives than in other types of disputes. Indeed, major-minor disputes have been the least likely to escalate to the use of force and, even then, war has been relatively unlikely. Minor-major disputes have a considerably higher propensity to involve the use of force, perhaps because in these cases the precipitating minor power has resolved to pursue its objectives even in the face of considerable odds. And finally, as we have noted, disputes involving only minor power participants have a very high likelihood of involving the use of force, but the probability of these disputes escalating to war has been quite small, suggesting that the limited military arsenals of such states have offered them few opportunities to sustain large-scale hostilities or that outside mediators have been able to prevent the escalation of hostilities to war.

This notion of opportunities to sustain large-scale hostilities spills over into the area of expanded disputes. Several factors suggest that multiparty disputes should be more likely than two-party disputes to escalate to war. First, multiparty disputes are likely to provide a larger aggregate of capabilities to sustain large-scale hostilities. Second, as we have already found, multiparty disputes are likely to involve major powers, the very states that have the greatest capabilities to sustain hostilities. And finally, the decision-making dynamics of multiparty disputes may make it difficult to control the escalatory potential of conflict spirals. These propositions seem to be supported by the data. Nearly 22 percent of multiparty disputes have resulted in wars; only slightly more than 5 percent of dyadic disputes have reached that level. Causal inferences about the relationship between dispute expansion (i.e., increase in the number of participants) and dispute escalation (i.e., increase in the level of hostility) must be handled with care, however; more dispute participants might provide greater capabilities to sustain large-scale hostilities, but sustained large-scale hostilities might attract additional participants or a third factor, such as particularly contentious issues, might both arouse many parties and lead to sustained hostilities. Whichever the causal direction, the data indicate that expansion and escalation are correlated and that as the number of participants in disputes has increased, so has the incidence of war (tau $c = .16$).

A similar and final link can be made between the duration and escalation of disputes. The median duration has increased significantly as the level of hostility has increased. For threats, displays, limited uses of force, and wars, the median dispute durations have been, respectively, 1.35, 32.25, 81.00, and 419.00 days ($\chi^2 = 102.44$; $p < .0001$). But, again, one must be careful about imputing causal direction.

Regional Distribution

The increase in the number of newly sovereign minor powers, as well as their geographic distribution, suggests that patterns of interstate dispute activity may differ across geographic regions. Indeed, it is generally accepted among traditional scholars of world politics that patterns of state behavior in more recently integrated regions of the global system differ along numerous dimensions. This belief is grounded in both theoretical and empirical factors. First, the formation of regions as subsystems of politically sovereign, interacting states took place in different historical epochs. Europe has maintained its essential political character and national subdivisions for over a century, as have Latin and North America. On the other hand, political independence for states in Africa, the Middle East, and much of Asia has been forged through turmoil and national political awareness largely in the second half of the twentieth century. The historical context in which statehood was achieved, as well as the length of time that states have been participants in the expanded Eurocentric political system, has produced different interpretations and differing responses to international challenges and opportunities.

Second, political, economic, and social development of states in Europe and the Americas has been, in general, gradual and evolutionary, while patterns of development in states in the more newly formed regions (Africa, the Middle East, and Asia) have been more rapid and revolutionary. In fact, many states in the more newly formed regions are still undergoing rending processes of modernization and change, still trying to define their role in the global economic and political community. Consequently, empirically observable differences exist across regions: differences in terms of national attributes such as political regimes, economic systems, and social stratification, which are related to differing patterns of foreign policy behavior (Wilkenfeld et al. 1980).

Finally, the capabilities of states to interact in regional and global affairs differ from region to region. Since most major powers have been concentrated in the European region and since, as we have noted, the conflict behavior of major powers differs from that of other states, it is reasonable to suspect cross-regional differences based upon the capabilities and perceived responsibilities of the state actors constituting the various regional subsystems.

To examine the data for cross-regional differences, we have adopted the global division set forth by Russett et al. (1968), namely, the Americas, Europe, the Middle East (including North Africa), Africa, and Asia, adding an extraregional category to incorporate disputes that have involved states from different regions. For the purposes of the current investigation, our categorization is based not on the loci of disputes but on the geographic locations of the disputants. Thus the Fashoda Crisis was a dispute between

European powers, while the Falkland Islands War between Great Britain and Argentina exemplifies an extraregional conflict.[18]

The distribution of disputes across geographic regions during each of our historical periods is much as we might expect (see table 6). American, European, and extraregional disputes were predominant until the conclusion of World War I. Considering that extraregional disputes in these early periods were by and large made up of major powers engaging states outside the major powers' regions, almost all militarized interstate disputes prior to 1919 were products of American and European politics. Following World War I, and particularly after World War II, both the distribution of sovereign states and the geographic locations of disputants became more diverse. Taking into account the number of states in each region, Asia and the Middle East have become the most conflict-prone regions during the nuclear era; Europe has been the least conflict prone. Perhaps the only surprising element in table 6 is the sizable and sustained proportion of extraregional disputes. Since interstate dispute activity is an indicator of interstate interaction, this proportion suggests that it is legitimate to look upon the interstate system throughout the past century and a half as being global (although asymmetric) in character.

Turning from the regional distribution of disputes across historical periods to the distribution of dispute types by region, the data reveal little that is unexpected. Regions with few or no major powers have had an overwhelming proportion of minor-minor disputes. In Europe, site of most major powers, 78 percent of all disputes have involved major power participation, with 22 percent of the disputes pitting major powers against one another. In extraregional disputes, major power disputants, as expected, have been involved in three-fourths of all conflicts reinforcing the notion that major powers are states possessing the capabilities and the interest to engage in extraregional affairs.[19]

In line with earlier findings concerning the association between major power participation and dispute expansion, we find that multiparty disputes have occurred most frequently in extraregional conflicts (41.7 percent) and in European disputes (37.2 percent). Disputes in other regions have been less

---

18. Two states, the Soviet Union (Russia) and Turkey (the Ottoman Empire) proved difficult to classify. In terms of their histories and their geographic locations, they sit astride regional divides. Consequently, we placed each of these states into two geographic regions. Disputes between the Soviet Union (Russia) and the European countries were considered European conflicts; disputes between the Soviet Union (Russia) and Asian countries were considered Asian conflicts. Similarly, Turkey (the Ottoman Empire) was sometimes considered Middle Eastern and at other times European. Disputes between the Soviet Union (Russia) and Turkey (the Ottoman Empire) were classified as European conflicts.

19. Of all extraregional disputes, 25 percent have been among minor powers. These disputes primarily have been between colonial states and states contiguous to their colonies, for example, Portugal and Zambia in 1966–69, and Holland and Indonesia in 1951, 1957, and 1959–61.

TABLE 6. Regional Distribution of Militarized Disputes, by Historical Periods

Geographic Region	Historical Period												Total	
	1816–48		1849–70		1871–90		1891–1918		1919–45		1946–76			
	N	%	N	%	N	%	N	%	N	%	N	%	N	%
Americas	10	18	24	26	26	39	49	29	23	16	46	12	183	19
Europe	29	52	31	34	21	31	63	37	86	48	31	8	261	27
Africa	0		0		0		0		0		45	12	45	5
Middle East	0		0		1		2		2	1	55	14	60	6
Asia	0		1		3	5	12	7	25	14	99	25	140	15
Extraregional	17	30	36	39	16	24	46	27	39	22	117	30	271	28
Total (%)	56	(6)	92	(10)	67	(7)	172	(18)	180	(19)	393	(41)	960	

than half as likely to expand. Extraregional, Middle Eastern, Asian, and European disputes have had the longest median durations (108, 91.5, 89, and 70 days, respectively); African and American disputes have had the shortest durations (33 and 32 days, respectively).

Finally, turning to the question of the severity of disputes in the different regions (table 7), we find that the use of force has been least prominent in European disputes (62.1 percent involved some use of force) and most prominent in Middle Eastern disputes (91.7 percent). However, the reverse has been true with regard to the resort to war: Europe has been the most war prone (15.7 percent of all disputes) and the Middle East (5.0 percent), the Americas (4.9 percent), and Africa the least war prone. This finding provides additional support for the proposition that minor powers, while considerably more likely to resort to the limited use of force, have been considerably less likely than major powers to resort to war.

In summarizing these findings, we can contrast interstate dispute activity within the long-established regional subsystems (Europe, the Americas, and the extraregional category) with that in the more newly formed regional subsystems (Africa, the Middle East, and Asia). Disputes in the newer subsystems have increased in number so that they now account for half of the interstate conflicts in the nuclear era. These African, Middle Eastern, and Asian disputes generally (74.7 percent) have pitted minor powers against one another, whereas disputes in the older subsystems more frequently (61.5 percent) involved the participation of major powers. Disputes in the newer regions have been significantly less likely to expand into multiparty conflicts (16.9 percent versus 32.1 percent, Z = 4.6, $p < .0001$) and have involved slightly fewer participants (on average, 2.3 vs. 2.7 disputants). Disputes in the newer regions have been somewhat more likely to have involved the use of force (83.3 percent versus 71.9 percent) but have been marginally less likely

TABLE 7.   Severity of Militarized Disputes, by Regions, 1816–1976

Geographic Region	Threat of Force N	Threat of Force %	Display of Force N	Display of Force %	Use of Force N	Use of Force %	War N	War %	Total N	Total %
Americas	9	4.9	37	20.2	128	69.9	9	4.9	183	19.1
Europe	22	8.4	77	29.5	121	46.4	41	15.7	261	27.2
Africa	8	17.8	4	8.9	33	73.3			45	4.7
Middle East	2	3.3	3	5.0	52	86.7	3	5.0	60	6.3
Asia	8	5.7	16	11.4	99	70.7	17	12.1	140	14.6
Extraregional	9	3.3	47	17.3	194	71.6	21	7.7	271	28.2
Total	58	6.0	184	19.2	627	65.3	91	9.5	960	100.0

Highest Level of Hostility Reached

to escalate to war (8.2 percent vs. 9.9 percent). In sum, there is evidence to support the notion of the behavioral uniqueness of regional subsystems as well as a shift in the severity and locus of interstate dispute activity. But these differences among regions appear to be by-products of the larger structural changes in the international system associated with the growth in the number of newly independent minor powers.

National Dispute Proneness and Enduring Rivalries

Having begun with broad brush strokes, it is time to identify and rank individual states according to the frequency of their dispute involvements and to identify enduring rivalries among pairs of states. In so doing, we will see how well the various patterns discussed in previous subsections are reflected in the behavioral profiles of individual states.

Throughout the article we have noted conflict-related differences between major and minor powers—in particular, the disproportionate frequency with which major powers participated in and initiated interstate disputes. Our findings concerning the frequency of such behavior are consistent with a variety of studies focusing on interstate wars that have determined that the most powerful states have tended to be the most war prone (see Rosenau and Hoggard 1974; Bremer 1980; Eberwein 1982). To illustrate the applicability of the "powerful and war prone" hypothesis to the dispute behavior of individual states, we have constructed table 8.

Table 8 lists the thirty most dispute-prone states in the interstate system, ranked in terms of the number of their dispute involvements during the 161 years of our temporal domain. The most striking findings in this table are that these thirty states have initiated over 70 percent ($N = 681$) and were primary targets in over 60 percent ($N = 587$) of all militarized interstate disputes. Equally important is that nine of the ten most dispute-prone states are, or have been, major powers.

In addition, table 8 shows that a high rank on total number of dispute involvements generally has implied that a state was active both as an initiator and as a primary target in interstate disputes. The correlation between the number of times a state initiated and the number of times it was a primary target in a dispute is high ($r = .80$). In this sense, the data in table 8 appear to challenge some conventional notions about revisionist and status quo states, a point to which we will return below.

Finally, table 8 reveals that the states that have been most often the initiators or primary targets in disputes also have been the most frequent joiners in ongoing disputes ($r = .83$). Consistent with our previous observations regarding patterns of dispute expansion, we find a high correlation between the number of times a given state has joined on the initiator's side and

TABLE 8. National Dispute Proneness: Initiation, Target, and Involvement Figures for the Most Dispute-Prone Nations, 1816–1976

Nation	Initiation				Target				Total		
	Number of Init.	Freq. Init.	Join Init.	Freq. Join	Number of Tar.	Freq. Tar.	Join Tar.	Freq. Join	Number Inv.	Freq. Inv.	Rank Inv.
U.K.	78	.484	24	.149	42	.261	37	.230	181	1.124	1
U.S.A	67	.416	18	.112	51	.317	24	.149	160	0.994	2
USSR	59	.369	22	.138	35	.219	15	.094	131	0.819	3
France	42	.267	36	.229	28	.178	21	.134	127	0.802	4
Germany	45	.346	16	.123	37	.285	9	.069	107	0.823	5
Italy	35	.217	19	.118	17	.106	10	.062	81	0.503	6
Turkey	14	.087	8	.050	41	.255	14	.087	77	0.478	7
China	36	.308	5	.043	26	.222	3	.026	70	0.598	8
Japan	20	.180	2	.018	25	.225	8	.072	55	0.495	9
Austria-Hungary[a]	18	.124	13	.090	11	.076	10	.069	52	0.359	10
Peru	25	.180	4	.029	14	.101	4	.029	47	0.338	11
Israel	25	.862	0	.000	19	.655	1	.034	45	1.552	12
Greece	19	.130	3	.021	15	.103	6	.041	43	0.295	13

Country											
Chile	25	.181	0	.000	14	.101	3	.022	42	0.304	14.5
Argentina	17	.125	1	.007	21	.154	3	.022	42	0.309	14.5
Spain	13	.081	4	.025	17	.106	3	.019	37	0.230	16
Portugal	18	.112	1	.006	12	.075	1	.006	32	0.199	17.5
India	17	.567	0	.000	15	.500	0	.000	32	1.067	17.5
Ecuador	11	.089	2	.016	14	.114	1	.008	28	0.228	19
Brazil	11	.073	2	.013	14	.093	0	.000	27	0.179	21.5
Mexico	8	.055	2	.014	16	.110	1	.007	27	0.185	21.5
Holland	5	.032	5	.032	15	.096	2	.013	27	0.172	21.5
Pakistan	7	.233	1	.033	18	.600	1	.033	27	0.900	21.5
Yugoslavia	10	.103	2	.021	11	.113	3	.031	26	0.268	24.5
Thailand	12	.133	2	.022	8	.089	4	.044	26	0.289	24.5
Bolivia	11	.085	0	.000	12	.093	1	.008	24	0.186	26
Paraguay	9	.111	2	.025	12	.148	0	.000	23	0.284	28.5
Egypt	10	.152	0	.000	7	.106	6	.091	23	0.348	28.5
Bulgaria	7	.101	4	.058	6	.087	6	.087	23	0.333	28.5
Colombia	7	.048	1	.007	14	.096	1	.007	23	0.158	28.5

Note: Frequency figures were obtained by dividing the number of dispute involvements in the appropriate column by the number of years the given state has qualified as a system member.

[a]The figures for Austria-Hungary include the dispute involvement history of post-World War I Austria.

the number of times it has entered on the target's side ($r = .82$), suggesting that third-party entrants have not systematically favored the initiators or the targets in disputes.

There are, however, several features that seem to distinguish between the dispute profiles of major powers and those of minor powers. First, both the total number of dispute involvements and, particularly, the frequency of joining ongoing disputes have been considerably higher for major powers than for minor powers. Related to this is the fact that, with the exception of Japan, major powers have been more likely to initiate disputes than to have been targets, whereas minor powers have been, on average, equally likely to be initiator or targets.[20]

While the major powers have not differed from the minor powers in terms of patterns of support for initiators and targets in ongoing disputes, the former have tended to enter such disputes with a considerably higher frequency than the latter. This suggests that the perception of their global responsibilities for determining the nature of systemic or regional order may entice major powers to participate actively in disputes among third parties. Minor powers, on the other hand, may be less directly concerned by disputes among third parties or less able to intervene, hence the lower frequency of joining ongoing disputes.

One of the most illuminating insights from table 8 is the comparison between the raw numbers of dispute involvements for states and the frequency of their dispute involvements. Although major powers have ranked very high in terms of total numbers of dispute involvements, some of the states with the highest annual frequency of dispute involvements have been newly independent minor powers such as Israel, India, Pakistan, and several other African and Asian states.[21] While the correlation between the raw number of involvements and the annual frequency of involvements is statistically significant ($r = .60, p < .001$), it is not as high as one might expect given the "powerful and war prone" hypothesis. The importance of this finding lies in what it may portend for the future. The challenges to world peace in the contemporary era and in the near-term future do not derive solely from confrontations emanating from major power struggles, but also from conflicts among minor powers. These latter conflicts are equally pernicious, given the propensity of major powers to join ongoing disputes. If the frequency of national dispute proneness is any indicator, the trouble spots in the contemporary era and near-term

20. The mean initiator/target ratios are 1.46 and 0.98 for major powers and minor powers, respectively. This difference is statistically significant ($F = 7.49, \eta^2 = 0.21, p \leq .05$).

21. Among the other nations with a slightly lower absolute number, but high frequency, of conflict involvement are Rhodesia/Zimbabwe (13 dispute involvements, frequency of 1.083 disputes per year), Zambia (16 involvements, frequency of 1.231), Uganda (13 involvements, frequency of 0.867), North Vietnam (20 involvements, frequency of 0.870), and Cambodia/Kampuchea (20 involvements, frequency of 0.833).

future lie in the Middle East, Africa, and Asia, and, consequently, increased major power involvement in these regions is as potentially explosive as are the more salient, but infrequent, confrontations in Europe.

These impressions become increasingly pronounced when we examine the figures on enduring rivalries presented in table 9. Table 9 presents, for each region of the world and for extraregional relationships, the pairs (dyads) of states that most often have engaged in disputes with one another. There are no surprises in terms of the identity of these enduring rivalries. However, several points are worth noting. First, almost all of the states on our list of dispute-prone nations (table 8) have been involved in enduring rivalries (table 9). This is particularly noticeable for major powers, which have engaged persistently and frequently in conflicts with one another. In regions containing two or more major powers (i.e., Europe and Asia, as well as the extraregional category), the majority of enduring rivalries have been between major powers. Moreover, with the exception of the Turko-Greek rivalry in Europe and the Indo-Pakistani and Thai-Cambodian rivalries in Asia, all other rivalries in these two regions involved at least one major power. Note in this context that Turkey appears to have been a favorite target of hostilities in Europe and that it participated in many of the traditional European rivalries. The "sick man of Europe" does not appear to be an unfounded moniker.

The predominance of major power participation in enduring rivalries, however, should not overshadow the bitterness of enduring minor-minor rivalries. As was the case with the frequency of dispute proneness of newly independent states, the newly formed rivalries among minor powers in the Middle East, Africa, and Asia are the most frequently manifested and, hence, appear to be an important source of threat to world order.

Neither our examination of national dispute proneness nor our survey of enduring rivalries provides unambiguous support for the conventional division of states into revisionist (offensive) and status quo (defensive).[22] While a few, mainly powerful, states have engaged in the overwhelming proportion of interstate disputes, there appears to be no clear-cut distinction between those states that are to be found on the initiator's side and those that are to be found on the target's. Without delving into the details of individual disputes, it is not possible to make definitive statements about national dispositions toward restructuring or defending the extant order. But the simple, prima facie assumption that the initiators of disputes should by and large be revisionist states and the targets in disputes should largely be status quo states finds little sustenance in our data.

Finally, contrary to some previous investigations of interstate conflict, our findings seem to display marked consistency over time and across levels of

---

22. For an excellent theoretical rebuttal of the notions of revisionist and status quo states, see Cottam (1977).

TABLE 9. Enduring Rivalries, 1816–1976: The Most Dispute-Prone Dyads, by Regions

Region	Number of Disputes	Frequency of Disputes
Americas		
U.S.A-Mexico	20	0.137
Chile-Argentina	17	0.125
Peru-Ecuador	15	0.122
Bolivia-Paraguay	11	0.136
Chile-Peru	10	0.072
Europe		
U.K.-USSR/Russia	24	0.149
Turkey-Greece	23	0.158
USSR/Russia-Turkey	21	0.130
Italy-Turkey	17	0.106
France-Germany	16	0.123
U.K.-Turkey	16	0.099
France-Turkey	14	0.088
Austria-Hungary/Austria-Italy	12	0.083
France-USSR/Russia	12	0.075
France-Italy	11	0.069
U.K.-Germany	10	0.077
U.K.-France	9	0.056
Africa		
Zambia-Rhodesia	8	0.667
Somalia-Ethiopia	7	0.412
Middle East		
Israel-Syria	17	0.586
Israel-Egypt	12	0.414
Israel-Jordan	8	0.276
Asia		
India-Pakistan	18	0.600
Russia/USSR-Japan	18	0.162
China-Japan	13	0.117
Russia/USSR-China	13	0.111
Thailand-Cambodia	11	0.458
China-India	10	0.333
Extraregional		
U.S.A.-China	17	0.145
U.S.A.-USSR	16	0.099
U.S.A.-Spain	15	0.093
U.S.A.-U.K.	12	0.075
U.K.-Japan	11	0.099
France-China	9	0.077
U.K.-China	9	0.077
USSR-Iran	9	0.074

Note: Frequency figures were obtained by dividing the total number of disputes for any given dyad by the number of years that the "youngest" nation of the dyad qualified for system membership.

analysis. This consistency may be more a result of our descriptive emphasis than any methodological weaknesses in earlier conflict studies, and a closer analytic inquiry into the determinants of various dispute attributes undoubtedly would shed more light on this issue. The Correlates of War data and our findings also open the door to new avenues of investigation. For example, the identification of enduring rivalries provides at least a preliminary response to complaints concerning lack of knowledge about "international enemies" (Feste 1982) and suggests the centrality of this phenomenon in world politics, particularly among, but not exclusively limited to, the major powers.

Conclusions and Implications

Three themes have run throughout this essay. First, patterns of dispute behavior have been more persistent over time than we often assume. Second, when these patterns have changed, the changes have been evolutionary in nature and have paralleled changes in the size and composition of the interstate system. Third, despite the diversity of the political units that make up the interstate system, patterns of dispute behavior are generalizable across geographic boundaries. What do these themes suggest for the years ahead?

We have seen that historical periods traditionally have been marked by initial declines and subsequent increases in the numbers of interstate disputes, and the nuclear era has been no exception. As our data show, following an initial decline after World War II, there was a dramatic upswing in the frequency of militarized disputes through 1976. While our evidence is incomplete, the years since 1976 appear to have been highly disputatious. There have been seven interstate wars and a large number of very volatile subwar conflicts.[23] One contribution factor to dispute activity—the number of sovereign states in the system—appears to have leveled off, thereby relieving some upward pressure on absolute dispute frequency.[24] Another important factor—the degree of dissension on the "rules" of the international order—does not seem to have diminished. Thus we suspect that high absolute levels of dispute activity will prevail in the near-term future. If past trends are any

---

23. The seven wars have been the Somali-Ethiopian in the Ogaden (1977–78), Ugandan-Tanzanian (1978–79), Sino-Vietnamese (1979), Russo-Afghan (1979–89), Irani-Iraqi (1980–present), Falkland Islands (1982), and Israeli-Syrian in Lebanon (1982). Among the more salient subwar disputes have been the Zambian-Rhodesian (1977–78), Egyptian-Libyan (1977), Syrian-Israeli (1977–present), Syrian-Iraqi (1977–present), Vietnamese-Thai (1977–present), Peruvian-Ecuadorian (1978, 1981), Vietnamese-Laotian (1979), American-Iranian (1979–80), and Israeli-Iraqi (1981). See Small and Singer (1982) for information on post-1976 wars.

24. The number of states in the interstate system increased by an average of 2 percent per annum from 1945 through 1959, by over 4 percent per annum during the 1960s, and by only 1 percent per annum in the 1970s.

indicator, the real danger lies in the possibility that the current dissension may be manifested in global conflagration, a phenomenon that marked the end of the two preceding periods—the age of imperialism and the interwar era. The historical alternative has been a great power concert or condominium; a more cooperative restructuring that affords significant participation by other—governmental and nongovernmental—actors is largely without historical precedent.

Major powers traditionally have been both the primary challengers and the primary defenders of the international order; their technological capacity and demographic and military attributes provide them with both the incentives and the means to define the nature of that order. During the nuclear era, major power participation in militarized disputes has actually increased, relative to the proportion of the interstate system membership that they constitute. And, if anything, the large number of minor powers that have achieved their independence since 1946 has increased the arena for major power competition. Consequently, we can expect to see a continuance of active major power involvement in interstate disputes, especially as joiners in the numerous minor power conflicts.

We also can expect that the median duration of interstate disputes will not be significantly different in the future from what it has been in the past, despite changes in weapons technology and the increasing need for governments to maintain public support for foreign adventures. The fact that interstate disputes traditionally have been brief reduces the likelihood that public attentiveness to foreign affairs or opposition to foreign adventures will have a significant impact on the duration of most disputes. Similarly, because the great majority of interstate disputes never escalate to the large-scale use of military force, the impact of weapons technology on the duration of the average dispute seems to be minimal. Even with respect to war, a perusal of the seven cases of large-scale hostilities since 1976 reveals both very brief and relatively lengthy encounters. Thus, at this point, there seems to be little hard evidence to suggest that changes in military technology have had a significant and predictable impact on the duration of military engagements.

The data that we have point to a long-term trend of increased use of force in interstate disputes, associated with the growth in the number of sovereign minor powers. This trend has probably peaked, but it does not appear likely that it will decline anytime soon. However, with the large number of predicted minor-minor disputes in the years ahead, the proportion of disputes escalating to war should remain low, so long as major powers do not intervene on opposing sides. In the past, such interventions have been uncommon, but when they did occur, they dramatically increased the probability of war. The current propensity of the Chinese, Soviets, and Americans to back opposing protagonists in volatile Third World disputes does not bode well in a world of nuclear weapons, where the uncontrolled escalation of an initially limited dispute could prove calamitous.

The fact that the number of disputes among minor powers has increased significantly during the nuclear era has meant that the locus of interstate dispute activity has shifted from Europe to Asia, Africa, and the Middle East. States in these regions have managed to develop a number of enduring rivalries with remarkably high frequencies of dispute involvement. Six of seven wars since 1976 have erupted among states from these three regions, and many of the most volatile subwar disputes in the past few years have occurred there. Neither economic nor cultural ties have been effective in inhibiting the outbreak or escalation of these disputes. Given past trends and current turmoil, these more newly formed regions appear destined in the years immediately ahead to host large number of interstate disputes.

Our empirical findings suggest that it is not appropriate to view the nuclear era as somehow unique with regard to conflictive interactions among states. Undoubtedly, nuclear weapons have made a difference. National leaders have appeared more cautious when the utilization of such weapons has seemed possible. But most aspects of dispute behavior that we have examined show considerable continuity across historical eras. This is not to deny that changes have occurred, such as the shift in the locus of dispute activity. Rather, it is to suggest that, in many respects, states behave today pretty much as they did in the past; the differences are in the composition and size of the interstate system. In recent years, we have witnessed American forces fighting in Vietnam, Russian troops in combat in Afghanistan, Chinese soldiers undertaking punitive strikes against Vietnam, and British troops enforcing their claims in the South Atlantic. Smaller and more newly independent states also have sought to impose their claims by means of military force. The image of a British armada off the coast of Argentina and the struggle for those desolate islands that the British call the Falklands may strike one as remarkably "nineteenth centuryish." Yet these events bring home, as perhaps no scholarly discourse can, the constancy and timelessness of basic interstate relations. Technology has changed; the objectives, motives, and methods of states remain the same.

Militarized Interstate Crises

Russell J. Leng and J. David Singer

Introduction

This is a report on an ambitious effort to code and classify the moves and countermoves of states embroiled in militarized crises. We believe that it represents a step forward in providing a reliable base of descriptive data for students of interstate conflict. Although a number of published studies employing segments of the emerging Behavioral Correlates of War (BCOW) data set are in the public domain, only recently have the data been made accessible to researchers other than those associated with the Correlates of War (COW) Project.[1] This article presents an overview of the design and content of the data set and of its potential for examining interstate crisis behavior. But before turning to a closer look at the data, it may be useful to place it in perspective by describing the genesis of the BCOW data and its relationship to other "events data" sets.

The Theoretical Foundation

The Behavioral Correlates of War Project began in the spring of 1970 as a component of the Correlates of War Project, a broad-gauged effort to account for the incidence, magnitude, severity, and intensity of interstate war between 1816 and, at that time, 1965. The epistemological and methodological assumptions that have guided the COW Project have been described fully elsewhere (Singer 1972, 1976, and 1981). We will simply summarize its basic assumptions here.

Reprinted from the *International Studies Quarterly* 32, no. 2 (June 1988): 155–73. With permission of the International Studies Association, James F. Byrnes Building, University of South Carolina, Columbia, SC 29208 USA. ©1988 International Studies Association.

1. Preparation of the BCOW data for public distribution has been made possible by National Science Foundation grant no. SES-8418657 and the assistance of the Middlebury College academic computing center. The data set is available through the Interuniversity Consortium for Political and Social Research (ICPSR), Ann Arbor, Michigan.

Given the absence of any widely accepted empirical theory on interstate conflict and war, the COW Project has taken a self-consciously multi-theoretical and inductive approach to examining alternative explanations of war. It has, however, been guided by certain a priori theoretical assumptions. One such assumption is that there has been considerable homogeneity in the political beliefs and decision rules of foreign-policy makers across nations and decades over the past century and two-thirds. This has led to an early focus on systemic variables and dyadic relationships in an attempt to account for the variation in the conflict behavior of nations, with the investigation of variations at the decisional and national levels left for a later phase of the project.

Our assumption of relative homogeneity in the foreign policy beliefs of national leaders engaged in conflict is derived from the premise that a preoc-cupation with maximizing national autonomy, guided by a realpolitik view of interstate conflict behavior, has been shared by national leaders throughout the modern state system (Leng 1980 and 1983). That is, we assume that out of a historically established tradition there has grown an implicit consensus among statesmen that views interstate conflict as dictated by considerations of power politics.[2] We do not presume that this image is necessarily an accurate por-trayal of international reality in the sense in which classical realists (Mor-genthau 1946 and 1948; Herz 1951) have portrayed it, nor do we consider the assumptions that we do make regarding the views of policymakers to be appropriate for relations among nations in more peaceful circumstances. We argue only that a realpolitik perspective identifies the key variables to which policymakers historically have directed their attention in the course of dis-putes in which their security is threatened. Shedding light on the relative descriptive and prescriptive validity of these realpolitik images of interstate conflict is one of the major purposes for which the BCOW data are designed.

In sum, our agnosticism with regard to the superiority of any particular empirical model of interstate conflict behavior has led to a "multitheoretical" typology of state actions that would permit the testing of a number of rival models of interstate conflict behavior. Nevertheless, beginning with our focus on militarized interstate crises, with states treated as unitary, purposive actors, and with the design of the coding scheme to test hypotheses relating to their attempts to influence each other's behavior, the data set reflects our preoc-cupation with conflict and war, and with testing realpolitik assumptions about conflict bargaining.

In this regard, we have been particularly interested in obtaining more

---

2. In this respect, we are most interested in that side of classical realism which Ashley (1981, 211) has called "practical realism," the aim of which is "to undertake interpretations that make possible the orientation of action within a common tradition," as opposed to the more deterministic aspect of realism as a set of objective laws governing interstate behavior.

microscopic descriptions of conflict bargaining than was possible with earlier event data coding schemes. Beginning with Singer's (1963a) model of internation influence, and informed by efforts to construct action-response models (Holsti, North, and Brody 1968), we designed the BCOW coding scheme to allow for the fullest possible description of influence attempt-response sequences (Leng 1980). The design of this portion of the coding scheme has also been influenced by the literature of conflict strategists, in particular Schelling (1960).

Relationship to Extant Events Data Sets

Our interest in detailed coded descriptions of the interactions of states in militarized crises has led to an event data approach, as distinct from more qualitative crisis data sets, such as those of Brecher, Wilkenfeld, and Moser (1988), or Snyder and Diesing (1977), with their strong emphases on perceptual phenomena. In constructing the BCOW coding scheme, we borrowed from a number of efforts at describing small-group interaction (Bales 1951; Homans 1958; and Longabaugh 1963), as well as the then extant international events data projects, particularly McClelland's (1968) World Event/Interaction Survey (WEIS), and Corson's (1971) East-West interaction project. For example, we began with the WEIS approach to the identification of international acts as those which were "newsworthy," and broadened the concept to include those interstate actions which were of sufficient importance to be reported by diplomatic historians. Corson's efforts to develop a coding scheme that included a means of continuously tracking ongoing physical actions beyond the day on which they were initiated became the starting point for our coding of the "tempo" of all nonverbal actions, which is described below.

Today the WEIS and Conflict and Peace Data Bank (COPDAB) (Azar 1971) data sets constitute the two most widely used sources of behavioral international events data. Each of these data sets attempts to obtain a global coverage of interstate events on a day-to-day basis. The data sets overlap to some extent in their temporal coverage, with the publicly available WEIS data extending from 1966 to 1977, and COPDAB extending from 1948 to 1978. The two differ considerably, however, in their approaches to describing international behavior and interaction. The WEIS project focuses on qualitative distinctions among sixty-three action types; the COPDAB project limits the qualitative distinctions to just five broad types, in favor of scaling the "content intensity" (Azar 1971) of each event. While comparisons of the BCOW data set with these and other events data sets appear in Leng (1979), a brief summary of the most distinctive differences may provide a useful perspective on the discussion of the BCOW data that follows.

The most obvious difference is in the domain of interstate interactions covered, with WEIS and COPDAB providing day-to-day global coverage in the post–World War II era, and the BCOW scheme focusing on a sample of interstate crises occurring between 1816 and the present. BCOW's relatively small sample of well-defined disputes, with considerably fewer actors, reflects not only the BCOW concern with crisis behavior, but also our attempt to obtain a more fine-screened description of interstate conflict behavior. The WEIS data set includes 91,240 events for its global survey of *all* interstate events for the period 1966–78; the BCOW data set includes 25,415 events for just thirty-eight crises. The greater density of BCOW coverage reflects use of multiple sources that is made possible by the narrower scope of the coverage.

The BCOW data resemble the WEIS data and differ from the COPDAB data in opting for a nominal categorization of actions by types, rather than scaling actions on one or another dimension at the data generation stage. In analyzing the data we have adopted procedures to classify actions according to their impact on the target and their intensity, but this is not attempted at the data-generation stage. We have tried to minimize the amount of inference regarding the motives of state actors or the effects of their actions on targets at the data-generation stage.

This is not to say that the BCOW data present a "purely descriptive" account of crisis behavior. The categories of action descriptors and, indeed, our conception of what constitutes a crisis, reflect the theoretical views mentioned above. The objective is to reduce the amount of explanatory inference that must be made by the coder, given the extent to which the common labeling of international actions is laden with interpretation. What one source labels an "ultimatum," another sees as a mere "warning." What one labels an "agreement," another describes as a "conditional acceptance." Thus the coding scheme avoids reliance upon the interpretive labels that reporters and historians attach to events in favor of categorizing each event according to its behavior content. For example, actions are not categorized as "ultimatums" or "warnings" in the coding scheme. Instead there are categories describing statements "requesting" and "intending" action, with descriptors of the conditions under which the action would be taken and a complete description of the action requested or intended.

At the modeling and analysis stages of the research, combinations of requested and intended actions may be labeled "warnings," "threats," or "ultimatums" reflecting the *analyst's* definition of the components of these types of events, as well as varieties of each. The coding scheme leaves that choice to the analyst, rather than rely on the meaning attached to the event by the source or by the coder. In sum, within the constraints of our own beliefs regarding the content of international actions, our objective is to describe the overt moves of the protagonist governments and leave judgments as to the motives of the actors and the consequences of the sequence of moves to the analysis phase of the research process.[3]

The BCOW data differ from WEIS and COPDAB data in the description of those physical actions which extend beyond a single day, such as military alerts or ongoing negotiations. Following the lead of Corson (1971), we have included a description of the "tempo" of action that allows us to track these ongoing actions from the day they begin until the day they end, as well as note increases or decreases in the magnitude of certain activities, such as the movement from a lower to a higher alert status or the upgrading of negotiations by sending in a higher ranking government official. This yields more valid descriptions of the patterns of interaction in evolving crises than that obtained from identifying the presence of such activities only on the day that they begin.

A less desirable consequence of the last two properties of the data set has been to complicate the descriptions of state actions to the point where counting, weighting, and scaling events require software designed specifically for the BCOW data. A general-purpose counting and scaling program (CRISIS) accompanies the data distributed through the ICPSR.

An Overview of the Data

The Spatial-Temporal Domain. The temporal boundaries for the BCOW Project are the same as those for the Correlates of War Project: 1816–present. (The data currently available through the ICPSR extend only through 1972.) Within this period one can discern at least three major diplomatic environments: (1) the traditional multipolar balance-of-power system of the nineteenth century, (2) the interwar period that marked the beginning of parliamentary diplomacy and the experiment with collective security in the League of Nations, as well as the rise of ideological states, and (3) after World War II, the rise of the superpowers, the dawn of the nuclear age, and the entrance of numerous newly independent states to the interstate system.

With these differences in mind, the data sample has been stratified to include a representative number of interstate crises that either did or did not end in war in each of three eras: 1816–1919, 1920–45, and 1946–75. The distribution of cases across these three eras is proportional to that appearing in

---

3. For each action appearing in the data file, we have appended a code describing the "immediate impact" of the action on the target state. This description is derived deductively from our views regarding the "impact" of particular action types; for example, the mobilization of military forces is assumed to have a negative impact on the target, while supplying economic assistance is assumed to be positive. Other users can disregard these codes and attach whatever meanings they wish to the actions described.

the population of "militarized interstate disputes" (MID) compiled by the COW Project (Gochman and Maoz 1984, 592).[4]

Types of Disputes

The unit of analysis is the dispute. A militarized interstate crisis falls near the upper end of a ladder of increasing belligerence that extends from (1) an interstate dispute, to (2) a militarized interstate dispute, to (3) a militarized interstate crisis, to (4) an interstate war.

The distinctions among these levels of belligerence are based on variations in the observed dispute *behavior* of the participants, rather than their perceptions or motivations, although these may well be the sources of the observed behavior, a point to which we shall return in discussing the operational definition of a militarized interstate crisis.

At the lowest level of belligerence are *interstate disputes,* that is, disputes with at least one member of the interstate system, as defined by Small and Singer (1982), on each side. Disputes, of course, are prevalent among members of the interstate system, and we have made no attempt to catalogue their occurrence over the past century and two-thirds. The first step up the ladder is from a mere dispute to a *militarized interstate dispute;* that is, to a dispute that includes the threat, display, or use of force by at least one of the participants (Gochman and Maoz 1984). This provides an operational criterion to identify those disputes in which the threat of war becomes explicit and overt. It is also a distinction that is consistent with traditional views of state behavior, including Article 2(4) of the United Nations Charter, which singles out the "threat or use of force" as contrary to the purposes of the charter.

The population and coding criteria for militarized interstate disputes occurring between 1816 and 1976 are discussed in Gochman and Maoz (1984). Not all such disputes reach the level of belligerence that we associate with a militarized interstate crisis. If, for example, one state reacts forcefully to a perceived transgression by another, and the matter is quickly resolved with an apology from the presumed transgressor or through a clarification of a misunderstanding, there is no interstate crisis, although the situation may become a foreign policy crisis for one or both of the states. By the same token, an interstate crisis may, or may not, represent a crisis for the regional or global system.

A militarized dispute evolves into a *militarized interstate crisis* when a member of the interstate system on each side of the dispute indicates by its

---

4. The distribution of cases for the three periods in the current BCOW sample is seventeen, eight, and thirteen. If the MID data set were shrunk to a sample of forty, the distribution across the three periods would be sixteen, eight, and sixteen. It should be kept in mind, however, that we have only tentatively identified the proportion of MID cases that qualify as crises.

actions its willingness to go to war to defend its interests or to obtain its objectives. This definition departs from several current definitions of crises, which are based on the *perceptions* of foreign policy makers (Brecher 1977; Snyder and Diesing 1977). It is, however, consistent with the COW approach to describing interstate conflict by focusing on the dispute as the level of analysis and basing operational indicators on observable behavior.

The sufficient conditions for classifying a militarized dispute as a crisis vary considerably among researchers, but there is consensus that a necessary distinguishing feature is a dangerously high probability of war (Buchan 1964; Bell 1971; Brecher 1977; Snyder and Diesing 1977). There can be many reasons why states find themselves in such a situation, but certainly there must be a perception that the interests at stake are serious enough to signal a willingness to risk war to defend or obtain them, even if the perceived high stakes are the actor's reputation for demonstrating resolve in a crisis.

Our operational indicator of the mutual perception of a dangerously high probability of war is the presence of a threat of force, display of force, or the use of force by both sides. If one side challenges, the other must resist for the dispute to qualify as a crisis; 593 (62 percent) of the 965 cases of militarized interstate disputes observed between 1816 and 1976 meet this criterion. The distinction is supported by observable difference between the two subsets. Those militarized disputes in which threats, displays, or uses of force are reciprocated reach statistically significantly higher ($p = .0001$)[5] scores along three salient dimensions: (1) the number of dispute-connected fatalities, (2) the peak level of hostility displayed by the first party to threaten force, and (3) the duration of the dispute from the first threat of force to its termination.

Given these findings, it may be that the reciprocation of the threat, display, or use of force is a sufficient criterion for identifying the population of crises; however, there is a second commonly cited behavioral manifestation of a crisis that ought to be considered: an unusually high intensity of interaction between the participants on the two sides (McClelland 1961; Zinnes, Zinnes, and McClure 1972; Snyder and Diesing 1977). The perceptual phenomenon most often associated with this is a sense of time pressure, that is, pressure to act quickly because of the magnitude of the foreign policy problem (Hermann 1972; Brecher 1977). There is a perceived need to take military action to prepare for the possibility of war, or to intensify diplomatic activities to avoid war.

Devising an operational definition of this concept raises several difficult questions, beginning with what actions, taken when, and by whom, should be included, and ending with the issue of determining a threshold to distinguish between "normal" interaction and "unusually intense" interaction (see

---

5. Using Cramer's *phi* as the measure of statistical significance.

Gochman and Leng 1987). In the absence of any convincing a priori reasons for making these determinations, we are moving inductively in deciding whether such an additional criterion is necessary and, if so, how and where to set the threshold. In the meantime, for the purposes of moving ahead with the data-generation process, not to mention obtaining a large enough sample of fully coded cases to test various potential intensity measures, we have coded all those disputes falling into the sample that meet the reciprocated threat, display, or use of force criterion.[6]

Boundaries and Phases of Crises

A crisis begins with a specific precipitant event. The term "specific precipitant" is borrowed from Snyder and Diesing (1977, 11–12), who define it as "a particular and especially provocative act." Operationally, we define a precipitant event as having at least one of the following attributes: (1) an explicit threat, display, or use of force; (2) a challenge to the vital interests of the target, that is, its territorial integrity, political independence, or any foreign possessions or rights; or (3) a serious affront to the dignity or prestige of the target state. The specific precipitant is identified from the accounts of diplomatic historians.

The identification of the termination of a crisis begins by distinguishing between those crises that evolve to war and those that do not. The outbreak of war moves the dispute another step up the ladder to an interstate war, with the Small and Singer (1982) criteria used to identify the onset of war. The termination dates for both wars and nonwar crises are classified according to whether or not the two sides reach a diplomatic settlement, or the crisis or war ends with no settlement (see Maoz 1982).

Settlements are identified by the presence of a treaty or other written agreement, such as a joint communiqué, by an exchange of letters, or by an explicit verbal understanding. When no settlement is reached, a crisis is considered terminated if no new threats, displays, or uses of force occur for six months.

The crisis outcome for each participant is classified as *win, lose,* or *tie.* When a crisis ends in a settlement, a tie represents a compromise agreement; when there is no settlement, a tie represents a stalemate.

Sample Selection

When the BCOW Project was launched in 1970, no reliable list of the population of militarized crises existed. The long-term solution to that problem was

---

6. We started with an accompanying, arbitrarily low, activity threshold of fifty total interactions for all participants, but found that this excluded none of the cases meeting the first criterion which appeared in the list of disputes from which we were selecting the sample.

to construct the list of candidate crises in the MID data set, but that quickly became a major project in its own right. And even after it was completed, we would need a sample of fully coded cases to consider possible intensity measures.

This dilemma, along with our desire to test the reliability and validity of the BCOW typology and to undertake some preliminary studies, prompted us to create a tentative list of the population of crises based on disputes that diplomatic historians and political scientists classified as crises. From this list, we drew a sample from those cases with reciprocal threats, displays, or uses of force. The thirty-eight cases in the data set available from the ICPSR represent this sample. With the exception of four cases,[7] they were selected randomly from a tentative list of the population of crises compiled from the Singer and Small (1972) list of interstate wars, initially augmented by Dupuy and Dupuy (1977) for the 1966–72 period, and a list of nonwar crises extracted from Langer's *Encyclopedia of World History* (1972), supplemented for the post–World War II period by qualifying interstate disputes drawn from Butterworth (1976).[8] A list of the crises making up the sample appears in table 1.

The Typology and Coding Scheme

There are scientific requirements that all typologies share in common: the categories must be constructed along explicit descriptive dimensions; they must be mutually exclusive; and they must be logically exhaustive. And if the typology is to serve as the basis for the generation of reproducible data, the definitions of categories must be operational.

Beyond meeting these basic requirements, the BCOW typology is designed to be fine-screened enough to distinguish among a wide range of cooperative and conflictive interstate actions, to allow their aggregation into larger classes to test particular hypotheses, to provide a sensitive measure of the mix and tempo of behavior within given time intervals, and to facilitate the observation of influence attempts and responses during the course of a crisis.

The coding of each action begins with the date on which the action occurs, the actor, the target, the location, whether the actor was acting unilaterally or with another state, and the "tempo" of the action. As we suggested above, the tempo describes whether the action began and ended on that date, or a continuing action is starting, increasing in intensity, decreasing, or

---

7. The Palestine War crisis, 1947–48; the Berlin Wall crisis, 1961; the Six Day War crisis, 1967; and the Bangladesh War crisis, 1971, were all chosen to complete sets of recurring crises for a particular study (Leng 1983).

8. Coverage in Langer (1972) becomes sparse after 1945, especially where newly independent states are concerned. Butterworth (1976) includes many cases that fall short of the threat-of-force criterion, as well as cases that are more properly classified as civil or colonial disputes.

TABLE 1. Sample of Interstate Crises, 1816–1975

Crisis Name	Major Participants		Begin-End (year/month/day)
	Side A	Side B	
1. Pastry War	France	Mexico	1838/3/2–1839/3/9
2. 2d Schleswig-Holstein War*	Prussia Austria-Hungary	Denmark	1863/3/30–1864/7/20
3. Russo-Turkish War*	Russia	Turkey	1876/9/1–1878/3/3
4. British-Russian crisis	Britain	Russia	1877/5/6–1878/5/30
5. British-Portuguese crisis	Britain	Portugal	1889/8/19–1890/1/12
6. Spanish-American War*	Spain	United States	1898/2/15–1898/8/12
7. Fashoda crisis	Britain	France	1898/7/10–1898/12/4
8. 1st Moroccan crisis	France	Germany	1904/10/3–1906/3/31
9. 2d Central American War*	Honduras Salvador	Nicaragua	1906/12/?–1907/4/23
10. Bosnian crisis	Austria-Hungary Germany Turkey	Serbia Russia	1908/10/6–1909/3/31
11. 2d Moroccan crisis	France Britain	Germany	1911/5/21–1911/11/4
12. 1st Balkan War*	Serbia Bulgaria Greece	Turkey	1912/5/29–1913/5/30
13. 2d Balkan War*	Bulgaria	Rumania Greece Serbia Turkey	1913/2/20–1913/8/10
14. Pre–World War I	Serbia	Austria-Hungary	1914/6/28–1914/7/29
15. Pre–World War I	Austria-Hungary Germany	Russia	1914/6/28–1914/8/6
16. Pre–World War I	Britain France	Germany	1914/6/28–1914/8/4
17. Teschen crisis	Czechoslovakia	Poland	1918/12/10– 1920/7/28
18. Chaco dispute	Bolivia	Paraguay	1927/2/25–1930/5/1
19. Chaco War	Bolivia	Paraguay	1932/4/6–1932/6/15
20. Italo-Ethiopian War*	Ethiopia	Italy	1934/11/22–1936/5/9
21. Rhineland crisis	Britain France Belgium	Germany	1936/3/7–1936/10/31
22. Anschluss crisis	Austrai	Germany	1938/2/12–1938/3/12
23. Munich crisis	Czechoslovakia Britain France	Germany	1938/2/20–1938/9/30
24. Polish-Lithuanian crisis	Lithuania	Poland	1938/3/12–1938/3/31

TABLE 1—*Continued*

Crisis Name	Major Participants		Begin-End
	Side A	Side B	(year/month/day)
25. Danzig crisis (pre-World War II)	Germany	Poland Britain France	1938/10/24–1939/9/1
26. Italo-French crisis	Italy Germany	France	1938/11/30–1939/9/3
27. 1st Kashmir War*	India	Pakistan	1947/10/22–1949/1/1
28. Palestine War	Egypt Iraq Lebanon Syria Transjordan	Israel	1947/8/31–1948/5/15
29. Berlin blockade	Britain France United States	USSR	1948/6/7–1949/5/12
30. Trieste crisis	Italy	Yugoslavia	1953/7/16–1954/10/5
31. Suez crisis	Egypt	Britain France Israel	1956/7/26– 1956/11/15
32. Berlin Wall crisis	United States Britain France West Germany	USSR East Germany	1961/6/4–1961/11/9
33. Cuban Missile crisis	United States	USSR Cuba	1962/10/14– 1962/11/20
34. Cyprus crisis	Greece	Turkey	1963/11/30– 1964/9/15
35. 2d Kashmir War	India	Pakistan	1964/12/21–1965/8/5
36. Rann of Kutch	India	Pakistan	1965/3/20–1965/6/30
37. Six Day War*	Egypt Jordan Syria	Israel	1966/11/5–1967/6/10
38. Bangladesh War*	India	Pakistan	1971/3/15– 1971/12/17

*Crises ending in war that have been coded through to the end of the war.

stopping. This provides a continuing index of the presence and variations in the intensity of ongoing physical actions.

From this point on, the typology is constructed in the form of the hierarchical choice tree depicted in figure 1. The next branching distinguishes between physical and verbal actions. Physical actions are categorized according to the resource that the actor brings to bear—military, economic, diplo-

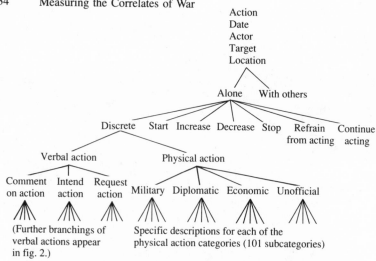

Fig. 1. BCOW Typology: hierarchical choice tree. We present the sub-categorization for only the leftmost branch when the subcategorization is the same for all branches.

matic, or unofficial. Then each of these categories branches into more specific descriptions of the act. In the case of diplomatic actions, some of the possibilities would be to consult, negotiate, declare neutrality, or change the status of diplomatic relations. Military actions include such categories as alert, blockade, clash, show-of-force, and military assistance, while economic categories include change in trade relations, economic assistance, and nationalization of foreign property. The "unofficial" category refers to actions for which the government does not take official responsibility, such as anti-foreign demonstrations, assassinations, or subversive activities. A list of the 101 types of specific descriptions for physical actions appears in appendix B.

We now will move back up the choice tree to consider verbal actions. Our interest in the conflict bargaining process has led to an innovation in the "double-coding" of all verbal actions to allow both a full line of description of how these actions are communicated to the target state, and a second line describing what is communicated. We begin by branching into the three basic types of verbal actions displayed in figure 2: (1) comments on actions or situations, (2) requests or demands for action (or inaction) by the target, and (3) intentions, that is, statements indicating that under certain conditions, the actor intends to take certain actions.

The first line of coded information describes the attributes of the verbal act per se, for example, whether a state's evaluative comments indicate approval or disapproval, or whether or not demands are accompanied by inducements from the actor, or the extent of a state's verbal commitment to carry out its intended actions. The second line of coded information describes what

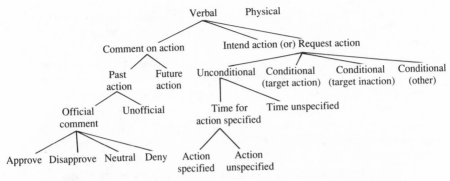

Fig. 2. BCOW verbal action subcategories. After reaching the final branching, the coder returns to the start of the choice tree (fig. 1) and fully describes the action commented upon, intended, or requested by the actor. We present the subcategorization for only the leftmost branch of the tree when the subcategorization is the same for all branches. The branchings for "intend" action and "request" action are the same. They refer to the action intended by the actor or requested of the target.

action the state is commenting on, requesting, or intending to carry out. This line is the key to tracing whether threats are carried out, promises kept, or demands met. Thus, it becomes the key to analyzing influence attempt–response sequences, where influence attempts are defined as requests coupled with positive and/or negative intended actions. The first line of description enables the investigator to compare different types of requests or inducements: for example, to test the association of the specificity of an actor's commitment to act with the target's compliance with demands coupled with what the analyst has classified as threats and/or promises.

The Coded Data

A detailed description of the procedures for coding international actions, along with step-by-step instructions, appears in the *User's Manual* (Leng 1987). The *User's Manual* also contains summary narrative accounts, along with descriptive and technical data for each of the cases in the sample, as well as instructions for using the CRISIS program for counting, categorizing, and scaling actions. A sample of a summary account for one case appears as appendix A.

Intercoder Reliability

Before leaving this section, some mention should be made about the reliability of the data. For each case, the coder constructs verbal chronologies from available historical monographs, archival sources, and press accounts. Then the several verbal chronologies are combined, with duplicate actions culled and discrepancies reconciled. The resulting single, multiple-source chronology is then coded according to the scheme that has just been described.

Intercoder reliability tests run for twelve pair of coders using the fourth, fifth, or sixth editions of the *Coder's Manual* and working from prepared chronologies (Leng 1986a) have yielded a mean score of .94, using Scott's π (Holsti 1969, 140–46). These scores may overstate the reliability of the data, however, as the identification of the events as codable actions takes place at the chronology stage, as does the identification of actors and targets. Lower scores have been obtained for more complex coding categories; mean score for coding the tempo of action, for example, is .84. The data have been cleaned and debugged prior to their public release. This is not to claim that there are no errors in the current data set of over 25,000 events, but every effort has been made to produce data that are reliable and error free.

Using the Data: Methods and Findings

However rich and fine-grained the BCOW data set may be, the true measure of its worth is in its ability to produce data that will enable us to answer significant political questions. Research on the Behavioral Correlates of War has grown with the data set, with some preliminary studies conducted with smaller samples of cases (Leng and Goodsell 1974; Leng 1980). We have also followed the tradition of the Correlates of War Project by beginning with essentially descriptive analyses of patterns of interstate action, and later moving incrementally toward more complex questions and techniques. By summarizing some of the research completed to date, we can present a sense of the potential of the data set, as well as describe some of the techniques that have been used in analyzing it. A flexible interactive computer program (CRISIS) for counting and scaling the data is available with the BCOW data set.[9]

Patterns of Interaction in Crises

One of our first findings (Leng and Goodsell 1974), which has been confirmed by subsequent studies (Leng and Wheeler 1979), is the high degree of reciprocity in crisis behavior, both in the types of actions employed and the

---

9. Because of the complexity of the data set, with its sensitivity to changes in the tempo of ongoing actions and the "double coding" of verbal actions, the CRISIS program is a prerequisite for almost any analysis of the data. CRISIS is an interactive program that offers the user considerable flexibility in the choice of crises, actors and targets, time intervals, particular categories of actions, and procedures for scaling the data. The program, written in VAX-11 PASCAL, is included with the tape of the data available at ICPSR, Ann Arbor, Michigan.

magnitude of positive or negative actions. These studies support the hypothesis that there is a fairly consistent increase in the magnitude of conflictive behavior following the first threat of force, thus adding credence to our choice of this event to serve as an important break-point between phases of evolving crises.

In subsequent studies (Leng 1986b) we have experimented with constructing typologies of crises based on their behavioral characteristics. We have settled on two salient dimensions—reciprocity and escalation—to produce six basic behavioral types. The findings from these studies suggest that disputes in which reciprocity and escalation are high are the most likely to lead to war, whereas those that score lowest on both dimensions are the least likely to end in war. Perhaps of more immediate relevance to the prospective user of the BCOW data, we also found a high degree of consistency between our classifications among the six behavioral types based on operational measures of the BCOW data, and the impressions of diplomatic historians as to the nature of the interaction between the two sides.

Contextual Predictors to Patterns of Interaction

Our research to date (Gochman and Leng 1983) suggests a positive association between the presence of vital issues at stake (threats to the territorial integrity or political independence of the target) and/or the use of physical threats of force, and greater escalation following the first threat of force. We also have found that much of the variation in dispute outcomes, for disputes falling within the six basic behavioral types identified in earlier studies, was associated with the presence or absence of vital issues and the participation of major powers. The presence of vital issues is positively associated with war outcomes; the participation of major powers, either as adversaries or as mediators, is positively associated with nonwar outcomes in disputes between states relatively evenly matched in military capabilities.

Crisis Bargaining Tactics

The unique potential of the BCOW data was exploited more fully when we turned to an examination of the interactions of states within crises. We began with stimulus-response models to test the association between types of influence attempts (request action plus an inducement in the form of an intended action) by State *A,* and types of responses by State *B* (Leng 1980). The findings indicated that what action is requested is less salient than how it is requested (what inducements accompany the request) in determining the response. Moreover, we have found that how an inducement is presented, that is, how specifically the actor makes the commitment to carry it out, is a powerful predictor of how the target will respond. While threats are generally more effective than promises alone, carrot-and-stick influence attempts combining positive and negative inducements are most effective in crises between evenly matched states, a finding that is particularly striking in a later study of crisis bargaining between the United States and the USSR (Leng 1984). We also found that in crises between equals, the more specific the commitment to carry out the threat, the greater the likelihood of a defiant response. In fact, in the U.S.-Soviet study we found that less specific threats, or warnings, were more likely to produce positive responses than more specific and more severe threats.

Crisis Influence Strategies

Beyond the effects of particular types of influence attempts, the detailed coding of verbal actions has been exploited to gauge the relative effectiveness of the overall influence strategies employed by states over the course of a crisis (Leng and Wheeler 1979; Leng 1984). Our identification of the predominant influence strategy employed by State A has been based on its choice of inducements (threats, promises, or carrot-and-stick) following particular responses by State B. That is, if B ignores an influence attempt by A that coupled its request with a warning, does A couple its next request with an appeasing promise, or a bullying ultimatum? The predominant influence strategy is based on the aggregate of A's choices over the course of the crisis or a phase of the crisis. The interested reader can find a full description of the classification scheme in Leng and Wheeler (1979, 657–71).

The results from this phase of the research have been particularly suggestive, pointing to a high association between predominantly coercive, "bullying" influence strategies and war. The most effective strategy overall, and particularly in disputes between relative equals, is a reciprocating, or "firm-but-fair," strategy that combines occasional positive initiatives with "tit-for-tat" matches of the inducements employed by the target (Leng and Wheeler 1979; Leng 1984). This is consistent with the suggestive results obtained through experiments in social psychology (Esser and Komorita 1975), repeated plays of Prisoner's Dilemma games (Axelrod 1984), and, more recently, data-based research on extended deterrence (Huth and Russett 1988).

Changes in Strategies and Tactics in Recurrent Crises

We mentioned earlier that four crises from the post–World War II era were specifically selected in order to permit an examination of pairs of states engaged in three successive crises. The findings in a study of three pairs of evenly matched states (Leng 1983) indicate that the relative victor in one crisis is likely to employ the same influence strategy in the next confrontation with the same adversary. On the other hand, states dissatisfied with the outcome of the previous crisis are likely to switch to a more coercive bargaining strategy the next time. And when they do, the previous winner follows suit. Consequently each successive crisis becomes more bellicose. Comparable results using different data have recently been obtained by Huth and Russett (1988).

A Comparison with a Qualitative Study

Finally, thanks to some overlap in the selection of cases in our sample with a comparative qualitative study of crisis behavior by Snyder and Diesing (1977), we were able to conduct an unusual direct comparison between quantitative and qualitative crisis research (Leng and Walker 1982). Although some interesting differences emerged in the findings from the two studies, we found a remarkable consistency in the selection of predominant influence strategies despite the appreciably different methods of observation employed in the two studies.

A Note on Methods

We have employed a wide range of statistical techniques in analyzing the BCOW data. The earlier studies of patterns of interaction in crises, crisis types, and influence tactics have relied primarily on simple bivariate correlations, difference of means tests, curve smoothing techniques, and cross-tabular analysis employing tests of statistical significance. Some of the more recent analyses have employed more sophisticated techniques, including a Box-Tiao (1975) approach to modeling time series with interventions.

Concluding Remarks

The variety of analyses that have been performed to date should give the potential user of the BCOW data some sense of their flexibility and research potential. As for the findings themselves, none is conclusive; nevertheless, the cumulative nature of the results, along with their logical consistency, is promising.

In certain respects, the findings are consistent with a realpolitik image of crisis bargaining. Crises escalate more rapidly when vital interests are at stake; threats are most likely to obtain compliance when they are credibly communicated; and crises are more likely to be resolved short of war when great powers are actively involved on both sides. But the most interesting findings run counter to the instrumentally rational bargaining suggested by realpolitik. The more specific the commitment to carry out a threat, the more likely it is to lead to a defiant response. Purely coercive influence strategies are highly associated with war outcomes, as are disputes that are high in escalation and in reciprocity. States that submit to coercion in one crisis are more likely to adopt more belligerent influence strategies in the next confrontation with the same adversary, particularly in confrontations between states of relatively equal military capabilities.

The findings to date indicate that the most effective influence attempts are those that employ carrot-and-stick inducements mixing credible threats with face-saving concessions. By the same token, the most effective overall crisis influence strategies are "reciprocating" strategies mixing tit-for-tat responses with occasional accommodative initiatives. Perhaps the prescription that these negative and positive findings provide is nothing more than that side of classical realism that stresses prudence—using one's power with care and giving the adversary its due. But that includes an understanding of limits, and of the virtues of restraint. If the data generation effort that has yielded these results does no more than confirm the continuing validity of such old-fashioned diplomatic truths in an age of competing global ideologies and nationalistic passions, the effort will have been more than justified.

Appendix A. Sample of Crisis Summary

The Pastry War Crisis: 1838–39

Dates coded: February 23, 1838, to April, 1839
Data file: PASTY.SRT
Total acts: 305

Participants
Side A: Mexico (070), *Mexican Federalists (897)
Side B: France (220), *French Nationals in Mexico (997)
Others: Britain (200), United States (002)

Other Locations
Gulf of Mexico (178), Demilitarized zone
Veracruz and environs (994), Disputed territory (996)

Sources
Blanchard, P., and A. D. Dauzats, *San Juan de Ulua ou Relation de l'expedition francaise au Mexique.*
Bocanegra, J. M. 1892. *Historia de Mexico Independiente: 1822–1846.* Mexico: Gobierno Federal en le Ex-Arzobispado.

de la Pena y Reyes, A. 1927. *La Primera Guerra entre Mexico y Francia.* Mexico City: Publications de la Secretaria de Relaciones Exteriores.

Key Dates
Precipitant event: March 2, 1838. The French fleet sails into Veracruz harbor.
First threat of force: March 2, 1838. French show of strength.
First hostilities: November 27, 1838. French forces attack at Veracruz.
Termination: March 9, 1839. Peace agreement reached; Mexico agrees to pay reparations.
Other Key Dates: March 21, 1838. First French ultimatum to Mexico, followed by blockade on April 16.
November 21, 1838. Second French ultimatum, followed by attack on Veracruz on November 27.
November 30, 1838. Mexico declares war on France.

Narrative Summary
Newly independent Mexico suffered from considerable civil unrest in the 1830s. French citizens, along with other foreigners, were victimized by the disturbances, including a baker, whose shop was ransacked and destroyed; hence the name of the Pastry War. On March 2, 1838, a French fleet sailed into Veracruz harbor and demanded, among other things, that Mexico pay $600,000 in reparations before April 15. Mexico refused the ultimatum, and the French blockaded Veracruz on April 16, 1838. Diplomatic attempts to alleviate the situation failed. On November 21, France issued an ultimatum giving Mexico until November 27 to meet French conditions or French forces would attack Veracruz. The conditions were not met; the French attacked, and, on November 30, Mexico declared war on France. In December a British agent, backed by the presence of a sizable British fleet anchored in Veracruz harbor, arrived to mediate the dispute. French and Mexican representatives met with the British mediator on March 7, 1838, and Mexico agreed to pay the $600,000 in reparations, as well as to grant France most favored nation status.

Coding Notes
1. Participants that are not members of the interstate system are identified by a preceding asterisk.
2. (178) as the location refers to the presence of French and British ships off the coast of Veracruz.
3. Acts #22, 36, 43, 50, and 260 refer to the Mexican refusal to recognize a change in French diplomatic representatives.
4. Acts #84–91, 137, 221, 224–25, 244, 251, 257–59, and 263 all refer to actions by the Mexican Federalist party. (996) indicates territory controlled by the Federalists.

Appendix B. Specific Descriptors for Physical Actions

Codes for these acts include five digits. The first digit (1, 2, or 3) is the physical action descriptor that appears in col. 25 of the BCOW data base. The second digit (col. 26) identifies the physical action type as (1) military, (2) diplomatic, (3) economic, or (4) unofficial. The last three digits (cols. 27–29) provide the specific descriptor of the action.

Military Actions
(11212)	International peacekeeping force
(11719)	Domestic military action (with verbal acts)
(11121)	Military advice or assistance
(11131)	Military coordination
(11333)	Alert
(11353)	Mobilization
(11413)	Evacuation
(11313)	Show of strength
(11363)	Antiguerrilla action
(11443)	Military intrusion
(11433)	Blockade
(11423)	Seizure
(11453)	Enter demilitarized zone
(11513)	Clash
(11523)	Attack
(11533)	Continuous military conflict
(11521)	Military withdrawal
(11663)	Take prisoners of war
(11673)	Inhumane actions or atrocities
(11633)	Military victory (partial)
(11643)	Military victory (total)
(11621)	Surrender
(11653)	Occupation
(21141)	Change in military assistance
(21111)	Military grant
(21121)	Sell or trade
(21133)	Change force level
(21143)	Change in combat force level
(21211)	Return
(21233)	Remove
(21311)	Supply nuclear weapons
(21333)	Remove nuclear weapons
(31121)	Permit foreign military passage
(31132)	Establish military base
(31133)	Fortify occupied territory

Diplomatic Actions
(12111)	Consult
(12121)	Negotiate
(12521)	Reach agreement

(12511)   Form alliance
(12361)   Peace settlement
(12142)   Mediate or arbitrate
(12152)   Guarantee agreement
(12223)   Violate international law
(12342)   Investigate
(12362)   Declare neutrality
(12161)   Change diplomatic relationship
(12631)   Attend international event
(12641)   Assume foreign kingship
(12533)   Break diplomatic agreement
(12363)   Declare war
(12131)   Provide diplomatic assistance
(12183)   Change in border restrictions
(12173)   Arrest or expel foreign representative
(12373)   Grant asylum
(12719)   Domestic political action
(12223)   Violate territory
(12232)   Conduct plebiscite
(12243)   Political intervention
(32111)   Grant or cede territory
(32132)   Colonize or claim territory
(32141)   Establish demilitarized zone
(32142)   Establish protectorate or trusteeship
(32163)   Declare independence
(32153)   Secede
(32143)   Annex territory
(32151)   Grant independence
(32161)   Integrate
(32173)   Partition
(32611)   Political concession

Economic Actions
(13111)   Consult
(13121)   Negotiate
(13131)   Advise
(13211)   Economic coordination
(13551)   Reach economic agreement
(23111)   Economic grant
(23121)   Sell or trade
(23131)   Loan
(23151)   Change in trade relations
(23163)   Confiscate or nationalize
(23171)   Economic integration
(23301)   Extend humanitarian aid or relief

(23141)   Change in economic assistance
(23211)   Return goods
(23223)   Remove goods
(23231)   Purchase payment
(23251)   Pay reparations
(23261)   Pay tribute
(33111)   Grant or lease economic concession
(33131)   Permit economic passage
(23719)   Domestic economic action (with verbal action)

Unofficial Actions
(14113)   Subversion or guerrilla activity
(14123)   Discrete attack
(14133)   Continuous combat
(14143)   Assassinate
(14151)   Consult
(14153)   Kidnap or hold hostage
(14213)   Antiforeign demonstration
(14223)   Antiforeign riot
(14251)   Proforeign demonstration
(14263)   Seize property
(14719)   Unofficial domestic action (with verbal action)

6
Conclusion

Evolution and Directions for Improvement in the Correlates of War Project Methodologies

Frank Whelon Wayman and J. David Singer

Having recently celebrated its silver anniversary and commenced its second quarter-century, the Correlates of War Project is one of the few social science research projects that has survived to maturity. Consequently, the Project methodologies have gone through the metamorphoses of youth and adolescence, in response to constructive criticism, normal professional growth, and the continually developing capabilities of modern social science. The essays in this anthology, a representative cross-section of some of the Project's classic, data-oriented methodological studies, are stepping stones on a journey of discovery, whose future path cannot be fully seen from today's vantage point, but whose general compass direction can be tentatively sketched out— though undoubtedly in a slightly different way by each of the sojourners.

The travelers on this particular journey have been criticized for wandering off the proper scientific path. The gist of the criticism is that the project has been unduly concerned with constructing indicators, generating data, and describing the trends and periodicities in war and its putative causes. As for the most important academic job—of explaining war—some critics feel that this has been insufficiently attended to, and insofar as it has, through a strategy that is unduly inductive and insufficiently deductive. In this chapter we wish to deal with the concerns of these critics, by focusing on the ways in which we have best contributed, and might in the future, best contribute— through the measurement of key concepts—to the goals of explaining and predicting war.

Vasquez (1987) identifies about two dozen "core members" of the Correlates of War Project—the people who have worked directly at the Project headquarters—plus another fifteen or so *popuchiki,* or "fellow travelers," who constitute "an invisible college" around the Project. It is the former group whose work is largely represented in this volume, and whose evolution

---

1. Nonetheless, we occasionally have reason to allude to the works of the fellow travelers and other colleagues in the quantitative international security studies community.

we are tracing here.[1] They represent a sizable concentration, perhaps a plurality, of scholars doing data-based research in international politics. Of 217 quantitative-empirical studies published in world politics journals between 1973 and 1986, one-fifth (forty-one articles) had one of the core members as sole or first author (Gibbs and Singer, forthcoming). A similar portion (thirty-nine articles) were by members of the COW "invisible college"—the scholars who use COW data, and who are often the Project's most constructive critics. If one believes in the importance of quantitative historical research, one will naturally be concerned about the development of such a project, which has been large enough to affect almost half of the scholarship in the field during the last two decades. When a project represents the creative energies of so many scholars, it would be presumptuous to play the pontiff, and dictate the direction in which researchers will chose to go. Here, we try to strike a middle course between agnosticism and pontification, and sketch out some ways in which the Project has been evolving, along with some promising new directions.

Levels of Analysis: From System to Dyad

A glance at the contents of this volume, and the dates of publication of the essays within it, will indicate how the Project has evolved over its history. The Project began with a focus on national capabilities, military alliances, systemic capability concentration, and systemic patterns of alliance polarization, in an age when international relations theorists were focusing their attention on the dominant realist paradigm, with its emphasis on capabilities and coalitions.

That theoretical literature was expressed in the form of deterministic hypotheses (Keohane 1983), leading to hypothesized high correlations between systemic characteristics and war. The empirical literature on polarity (as surveyed by Wayman 1984 and by Wayman and Morgan in this volume) has produced surprisingly weak and inconsistent relationships. This suggests that the systems level may not be the best or only place to look for explanations. While the realist literature is not explicitly theoretical enough to be demolished by this, it is true that the hypothesized relationships are not as strong as that literature of twenty years ago led one to expect.

Whereas the outlook of that time led one to expect that the systemic level would be more important than the dyadic, it appears now that it might be the other way around. At least three dyadic relationships appear strong enough that some scholars have argued they are deterministic: democratic dyads do not fight each other (Rummel 1983); overwhelming preponderance guarantees peace (Weede 1976); and power transitions between the two leading powers lead to war (Organski and Kugler 1980). No findings of anywhere close to that degree of strength have been found in the systems level literature. Strong findings have also been discovered at the dyadic level by Wallace (1982) and by Bueno de Mesquita (1981 and as refined in several subsequent journal articles).

Operating at the dyadic level can create two problems of independence of cases. First, wars (and disputes) between two opposing coalitions are often treated statistically as many dyadic wars, and if not handled sensibly this can create serious analytic problems (Ray 1990). Second, wars between two parties are often the result of a chain of previous disputes, and even wars, embedded in an enduring rivalry.

One way around the latter problem is the study of repeated crises (Leng 1983) and enduring rivalries (Wayman 1989). In such approaches, the onset of war is explained as the consequence of a chain of disputes, dispute behavior, and dispute outcomes between a pair of nations. As Russett has put it, "Some people talk about dependence between events and Galton's problem as an obstacle. It could be viewed as a chance to learn something really new and exciting about contagion, learning, and the use of precedents in interstate behavior" (quoted in Wayman 1988).

Knowledge and Policy Prediction

At the recent American Political Science Association symposium on the Project's next twenty-five years, Bruce Russett cut to the heart of the matter in saying, "The *explicit* task before us is what COW should do for the next twenty-five years. The *implicit* task is what international relations theory should do for the next twenty-five years." The goal we all share is a theory of world politics that would explain interstate behavior and thus allow us to— inter alia—predict the outbreak of international conflict and its escalation to war. In the real world, however, we fall short of that ideal. As Paul Diehl put it in his text organizing the symposium, "Although few serious research efforts can be labeled purely inductive or deductive, the COW Project has tended to tilt toward the former. . . . One avenue to pursue is the marriage of formal modeling with empirical testing (Bueno de Mesquita 1985). This may seem like an obvious strategy, but one only has to look at the leading journals to realize that this marriage is rarely consummated" (Diehl 1988, 2).

The fundamental problem here is that we do not have a widely shared model—not to mention one or more competing theories—that explains war. Moreover, many of the project scholars are strongly committed to the somewhat utopian but understandable objective of finding leading indicators of war and applying them in our lifetime, even before the emergence of a satisfactory theoretical explanation. This preoccupation led Singer and Wallace to launch the early warning indicators movement, which had six goals:

1. Identify a . . . condition . . . whose social undesirability . . . can be reasonably demonstrated.

2. Measure with high reliability . . . that condition.
3. Identify and measure one or more predictor conditions or events that might be expected . . . to regularly precede the outcome condition or event.
4. Demonstrate the extent to which such an association has obtained . . . in the international system of the past.
5. Clearly articulate the ways in which some or all policymakers could, if they chose, utilize such predictive indicators to reduce the incidence of interstate war.
6. Clearly articulate the normative and pragmatic considerations that might, at the same time, make the utilization of such indicators detrimental to the interests or needs of any affected parties. (1979, 13)

This search for early warning indicators of war, while inspired as much by the engineering as the scientific spirit, is hardly an antitheoretical enterprise. As Vasquez (1987) has observed, the project has focused on measuring variables (such as national capabilities, alliance commitments, and contiguities) that are key components of the realpolitik paradigm of international affairs. For instance, realists such as Morgenthau (1967) have argued that the most important foreign policy decisions of status quo states involve identifying revisionist states (those who are intent on overthrowing the established international order, even by force), and then thwarting their ambitions by arms buildups and alliances that force the revisionists to back down in the face of superior forces. Wallace (1982) tested the underlying hypothesis that revisionist states would be deterred by superior capabilities on the status quo side, and he found that the hypothesis was not supported by the evidence. While not guided by a formal theory, Wallace's research was typical of much COW research in that it was motivated by a focus on the implications of the dominant realist paradigm.

The debate at that symposium (Wayman 1988) captured many of the premises underlying such COW investigations into the realist paradigm. Singer began by articulating the reasons for investigating the validity of the realpolitik framework: "Realism is not a theory, nor is the preferred label—realpolitik. By the latter, we mean to convey only the acceptance of a set of hunches that seem to have carried the field relatively far along in its early stages. Elites, while spending much time protecting their own domestic position and enjoying life, *do* devote a fair amount of energy and competence to preventing the erosion of territory, status, and related values, and capabilities and coalitions are important in the game the elites play. I see the preservation of autonomy, sovereignty, and options as the goal of major and regional-dominant powers." Many scholars see this paradigm as not only the dominant scientific paradigm in world politics, but also as a guide to policy. However flawed, it has helped shape national security policies for centuries, and its hypotheses are thus worth testing if one is interested in public policy. But, paradoxically, the adoption of the realist paradigm by policymakers makes it imperative to emphasize that testing these hypotheses is not the same as believing that they should guide policy; as Singer noted, "the decision to build data sets to test realpolitik hypotheses is not an endorsement of realism as a normative model of how states *ought to* behave."

Vasquez agreed that realpolitik was of central importance because it represents the dominant conventional wisdom:

Realism is a set of learned behaviors. Because they have been learned by a large number of national security officials, realism is pertinent. Hence, variables drawn from the realist perspective, in the Correlates of War Project, can predict a range of foreign policy acts. But we need to focus on the circumstances in which realism is learned. Realism tells us how countries behave on the brink of war, but little on how to create the conditions of peace. I'd like to see more on learning and precedents and social psychology rather than realism and rational choice. I'd also like to see more on issues, such as territory. I think rivalry, such as discussed by Diehl, could be linked to issues. (quoted in Wayman 1988)

Russett went on to indicate the considerable extent to which COW findings had undermined the support for realpolitik in at least parts of the academic community:

Realism is not a theory, probably/perhaps not even a paradigm. Certainly it is the dominant set of prejudices. For that reason, you should not throw it out—if for no other reason than to establish its limitations. An indictment of realism is seen in the mixed results of the polarity literature, a la Waltz, etc.—Wayman has reviewed this and gone beyond just a review to do some analysis. The realist theoretical literature on polarity seems to lack any consistent empirical support. (quoted in Wayman 1988)

Paradigms can only be overturned (or revised) if the scholarly community attends to the accumulating evidence that reveals their shortcomings, and policies based on them will never be modified if those in the policy community ignore the ongoing investigations in the scientific subculture. Paradoxically, while the realpolitik framework was developed as a guide to national security policy, and while foreign policy makers have been heavily influenced by it, still the COW findings on realpolitik have had little effect on debates about international security affairs. For instance, even the efforts of the National Academy of Sciences to study nuclear deterrence (Rusten and Stern

1987) have, with rare exceptions (Levy 1988), focused on deterrence analysis and case studies, rather than such relevant empirical tests as Blechman and Kaplan (1978); Wallace (1979 and 1982); Maoz (1982); Diehl (1983); Leng (1983); and Wayman, Singer and Goertz (1983).

Newer studies may be harder to ignore. In particular, one recent investigation (by scholars in the "invisible college" around the COW Project) is an excellent model of policy-relevant hypothesis testing. Huth, alone (1988) and with Russett (1984), has constructed a multivariate, static model of extended, immediate deterrence. This has shed light on such important policy questions as what factors (e.g., formal military alliances) contribute to effective deterrence, by utilizing and building on the COW militarized interstate dispute data set. That data set records all militarized interstate disputes—defined as instances in which there was an explicit threat to use force, display of force, or use of force between two members of the interstate system since 1816. They measure a deterrence encounter by looking, first, for an explicit verbal threat to use force or a display of force by the potential attacker, and subsequently, a threat to use force or display of force by a defender of the potential target (Huth 1988, 23–24). Their approach, however, has been criticized by Lebow and Stein (1989), who prefer to measure a deterrence encounter by looking for the highly elusive "intent to attack." We believe that the Lebow and Stein approach (which would be excellent if there were no measurement problems) remains intractable given the near impossibility of validly inferring foreign policymakers' intentions. Their statements about their intentions will often be self-serving, and, as we know from decades of survey research, memories of political decisions will be distorted by selective recall if made long after the event. And even if made in private diaries and at the time of the deterrent encounter, policymakers' statements may be both self-deluding and irrelevant, because human thought processes, partially subconscious, are obscured from normal awareness. Huth and Russett thus put the study of deterrence on a sounder scientific basis, and hold out the promise that quantitative empirical studies may play a more central role in the application of world politics research to current international security affairs.

One issue in applying COW project findings to policy questions such as nuclear deterrence is specifying exactly what difference nuclear weapons make, and how findings from the pre–nuclear age can be applied to the nuclear powers (Singer 1990). For instance, in a sample of enduring rivalries, Leng (1983) finds that the more frequently militarized disputes recur, the greater the likelihood of war, with the fourth dispute going to war in five out of six cases. It is interesting, however, that the one exception to the rule is the Cuban missiles crisis—the one involving nuclear deterrence and the high risk of Armageddon. Obviously, one could argue that, since the urgency of avoiding war is much greater in the nuclear age, the risk of recurrent crises escalating to war in MAD circumstances is much lower than this. Indeed, the N of a study like Leng's is small enough that the distinction between empirical research like his and properly conducted comparative case studies begins to blur: there is only one case of a nuclear-armed enduring rivalry in Leng's study. The updating of the COW data base through the late 1980s, as funded by Data Development for International Research (DDIR), will improve this situation by enlarging the number of cases of militarized disputes involving nuclear powers. Leng's study of the Behavioral Correlates of War, as reviewed by Leng and Singer in this volume, is also helpful, because it allows statistical comparisons of patterns of covariance within specific prenuclear and postnuclear disputes.

Even if there were no problem in comparing the pre- and post-1945 worlds (Blainey 1988, 267–90; Mueller 1988), the Correlates of War findings to date have not produced the kind of clear and unambiguous signals that would tell foreign policy makers what to do in foreign policy. When people in government ask, "Do you think we should base U.S. foreign policy on these COW models and findings?" we believe it appropriate to reply, "That would be premature. These results are too tentative, but you should be aware of them because they can reduce the probability of buying into the conventional wisdom of the moment."

From Correlation to Causal Inference

Correlates of War studies frequently have begun by taking a hypothesis from a dominant paradigm, scholarly or political, and then proceeding to empirically test the extent to which the hypothesized association does exist. Thus, in a fairly typical COW study, Wallace (1982) tests two hypotheses: the hawkish hypothesis, discussed above, that superior force will deter a revisionist state, and the dovish hypothesis that arms races (which often result from an arms buildup designed to attain superior force) cause wars. He finds support for the dovish, but not for the hawkish, hypothesis, and thus questions whether national security policies of arms acquisition have tended too far in a hawkish direction over the period from the Congress of Vienna to our time.

To reach such an inference that a policy "causes" war, or increases the risk of war, one must go through a rigorous process of reasoning and testing. From the time of John Stuart Mill to the present (Cook and Campbell 1979, 18, 31), these processes have been described in terms of three requirements: a postulated cause has to precede the effect in time (or at least occur simultaneously with it, rather than come after it); the cause and effect have to covary (that is, be statistically related); and other explanations of the cause and effect relationship (that the supposed effect is really a cause, or that some third factor is the cause) have to be eliminated by some scientific procedure involving experimental or statistical controls. For instance, Wallace (1979) finds that arms races are strongly associated with the escalation of interstate disputes to war. One might say that he has established a correlate of war. Are arms races not just a correlate, but a cause of war? Wallace's work in establishing the correlation is a crucial first step, but only a first step, in the journey to such a conclusion. At the time the COW Project was launched, even this first step had not been taken (with rare exceptions), and so it was natural to call the project the Correlates of War. Today, as our correlational knowledge has expanded, it becomes important to take the next steps, and ascertain the degree to which these correlations permit of causal inference.

We agree with Cook and Campbell (1979, 12–13; cf. Bueno de Mesquita 1981, 4–5) that there is no reason to search for necessary or sufficient conditions for war. We are, instead, searching for variables that are positively correlated with the onset of war, and ascertaining whether the association seems causal, controlling for plausible rival hypotheses. Such controls can be introduced through control groups, through statistical controls in cross-sectional designs, or through analysis of change over time (Campbell and Stanley 1966; Singer 1977). Obviously, control groups are often a problem in global affairs, where we lack the luxury of the physical or psychological laboratory experiment. Attention has, therefore, largely shifted to the latter two approaches.

Ultimately, causation cannot be observed (Hume 1739), and there are threats to the validity of any causal inference (Cook and Campbell 1979). While threats to "internal validity" are especially hard to overcome outside of a laboratory experiment, techniques have been established for making causal inferences from statistical evidence when one has measures of all relevant variables in a cross-section of time, or panel or time series data (Cook and Campbell 1979).

In the typical Correlates of War study, a correlation is detected, say, between an increasingly bipolarized alliance structure and the onset of war (Wayman 1984). A possible causal inference would be that bipolarization "causes" war, because bipolarization reduces the number of cross-cutting cleavages and increases the amount of hostile attention devoted to the rival state or coalition (Deutsch and Singer 1964). A threat to the validity of this causal inference is that a third factor may be affecting the relationship between the two correlated variables (polarization and war).

For example, an advantage, or perceived advantage, possessed by the offense may "cause" both alliance bipolarization (as coalitions are formed against threatening revisionist states) and war. It is appropriate to determine whether the relationship will weaken, partially or all the way to zero, when we control for other variables that may have covaried with the initial two variables, as is done in multiple regression analysis, probit analysis, path analysis, causal modeling, and structural equation models such as two-stage least-squares (Duncan 1975).[2] An excellent example of such work in our field is Huth and Russett's (1984) study—already discussed—of what makes deterrence effective. Unfortunately, there are many obstacles in the way of such work. First, the third variable—the offensive/defensive balance in our example—may be multidimensional and practically unmeasurable (as argued by Levy 1983). Even if other proper control variable(s) can be measured, multicollinearity can make such controls inapplicable in many studies (Wayman, Singer, and Goertz 1983). There is also the problem of lost degrees of freedom, which could reduce the number of cases in each cell to less than even the one case per cell accepted by the comparative case method (George and Smoke 1989). This small N with which we work, as well as the lack of adequate instrumental variables, renders two-stage least-squares inappropriate in most studies, and thus makes it especially difficult to estimate causal effects when a theoretical model indicates there should be reciprocal causation.

An alternative way to improve internal validity is to move away from cross-sectional data and to examine processes over time. Such "diachronic" studies, and time-series analysis in particular, is a natural focus of COW research, since the COW data sets extend over a much longer period of time (170 years and growing) than most social science data sets. In order to do such analyses, however, the COW data sets must be reaggregated in the time-series mode; such an approach has long been recommended (Moul 1973), and has begun to bear fruit (Wayman 1990). While some analytic techniques such as studying contagion with the Poisson distribution have been criticized as atheoretical (Goertz 1988), other procedures such as waiting times analysis are being brought to bear on the analysis of data over time (Williamson, Warner, and Hopkins 1988).

Reliable and Valid Indicators

The more reliable and valid one's measures of key concepts are, the more likely that these causal inference procedures will succeed. A *reliable* measure consistently gives the same or at least similar results with repeated observations of the same phenomenon, while a *valid* measure detects what it was supposed to detect, rather than something else. For example, a reliable IQ test gives about the same result each time the same person takes it. A valid IQ test would actually measure intelligence, rather than something like degree of sophistication or parental social class. Reliability is a necessary, but not

---

2. This process may be further complicated by the need to use multiple indicators for underlying concepts that cannot be directly observed (Coombs 1964; Rummel 1970; Kruskal and Wish 1978; Bollen 1989).

sufficient, condition for validity. While there is basic agreement on these basic points, there is much less attention to them in the study of world politics than in fields such as social psychology or survey research. How this is related to COW research is examined in the following sections, in the context of different approaches to validity.

According to the literature on convergent and discriminant validity, good measures of the same concept should have a high intercorrelation, and should be more weakly correlated with measures of other concepts (Campbell and Fiske 1959). Wayman and Morgan, in this volume, apply this idea to the extensive literature on the polarity and polarization of the international system. They find that the intercorrelations among a dozen indicators of polarity are surprisingly weak, and they find that the strong correlations that do exist can be attributed to a few underlying factors. These results, while important, leave the reader to ponder to what extent the problem is with the theoretical and conceptual work on polarity, and to what extent it is due to measurement inadequacies (see Carmines and Zeller 1979, 63–69; Bollen 1989).[3]

It may be that strong relationships exist between system characteristics and war, but that our measures of system characteristics are invalid. For instance, we do not have any direct measures of when the system is dominated by the cross-cutting cleavages and divided attention emphasized by Deutsch and Singer (1964), and we have been forced to assume a high positive correlation between these systems characteristics and various measures of alliance polarization (Wayman 1984). Not surprisingly, then, Bueno de Mesquita observed that "the standard polarity and polarization measure did not work well in the analysis that Lalman and I did, so we need to develop a better theory and measurement of systemic influences." (Bueno de Mesquita and Lalman 1987; Wayman 1988).

One way to proceed would be to hypothesize that systemic forces are constraints that can alter the likelihood of a dispute escalating to war. Then, given the onset of a dispute, one could measure the degree of capability concentration, the existence of cross-cutting cleavages, and other systemic attributes, not for the system as a whole, but for the great power actors and regional actors pertinent to the particular pair of disputing states.

A methodological problem we face is that the standard procedures for

---

3. CON, discussed in this volume and designed decades ago to measure systemic power concentration, has remained a cornerstone of several COW studies of polarity. CON was designed to measure power concentration better than rival indices of inequality such as GINI. Recent new indicators of inequality (Midlarsky 1988; Muller et al. 1989) may someday shed better light on the validity of CON as a measure of systemic power concentration. More likely, however, it will be necessary to measure other aspects of system structure than just polarity and polarization. One potential approach, focusing on spheres of influence and the weight, scope, and domain of power (see Deutsch 1978, 28–43), is discussed in the last pages of this chapter.

assessing validity (Cronbach 1970; Carmines and Zeller 1979) are often difficult to apply in our empirical domain (see Gurr 1972, 44–49, for a useful discussion of these problems). Methodology texts commonly discuss content validity, predictive validity, and construct validity. *Content validity* is based on the assumption that the universe of material under study is agreed upon, and then involves taking valid samples of that universe. Thus, a geography test is valid if the teacher has selected questions that give equal emphasis to each of the readings in the course. This type of validity is rarely applicable to research in international relations. One application is the COW capabilities data set, made up of three facets of national capabilities: demographic, economic, and military. The assumption is that national capabilities are based on people, productivity, and military prowess, and to insure balance among them, the COW project uses a "sample" of two indicators of each. The consequent six measures are then aggregated into an overall national capabilities score, in which the three facets receive equal emphasis. Stoll (1984b) asks whether such a sampling of indicators, giving an equal emphasis to military, economic, and demographic factors, is appropriate, suggesting that a more valid indicator might emerge if military or economic facets received greater emphasis. But he finds that the rank-order of nation-states changes little if one changes the weighting, as when he doubles or triples the importance of one facet compared to the other two.[4]

In *predictive validity* (sometimes called criterion-oriented validity), "decisions are based on . . . future performance as predicted from" the indicator (Cronbach 1970, 122). By this standard, college board tests are considered valid to the extent that they accurately predict success in college. An early warning indicator of war would be valid if it were highly correlated with the future outbreak of war. Thus, Wallace (1979) justifies his studies of arms races and war on the impressive grounds that his indicator of the existence of an arms race is highly correlated with escalation of disputes to war. But such predictive validity is not very useful outside of the early warning indicators movement. For instance, if one were trying to validly measure the polarity of the international system, one would not necessarily conclude that one indicator was more valid than the others just because it had the highest correlation with the onset of war. After all, for theoretical reasons, one might have predicted a low correlation between polarity and war, and hence a very high correlation would not be a sign that polarity had been properly measured.

---

4. Stoll's approach cannot get at the more subtle question, discussed at COW seminars, of whether a fourth dimension, such as technology, might someday merit inclusion. Przezworski and Teune (1970) discuss techniques for incorporating equivalent measures in a data set when changes of time or space render new variables (such as GNP or computer chip production) more pertinent than they had previously been.

Construct validity is an alternative approach that makes theory central to the validation process. When one is trying to measure a theoretical construct, such as anxiety, one turns to theories of anxiety to see what they predict will be the relationship between anxiety and a host of other variables. One then considers a measure of anxiety to be valid to the extent that the predicted relationships hold. This may work in psychology, but in the study of war and peace, in how many cases is there a clear and unchallenged theoretical prediction about the direction, let alone the magnitude, of the correlation between two variables?

The weakness of construct validation is indicative of the weakness of theory in our field. There are not enough clear and precise theoretical predictions to allow a construct validation approach to operate. There have been recent advances in game theory, which some consider to be one of the more promising scholarly tools in the social sciences. A problem, however, is that game theory, including the sequential game version (Powell 1987) is more accurately called game calculus. We prefer to retain the word *theory* for a chain of deductions that has, at least, clear operational referents to the world of observations and data. The sequential game studies, in contrast, seem to be primarily of heuristic value, in that it is extremely difficult to see how they could be operationalized, even for a set of measures of the cold war era and superpower rivalry, let alone the globe from 1816 to the present. Indeed, the work of Powell implicitly does a great deal to raise methodological and substantive doubts about prior applications of (presequential) game theory to historical interstate crises (e.g., Snyder and Diesing 1977). We believe the gap between purely heuristic theoretical work and nontheoretical empirical work would be reduced if we were more knowledgeable about and experienced in both traditions. This is not a panacea, however. As the work of Bueno de Mesquita (1981) indicates, attempts to operationalize rational choice models, commendable as they are, run into the problem of slippage between the theoretical concept and its measurement. For example, it is arguable whether the convergence between two countries' utilities is properly measured by his indicator of similar alliance patterns.

Auxiliary Validity

Hubert Blalock spoke of "auxiliary theory" as the assumptions and inferences one makes in deciding how to operationalize a theoretical concept. We believe it is useful to introduce the concept of auxiliary validity to refer to questions about validity that arise from a critique of an author's auxiliary theory. The purpose of this term is to help fill the gap between the standard textbook terms of content, construct, and predictive validity, on the one hand, and the validation process as described by students of macropolitical research (Gurr 1972), on the other.

Even more than the debate between Bueno de Mesquita and his critics, that which engages Wallace (1979) and his critics (e.g., Diehl 1983) hinges on these matters of auxiliary validity. The former has established that his measure of arms races is an excellent early warning indicator of war; that is, it has good predictive validity, in that there is a high correlation between arms races and the subsequent onset of war. No one debates these points. It is widely recognized that the thing Wallace has measured does indeed have awesome predictive power in discriminating between disputes that will and will not escalate to war. The debate ensues, however, because it is very difficult to measure the presence of an arms race, and not everyone agrees that what Wallace is measuring is an arms race. A problem is that construct validity is not really relevant to this issue, because we do not have theoretical agreement on whether any phenomena (e.g., war) should be correlated to any specific degree with arms races. Diehl and Wallace agree that, conceptually, an arms race involves a mutual arms buildup, but a key question is whether Wallace's indicator does or does not code as arms races those cases in which only one party is building up arms. There is no good term in the literature for this kind of argument about validity, as the available phrase, *face validity*, is often used disparagingly to refer to reliance on the judgments and hunches of "experts." It might be better to use the term *auxiliary validity*, since these debates are not about whether Wallace or Diehl has better intuition, but rather about whether Wallace's or Diehl's "auxiliary theory" or operationalization of "arms race" has the proper mathematical form to distinguish between unilateral arms buildups and true arms races.

There are four components of an assessment of auxiliary validity:

1. Does the measure of the concept have logical or mathematical flaws, so that one can deduce that it cannot measure what it is designed to measure in the cases under study? The last point is an important qualification because the operationalization, designed for a particular research project, only has to work for the cases that are being studied in that project.

2. Do the procedures for measuring the concept involve so many steps, and include so many seemingly ad hoc exceptions, each entailing a certain nonzero probability of error, that one begins to worry that, because of measurement error, selection bias, and/or self-deception of the principal investigator, the results of the operationalization may be far removed from the original concept?

3. Do the actual results obtained accord with what is known about the phenomena under study? Just as one would have little faith in an IQ test that Einstein flunked, one would have little faith in an arms race index that indicated an arms race between the USSR and Poland between 1950 and 1980. By the same token, one must view with

skepticism a measure of the polarity of the international system, if that measure treats a pole called NATO as equivalent to another pole made up of Finland and Mongolia (Wayman 1984).

4. Can the critic replicate the criticized study with corrected (more valid) measures, and show that the findings and conclusions need to be altered because of the changed measurement? This last point is important, because scholars such as Lebow and Stein (1989), in their criticism of the Huth and Russett studies of deterrence, only address steps one and three, and then seem to assume that this fourth step necessarily follows from their concerns about how accurately a deterrence encounter was measured in certain cases.

Models, Case Studies, and Hypothesis Testing

In the beginning of their chapter, Wayman and Morgan speak of how a discipline often advances in an iterative process in which a model is first formulated, then tested, and then reformulated based on the test results. In the social sciences, this process frequently begins with case studies, such as Thucydides' study of the Peloponnesian War, which engender a set of questions that stimulate theory building. In our view, sound theorizing will almost always involve multivariate modeling. Any bivariate social science hypothesis will be probabilistic, both theoretically, because of the ceteris paribus requirement in a multivariate model, and at the stage of testing, because of measurement error in one's auxiliary "theory" and operationalizations. Therefore, a social science hypothesis cannot be validated by a critical experiment involving only one case for each combination of the independent variables. Rather, such hypotheses will require a test that encompasses a larger number of cases, to provide statistical degrees of freedom. We will need to be involved with case studies first, and, second, a formal model, and then proceed to a third stage, quantitative tests. The process then cycles back to step one: if the tests show the model to be weak, one must examine the cases that do not fit in order to get clues from them of how to improve it; if the tests validate the model, then case studies applying the model can be taught to current and future practioners, such as students planning to enter government service.

In many areas of social science, the research process does operate this way, but the balance among case studies, modeling, and statistical testing does vary from field to field. In psychology, for instance, advances have been made both in heavily experimental fields such as learning and memory, in which laboratory experiments are conducted on large numbers of subjects, and in clinical psychology which proceeds through an emphasis on the detailed examination of individual cases. Political science exhibits a similar variety. In such fields as American politics, often dominated by voting studies, the examination of cases becomes secondary to the interaction between models (e.g., spatial models of party competition) and empirical tests (e.g., polling). In world politics, case studies have been dominant, and the empirical tests, exemplified by the COW Project, play a much more modest role, somewhat analagous to the role experimental psychology would have in a discipline dominated by Freudian clinicians. For instance, based on a recent survey of political science (Klingemann et al. 1989), one can identify the thirty-eight most frequently cited authors in world politics. Of these, only seven (Karl Deutsch, Ole Holsti, Kenneth Organski, Charles Ostrom, Rudolph Rummel, Bruce Russett, and J. David Singer) are primarily known for conducting statistical tests of hypotheses, and only three (Steven Brams, Robert Axelrod, and William Riker) are primarily known for construction of formal theories such as game theory. The remainder are scholars who focus on case studies or who construct models in a traditional, nonformal way. A recent forum in *World Politics* (Achen and Snidal 1989; George and Smoke 1989) reflects not only important advances in case studies, but also the weak, tertiary position of empirical testing in studies of international peace and security. As discussed in our section on knowledge and policy prediction, we devoutly hope that this will change, and that the recent improvements in scientific research will gradually help bring such change about.

The Next Phase

While it is clear that some mistakes were made, in the operationalization of the variables or in the data set generation, the net balance of a quarter-century of COW research seems to be one of qualified success. We have defined what some had said was undefinable, measured what some had said was unmeasurable, and tested what some had said was untestable to an extent beyond our earlier expectations and well beyond what had been attempted before. Thus, it should come as no surprise that we are now prepared to embark on a new round of index construction, leading to the generation of quite a few new data sets.

The theoretical context is that of our war-to-war model, in which we go from a "comparative statics" to a dynamic formulation. The argument, briefly stated, is that while many (perhaps most) postwar settlements of wars between major powers produce a relatively clear hierarchical ranking in the major power subsystem, as well as a clear set of alignments, neither the vertical nor the horizontal configuration is very durable. Eschewing for the moment the reasoning behind this generalization, we next postulate that these changes induce in those major powers that experience relative decline in capabilities or influence, and/or increasing isolation in the alliance picture, a set of behaviors intended to redress these emerging disadvantages. Central among these is a substantial increase in military allocation ratios, leading not only to reciprocal moves by others, but to a domestic process that incrementally diminishes the economic and social strengths of the society while redistributing internal economic and political power to the more militarized sectors. As the latter's influence increases vis-à-vis those with a broader conception of national security and well-being, the nation not only becomes embroiled in more frequent militarized disputes, but also experiences a declining rate of success, failing to prevail with greater frequency. Once these patterns set in, we postulate a self-amplifying process that frequently culminates in war.

Note that this model is not only indifferent to either issues or ideologies, but rather heavily rests on a number of variables often associated with political economy and the concept of militarization. Thus, our next round of indicators and data activity will focus on these concepts, discussed often but measured seldom. Further, the key concept of declining national influence that allegedly catalyzes such domestic processes has also resisted systematic measurement to date, and this will be attempted in the context of the traditional notion of "sphere of influence" as well as the more recent notions of "regime" and "dependencia." Thus, this model requires integration of our established data on such variables as capabilities, alliances, disputes, and wars with new data sets on international influence and domestic power concentrations, all incorporated into a process model that treats war as the outcome of a recurrent historical sequence.

This work, as well as COW work in general, would be enhanced by alterations in the dispute data set. Only about a hundred disputes have been coded on outcomes, and then only in terms of winner and loser. Win-lose-draw codes for the entire dispute data set, being completed by Zeev Maoz at Haifa in conjunction with a team at "COW Central" in Ann Arbor, are expected in the next year or so. But beyond this, it may be necessary to develop more detailed outcome codes, such as those that distinguish such outcomes as capitulation, appeasement, and negotiated settlement, each of which, theoretically, should have a quite different effect on the future course of an enduring rivalry. Maoz goes further:

> Dependence between events is a big problem that we need to worry about. . . . We need to do a more general job, incorporating conflict outcomes—not just who wins, but economic consequences, governmental changes, et cetera. Going into the black box of the state might be useful. Russett sees a link between economic decline and war, and Levy finds some support for the diversionary hypothesis. Treating the state as a black box served a purpose when we were operating at the systemic level, but needs to be reconsidered. (quoted in Wayman 1988)

Another need is for an improved understanding of what might be called the escalatory "ladder" from the mildest recorded threat of force to all-out war. Calling this a ladder implies that it is a unidimensional scale, with movement along it proceding in a straight line from one end to the other. But is it? A variety of techniques have been developed for examining such questions, and these techniques are routinely used in psychology, sociology, and many branches of political science, especially survey research and legislative studies (Coombs 1964; Rummel 1970; Kruskal and Wish 1978; Bollen 1989).

Maoz (1982, 217–25) attempted to construct a fourteen-point scale of dispute intensity, using all fourteen of the COW dispute incident categories. He concludes that war is the most severe type of military confrontation action, followed, in descending order, by declaration of war, blockade, occupation of territory, mobilization, seizure of material or military personnel, clash, other use of military force, show of force, threat to use force, threat to declare war, alert, threat to occupy territory, and threat to blockade. While Maoz's results are insightful, it remains questionable whether his methodology actually does produce the most valid indicator of dispute severity. His method is based on the assumption that the more frequently one type of military confrontation action is followed by another, the more similar they are in severity. For instance, in accord with the Tit-for-Tat hypothesis that one side will respond in kind to what the other side has just done, a blockade is most frequently followed by a blockade, a declaration of war by a declaration of war, and so on (Maoz 1982, 219). While this starting assumption is plausible, it is not clear that the algorithm used by Maoz provides an interval or even an ordinal scale of severity. For one thing, he uses a unique method, and he does not explain how and why his method differs from established methods of scaling, such as Coombsian unfolding analysis, Guttman scaling, factor analysis, or multidimensional scaling. Moreover, he does not provide any test of whether the scale he has produced is unidimensional or multidimensional, as all these other techniques routinely do. In short, while Maoz's putative scale may be able to predict the Markovian transition probabilities in the escalation of future disputes, it remains uncertain whether it is a valid scale of the severity of actions in disputes.

Given the lack of a widely accepted severity scale, the project has been forced back to a five-level, a priori index of dispute intensity: no codable activity, explicit threat to use force, display of force, use of force short of war, and war. Because it is based on a priori assumptions rather than a scaling procedure, this index is vulnerable to criticism. In this regard, it is logically similar to the COW alliance index (no alliance, neutrality pact, entente, and defense pact) that is also used as the basis for Bueno de Mesquita's measures of utility (1981). He assumes that it is possible to measure utilities, in his expected utility model, by measuring the similarity of nations' military alliance commitments. And the similarity of national alliance commitments is measured by an ordinal correlation coefficient, under the assumption (Bueno de Mesquita 1975b; 1981, 115) that military alliances can be rank-ordered in the a priori fashion of the COW project's early years: defense pacts, neutrality or nonaggression pacts, ententes, and no military alliance between the two states.

As Bueno de Mesquita puts it (1981, 115),

> I assume that defense pacts represent the most serious loss of auton-
> omy in that they require a declaration of war under the contingent condi-
> tions. . . . Neutrality or nonaggression pacts require the next greatest
> sacrifice of decision-making autonomy in that they deprive the signato-
> ries of the option of joining in the war. . . . Ententes require less sacri-
> fice of decision-making autonomy in that they require only consulta-
> tions . . . while not formally precluding any course of action. The no
> alliance condition, of course, requires no loss of autonomy.

As Machiavelli might have observed, however, these pacts do not involve loss of autonomy. They involve a promise to sacrifice one's autonomy. And states do not always keep their promises. Indeed, the one pertinent study (Sabrosky 1980) of whether allies do keep their word leads one to question the validity of Bueno de Mesquita's rank-ordering. Sabrosky measures the number of times allies lived up to their promises, and subtracts from this the number of times they violated the terms of their treaty. He then normalizes this difference by dividing it by the number of opportunities they had to live up to their agreements. He calls these ratios (which can vary from 1.0 when all agreements are kept to minus 1.0 when all agreements are broken) measures of alliance reliability. He finds that

> The nominally strongest class 1 (defense) pacts usually do have a
> relatively impressive wartime reliability. Yet the nominally weakest al-
> liance—class 3 (entente) also does well, and on one index of alliance
> reliability . . . it does *better* than the class 1 alliance. The intermediate
> class 2 (neutrality/nonaggression) pacts, however, consistently have the
> lowest wartime reliability scores of all classes of alliance. (Sabrosky
> 1980, 196)

In short, while ententes demand little of their signatories, the signatories typically live up to them. While neutrality/nonaggression pacts nominally demand more, they are honored more in the breach than the observance. After all, a neutrality or nonaggression pact is a public pledge that State A will not attack State B; why would such a pledge be necessary? If someone has to pledge not to attack, the pledge may be less a sign of friendship than an indicator that an attack might have been imminent. Sabrosky's findings, and this reasoning about nonaggression pledges, suggest that neutrality/ nonaggression pacts may have been ranked too highly by Bueno de Mesquita. If so, his rank-order correlations will tend to be contaminated by error, and so will tend to misstate the degree to which similar states have similar alliance bonds. If this error is random, it should tend to weaken the goodness of fit of his model. To the extent that he can improve this alliance indicator in future work, he will get slightly more accurate evidence on his expected utility model.

The questions raised by Maoz's study of the escalatory ladder are of similar importance. According to COW coding, dispute incidents can be ranked in severity from the mildest, threat of force; to the next level, display of force; to the most severe, use of force. While Maoz's (1982) results indicate that this is true on the average, he also finds specific exceptions. In particular, mobilization, a category of display of force, is, according to Maoz, *more* serious than three of the five uses of military force. On the other extreme, alert, which is another category of display of force, is *less* serious than one-half of the threats to use force. If Maoz is right, then the middle category (display) varies in seriousness much more than the others, so that it includes one very ominous move (mobilization) and one relatively benign one (alert). This could explain why some displays of force provoke no response, while others bring on war.

An improved incident severity scale could help close the gap between recent theoretical and empirical work. Powell's (1987) work on sequential games has emphasized the importance of choosing to escalate, de-escalate, or continue the existing level of tension in response to an opponent's prior move. A scale of severity of militarized incidents would be a step toward operationalizing such game-theoretic concepts. Leng's BCOW data would also have to be incorporated, however, because they go beyond militarized incidents to include equally important diplomatic acts. Huth (1988), building on the work of Leng and others, has already shown the value of categorizing an entire crisis according to the defender's policy of military escalation (policy of strength, Tit-for-Tat, or policy of caution) and diplomatic responsiveness (bluffing, firm-but-flexible, or conciliatory). Is it possible to go beyond such ordinal trichotomies for the defending side in entire crises? Is it possible to quantify, in time-series through the crises, iterated sequences of escalatory or de-escalatory moves and responses by both sides?

If so, is it appropriate to keep the military and diplomatic activities separate, as in Huth's work? McGinnis and Williams (1989) remind us that such compartmentalization can be unrealistic: "Rival states need not react in kind to each specific type of behavior, but can instead select from a wide range of policy instruments. As a consequence, no one policy area can be considered in isolation." But could a militarized dispute severity scale somehow be combined with a scale of diplomatic toughness (perhaps by normalizing each scale), so that sequences of mixed military and diplomatic incidents could be coded as escalatory, de-escalatory, or neither? With further work, answers to such questions could be an important benefit of improvements in COW's militarized incident severity index.

In criticizing such a priori alliance and incident severity indices, we need to strike a balance between rejecting them as flawed, on the one extreme, and failing to understand how they might be improved, on the other. It is our view that both the alliance index and the dispute intensity index have served the project well, but should not be seen as the final solution to our scale-construction problems. Especially with the dispute data set, which is so new and in many ways incomplete, we are only beginning to fully understand the dimensions of dispute severity. For instance, we need to distinguish between reciprocated and nonreciprocated disputes. About half of approximately one thousand COW militarized disputes are nonreciprocated, in the sense that the target makes no codable response to a threat, display, or use of force. Is reciprocation a second dimension of dispute intensity? In what ways is a reciprocated threat to use force more or less intense than a nonreciprocated display of force? Can any nonreciprocated dispute be considered an international crisis in the same sense that a reciprocated dispute is? Are all uses of force (seizure of territory, armed attack resulting in casualties) part of a unidimensional escalatory ladder? Such measurement questions have not yet been thoroughly addressed, and deserve more attention in the near future.

Summary

In this final chapter we have offered a fairly broad tour d'horizon of the Project's efforts and results, attending to that critical intersection of model and method. It should be clear that the link is an intimate one, and that neither we—nor others concerned with the development of a science of world politics—could have developed this range of indicators, generated so extensive a data base, and examined so broad an array of plausible correlates of war in a theoretical vacuum.

That we have addressed the theoretical foundations of our index construction and data analysis in so relaxed a manner throughout our books and articles is, thus, to be taken less as a sign of indifference than perhaps as a sign of agnosticism. In contrast to our obvious assertiveness regarding the importance of operational measurement and reproducible procedures, this agnosticism reflects our sense that neither plausibility nor logic can suffice for long as support for one or another theoretical position. While absolutely necessary to the scientific enterprise, they nevertheless still leave us in the dark as to the etiology of international war and the historical accuracy of contending explanations of the conflict process. To reiterate a familiar phrase, these remain empirical questions as we move through the "natural history" phase of the emerging science of world politics. Thus, we think it a bit premature to claim that we already have much in the way of theory, or to bask in the deductive elegance of models that we examine.

In sum, we fully accept the dictum that goodness of fit between the predictions of our models and the observed historical patterns does not constitute explanation, or as the cliche has it, "correlation is far from causation." Nor is there any intimation that an endless accumulation of correlational knowledge will assure the ultimate theoretical breakthrough. On the other hand, the most cursory examination of the literature in our discipline indicates that an overwhelming fraction of it largely ignores the indispensable role of reproducible evidence. Faced with the numerical dominance of prescientific research, now beginning to merge with the putatively postscientific (sometimes styled postpositivist or postmodern), it is little wonder that we reassert here our commitment to the epistemology of the "compleat scientist." We hope, therefore, that this unconventional collection of efforts to measure the correlates of war will stand as a reinforcement for those who already work in this part of the vineyard, and as a stimulus for those in other parts of this fertile valley.

References

Achen, C. H., and D. Snidal. 1989. "Rational Deterrence Theory and Comparative Case Studies." *World Politics* 41 (January): 143–69.

Adelman, M. A. 1959. "Differential Rates and Changes in Concentration." *Review of Economics and Statistics* 41 (February): 68–69.

Aitchison, J., and J. A. Brown. 1954. "On Criteria for Description of Income Distribution." *Metroeconomica* 6 (December): 88–107.

Alger, C. 1966. "Interaction and Negotiation in a Committee of the United Nations General Assembly." *Peace Research Society (International) Papers:* 141–69.

Alger, C., and S. Brams. 1967. "Patterns of Representation in National Capitals and Intergovernmental Organizations." *World Politics* 19:646–63.

Alker, H. 1964. "Dimensions of Conflict in the General Assembly." *American Political Science Review* 58 (September): 642–57.

Alker, H. 1965. *Mathematics and Politics.* New York: Macmillan.

Alker, H., and M. Midlarsky. 1985. "International Disputes Data: A Comparison of Approaches and Products, with Some Recommendations for the Future." *International Studies Notes* 12: 1–9.

Alker, H., and D. Puchala. 1968. "Trends in Economic Partnership: The North Atlantic Area, 1928–1963." In *Quantitative International Politics,* ed. J. D. Singer. New York: Free Press.

Alker, H., and B. Russett. 1964. "On Measuring Inequality." *Behavioral Science* 9 (July): 207–18.

Alker, H., and B. Russett. 1965. *World Politics in the General Assembly.* New Haven, CT: Yale University Press.

Alker, H., and F. Sherman. 1982. "Collective Security-Seeking Practices Since 1945." In *Managing International Crises,* ed. Daniel Frei. Beverly Hills: Sage Publications.

Allport, G. 1955. *Becoming.* New Haven, CT: Yale University Press.

Amemiya, E. C. 1963. "Measurement of Economic Differentiation." *Journal of Regional Science* 5 (Summer): 84–87.

Andreski, S. 1968. *Military Organization and Society.* Berkeley: University of California Press.

Arms Control and Disarmament Agency. 1983. *World Military Expenditures and Arms Transfers 1971–1980.* Washington: ACDA.

Ashley, R. K. 1981. "Political Realism and Human Interests." *International Studies Quarterly* 25:204–36.

Axelrod, R. A. 1984. *The Evolution of Cooperation.* New York: Basic Books.

Azar, E. 1971. *Conflict and Peace Data Bank: A Codebook.* University of North Carolina. Mimeo.

Bachi, R. 1956. "A Statistical Analysis of the Revival of Hebrew in Israel." In *Scripta Hierosolymitana,* ed. R. Bach. Jerusalem: Magnus.

Bairoch, P. 1974. "Europe's GNP, 1800–1970." *Journal of European Economic History* 3 (3): 557–608.

Bales, R. F. 1951. *Interaction Process Analysis: A Method for the Study of Small Groups.* Reading, MA: Addison-Wesley.

Banks, A. 1971. *Cross-Polity Time Series Data.* Cambridge, MA: MIT Press.

Banks, A., and R. Textor. 1963. *A Cross-Polity Survey.* Cambridge, MA: MIT Press.

Barber, Bernard. 1968. "Social Stratification." In *International Encyclopedia of the Social Sciences,* ed. D. C. Sills. New York: Macmillan.

Bell, C. 1971. *The Conventions of Crisis.* London: Oxford University Press.

Bell, W. 1954. "A Probability Model for the Measurement of Ecological Segregation." *Social Forces* 32 (May): 357–64.

Benoit, E., and H. Lubell. 1967. "The World Burden of National Defense." In *Disarmament and World Economic Interdependence,* ed. E. Benoit. New York: Columbia University Press.

Berelson, B. 1952. *Content Analysis in Communication Research.* Glencoe, IL: Free Press.

Blainey, G. 1988. *The Causes of War.* 3d ed. New York: Free Press.

Blair, J. M. 1956. "Statistical Measures of Concentration in Business." *Bulletin of Oxford University Institute of Statistics* 18 (November): 355–56.

Blalock, H. 1961. "Theory, Measurement, and Replication in the Social Sciences." *American Journal of Sociology* 66 (January): 342–47.

Blalock, H. 1968. "The Measurement Problem: The Gap between the Language of Theory and Research." In *Methodology in Social Research,* ed. H. Blalock and A. Blalock. New York: McGraw-Hill.

Blechman, B., and S. Kaplan. 1978. *Force without War.* Washington, D.C.: Brookings.

Blum, J., R. Cameron, and T. Barnes. 1970. *The European World Since 1815.* Boston: Little, Brown.

Bollen, K. 1989. *Structural Equations with Latent Variables.* New York: John Wiley.

Bornstedt, G. W., and Borgatta, E. F. eds. 1981. *Social Measurement.* Beverly Hills: Sage.

Box, G. E. P., and G. C. Tiao. 1975. "Intervention Analysis with Application to Economic and Environmental Problems." *Journal of the American Statistical Association* 70:70–72.

Brecher, M. 1977. "Toward a Theory of International Crisis Behavior." *International Studies Quarterly* 21:39–74.

Brecher, M., and J. Wilkenfeld. 1982. "Crises in World Politics. *World Politics* 34(3): 380–417.

Brecher, M., J. Wilkenfeld, and S. Moser. 1988. *Crises in the Twentieth Century.* New York: Pergamon Press.

Bremer, S. 1972. "Formal Alliance Clusters in the Interstate System: 1816–1965." Presented at the annual meeting of the American Political Science Association, Washington, D.C.

Bremer, S. 1980. "National Capabilities and War Proneness." In *The Correlates of War*, ed. J. D. Singer, vol. 2. New York: Free Press.

Brody, R. 1963. "Some Systemic Effects of the Spread of Nuclear Weapons Technology: A Study through Simulation of a Multinuclear Future." *Journal of Conflict Resolution* 7 (December): 663–753.

Buchan, A. 1964. *Crisis Management: The New Diplomacy*. Boulogne-sure-Seine: Atlantic Institute.

Bueno de Mesquita, B. 1973. "The Impact of Alliances on Industrial Development." East Lansing. Mimeo.

Bueno de Mesquita, B. 1975a. "The Effects of Systemic Polarity on the Probability and the Duration of War: Toward an Early Warning Indicator of War." Presented at the annual meeting of the International Studies Association.

Bueno de Mesquita, B. 1975b. "Measuring Systemic Polarity." *Journal of Conflict Resolution* 19 (2): 187–216.

Bueno de Mesquita, B. 1981. *The War Trap*. New Haven, CT: Yale University Press.

Bueno de Mesquita, B. 1984. "A Critique of 'A Critique of the War Trap.' " *Journal of Conflict Resolution* 28: 341–60.

Bueno de Mesquita, B. 1985. "Toward a Scientific Understanding of International Conflict: A Personal View." *International Studies Quarterly* 29:121–36.

Bueno de Mesquita, B., and D. Lalman. 1987. "System Norms, System Structure, and National Incentives for Peace." Presented at the annual meeting of the American Political Science Association, Chicago.

Bueno de Mesquita, B., and D. Lalman. 1988. "Systemic and Dyadic Explanations of War." *World Politics* 41:1–20.

Bueno de Mesquita, B., and J. D. Singer. 1973. "Alliances, Capabilities, and War: A Review and Synthesis." *Political Science Annual* 4:237–80.

Bull, H. 1977. *The Anarchical Society*. New York: Columbia University Press.

Butterworth, R. 1976. *Managing Interstate Conflict, 1945–74*. Pittsburgh: University Center for International Studies.

Campbell, D. 1958. "Common Fate, Similarity, and Other Indices of the Status of Aggregates of Persons as Social Entities." *Behavioral Science* 3:14–25.

Campbell, D., and D. Fiske 1959. "Convergent and Discriminant Validity by the Multitrait-Multimethod Matrix." *Psychological Bulletin* 56:81–105.

Campbell, D., and J. Stanley. 1966. *Experimental and Quasi-Experimental Designs for Research*. Chicago: Rand McNally.

Caporaso, J. 1976. "The External Consequences of Regional Integration for Pan-European Relations." *International Studies Quarterly* 20:341–92.

Carmines, E., and R. Zeller. 1979. *Reliability and Validity Assessment*. Beverly Hills: Sage.

Cattell, R., and W. Sullivan. 1962. "The Scientific Nature of Factors: A Demonstration by Cups of Coffee." *Behavioral Science* 7:184–93.

Choucri, N., and R. North. 1975. *Nations in Conflict*. San Francisco: W. H. Freeman.

Cioffi-Revilla, C. 1989. *The Scientific Measurement of International Conflict*. Boulder, CO: Center for International Relations.

Clark, R. 1971. *Einstein: The Life and Times*. New York: T. Y. Crowell.

Cook, T., and D. Campbell. 1979. *Quasi-Experimentation: Design and Analysis Issues for Field Settings*. Chicago: Rand McNally.

Coombs, C. 1964. *A Theory of Data*. New York: John Wiley.

Corson, W. 1971. *Measuring Conflict and Cooperation Intensity in East-West Relations: A Manual and Codebook*. University of Michigan, Institute for Social Research. Mimeo.

Cottam, R. 1977. *Foreign Policy Motivation*. Pittsburgh: University of Pittsburgh Press.

Cowgill, D. O., and M. S. Cowgill. 1951. "An Index of Segregation Based on Block Statistics." *American Sociological Review* 16 (December): 825–31.

Cronbach, L. 1970. *Essentials of Psychological Testing*. 3d ed. New York: Harper and Row.

Cronbach, L., and P. Meehl. 1955. "Construct Validity in Psychological Tests." *Psychological Bulletin* 52(4): 281–302.

Cusack, T., and W. Eberwein. 1982. "Prelude to War: Incidence, Escalation, and Intervention in International Disputes, 1900–1976." *International Interactions* 9 (March): 9–28.

Cusack, T., and M. Ward. 1981. "Military Spending in the United States, Soviet Union, and the People's Republic of China." *Journal of Conflict Resolution* 25(3): 429–69.

Cutright, P. 1967. "Inequality: a Cross-National Analysis." *American Sociological Review* 32 (August): 562–78.

Deutsch, K. W. 1966. "The Theoretical Basis of Data Programs." In *Comparing Nations*, ed. R. Merritt and S. Rokkan. New Haven, CT: Yale University Press.

Deutsch, K. W. 1969. "On Methodological Problems of Quantitative Research." In *Quantitative Ecological Analysis in the Social Sciences*, ed. M. Dogan and S. Rokkan. Cambridge, MA: MIT Press.

Deutsch, K. W. 1978. *The Analysis of International Relations*, 2d ed. Englewood Cliffs, NJ: Prentice-Hall.

Deutsch, K. W., and J. D. Singer. 1964. "Multipolar Power Systems and International Stability." *World Politics* 16:390–406.

Deutsch, K. W., J. D. Singer, and K. Smith. 1965. "The Organizing Efficiency of Theories: the N/V Ratio as a Crude Rank-Order Measure." *American Behavioral Scientist* 9 (October): 30–33.

Diehl, P. 1983. *Arms Races and the Outbreak of War*. Ph.D. diss. University of Michigan.

Diehl, P. 1985. "Arms Races to War: Testing Some Empirical Linkages." *Sociological Quarterly* 26(3): 331–49.

Diehl, P. 1988. "The Correlates of War Project: The Next Twenty-Five Years." Presented at the annual meeting of the American Political Science Association, Washington, D.C.

Diehl, P., and G. Goertz. 1985. "Trends in Military Allocations since 1816: What Goes Up Does Not Always Come Down." *Armed Forces and Society* 12(1): 134–44.

Doran, C. 1983. "War and Power Dynamics: Economic Underpinnings." *International Studies Quarterly* 27(4): 419–42.

Duncan, O. D. 1975. *Introduction to Structural Equation Models*. New York: Academic Press.

Duncan, O. D., and B. Duncan. 1955. "A Methodological Analysis of Segregation Indexes." *American Sociological Review* 20 (April): 210–17.

DuPuy, R., and T. DuPuy. 1977. *Encyclopedia of Military History*. New York: Harper and Row.

East, M. A. 1972. "Status Discrepancy and Violence in the International System: An Empirical Analysis." In *The Analysis of International Politics: Essays in Honor of Harold and Margaret Sprout*, ed. J. N. Rosenau, V. Davis, and M. A. East. New York: Free Press.

Eberwein, W. 1982. "The Seduction of Power: Serious International Disputes and the Power Status of Nations, 1900–1976." *International Interactions* 9 (March): 57–74.

Eckhart, W., and E. Azar. 1978. "Major World Conflicts and Interventions, 1945–1975." *International Interactions* 5 (January): 75–110.

Esser, J. K., and S. Komorita. 1975. "Reciprocity and Concession Making in Bargaining." *Journal of Personality and Social Psychology* 31:864–72.

Feste, K. 1982. "International Enemies." Presented at the annual meeting of the International Studies Association, Cincinnati.

Finkelstein, M., and R. M. Friedberg. 1967. "The Application of an Entropy Theory of Concentration to the Clayton Act." *Yale Law Journal*, March, 671–717.

Fucks, W. 1965. *Formeln zur Macht*. Stuttgart: Deutsche Verlaganstalt.

Galtung, J. 1964. "A Structural Theory of Aggression." *Journal of Peace Research* 1:95–119.

Galtung, J. 1966. "East-West Interaction Patterns." *Journal of Peace Research* 2:146–77.

George, A., and R. Smoke. 1989. "Deterrence and Foreign Policy." *World Politics* 41:170–82.

German, F. C. 1960. "A Tentative Evaluation of World Power." *Journal of Conflict Resolution* 4 (March): 138–44.

Ghiselli, E., J. Campbell, and S. Zedeck. 1981. *Measurement Theory for the Behavioral Sciences*. San Francisco: W. H. Freeman.

Gibbs, B., and J. D. Singer. Forthcoming. *Beyond Conjecture II: Abstracts of Data-Based Research in World Politics*. Westport, CT: Greenwood.

Gibbs, J. P., and H. L. Browning. 1966. "The Division of Labor, Technology, and the Organization of Production in Twelve Countries." *American Sociological Review* 31 (February): 81–92.

Gibbs, J. P., and W. T. Martin. 1962. "Urbanization, Technology, and Division of Labor: International Patterns." *American Sociological Review* 27 (October): 667–77.

Gini, C. 1912. *Variabilita e Multabilita*. Bologna.

Gleditsch, N. P. 1967. "Trends in World Airline Patterns," *Journal of Peace Research* 4:366–408.

Gochman, C. 1979. "Power and Influence (II)." In *International Security*, ed. C. Pirtle et al. Pittsburgh: University Center for International Studies.

Gochman, C., and R. Leng. 1983. "Realpolitik and the Road to War: An Analysis of Attributes and Behavior." *International Studies Quarterly* 27:97–120.

Gochman, C., and R. Leng. 1987. "Militarized Disputes, Incidents, and Crises:

Identification and Classification." Presented at the annual meeting of the International Studies Association, Washington, D.C.

Gochman, C., and Z. Maoz. 1984. "Militarized Interstate Disputes, 1816–1976: Procedures, Patterns, and Insights." *Journal of Conflict Resolution* 28:585–616.

Goertz, G. 1984. "Changing Parameters across Time and Space." Presented at the European Consortium for Political Research meetings, Salzburg.

Goertz, G. 1988. "Models of Conflict Intervention in Context." Ph.D. diss. University of Michigan.

Goldman, K. 1974. *Tension and Defense in Bipolar Europe.* Stockholm: Esselte Studium.

Gort, M. N.d. "Analysis of Stability and Change in Market Shares." *Journal of Political Economy* 71:51–63.

Gottschalf, L., and D. Lach. 1954. *Europe and the Modern World Since 1870.* Glenview, IL: Scott, Foresman.

Greenberg, J. 1956. "The Measurement of Linguistic Diversity." *Language* 32:109–15.

Gulick, E. V. 1955. *Europe's Classical Balance of Power.* Ithaca, NY: Cornell University Press.

Gurr, T. 1972. *Politimetrics.* Englewood Cliffs, NJ: Prentice-Hall.

Gurr, T. 1974. "The Neo-Alexandrians: A Review Essay on Data Handbooks in Political Science." *American Political Science Review* 68 (March): 243–52.

Guttmann, L. 1968. "A General Nonmetric Technique for Finding the Smallest Coordinate Space for a Configuration of Points. *Psychometrika* 33:469–506.

Haas, M. 1968. "International Subsystems: Stability and Polarity." Presented at the annual meeting of the American Political Science Association, Washington, D.C.

Haas, M. 1970. "International Subsystems: Stability and Polarity." *American Political Science Review* 64 (March): 98–123.

Haas, M. 1974. *International Conflict.* Indianapolis: Bobbs-Merrill.

Hall, M., and M. Tideman. 1967. "Measures of Concentration." *Journal of the American Statistical Association* 61:162–86.

Handel, M. 1981. *Weak States in the International System.* London: Frank Cass.

Harmon, H. 1976. *Modern Factor Analysis.* Chicago: University of Chicago Press.

Hart, J. 1974. "Symmetry and Polarization in the European International System, 1870–1879." *Journal of Peace Research* 11 (3): 229–44.

Hart, P. E. 1957. "On Measuring Concentration." *Bulletin of the Oxford University Institute of Statistics* 19 (August): 225.

Hart, P. E., and S. J. Prais. 1956. "The Analysis of Business Concentration: A Statistical Approach." *Journal of the Royal Statistical Society* 119:150–81.

Hays, W. 1963. *Statistics.* New York: Holt, Rinehart and Winston.

Hazelwood, L., and J. Hayes. 1976. *Planning for Problems in Crisis Management.* Arlington, VA: Defense Advanced Research Projects Agency.

Herfindahl, O. 1950. "Concentration in the Steel Industry." Ph.D. diss. Columbia University.

Hermann, C. F., ed. 1972. *International Crisis: Insights from Behavioral Research.* New York: Free Press.

Herz, J. 1951. *Political Realism and Political Idealism*. Chicago: University of Chicago Press.

Hexter, J. L., and J. W. Snow. 1970. "Entropy Measure of Relative Aggregate Concentration." *Southern Economic Journal* 36 (January): 239–43.

Holsti, K. J. 1966. "Resolving International Conflicts: A Taxonomy of Behavior and Some Figures on Procedures." *Journal of Conflict Resolution* 10 (September): 272–96.

Holsti, K. J. 1983. *International Politics*. Englewood, Cliffs, NJ: Prentice-Hall.

Holsti, O. 1969. *Content Analysis of the Social Sciences and Humanities*. Reading, MA: Addison-Wesley.

Holsti, O., R. North, and R. Brody. 1968. "Perception and Action in the 1914 Crisis." In *Quantitative International Politics*, ed. J. D. Singer. New York: Free Press.

Homans, G. C. 1958. "Social Behavior as Exchange." *American Journal of Sociology* 63:597–606.

Hornseth, R. A. 1947. "A Note on 'The Measurement of Ecological Segregation' by Julius Jahn, Calvin F. Schmid, and Clarence Schrag." *American Sociological Review* 12 (October): 603–4.

Horvath, J. 1970. "Suggestion for a Comprehensive Measure of Concentration." *Southern Economic Journal* 36 (April): 446–52.

Hume, D. [1739] 1888. *A Treatise of Human Nature*. Reprint. Oxford: Oxford University Press.

Huth, P. 1988. *Extended Deterrence and the Prevention of War*. New Haven, CT: Yale University Press.

Huth, P. N.d. "Cases of Extended-Immediate Deterrence, 1885–1983." University of Michigan. Mimeo.

Huth, P., and B. Russett. 1984. "What Makes Deterrence Work? Cases from 1900 to 1980." *World Politics* 36:496–526.

Huth, P., and B. Russett. 1988. "Deterrence Failure and Escalation to War." *International Studies Quarterly* 32 (1): 29–46.

Ijiri, Y., and H. A. Simon. 1964. "Business Firm Growth and Size." *American Economic Review* 54 (March): 77–89.

Inglehart, R. 1985. "Aggregate Stability and Individual-Level Flux in Mass Belief Systems: The Level of Analysis Paradox." *American Political Science Review* 79:97–116.

International Monetary Fund. 1982. *International Financial Statistics*. Washington, DC: IMF.

Jahn, J. A. 1950. "The Measurement of Ecological Segregation: Derivation of an Index Based on the Criterion of Reproducibility." *American Sociological Review* 15 (February): 100–104.

Jahn, J. A., C. F. Schmid, and C. Schrag. 1947. "The Measurement of Ecological Segregation." *American Sociological Review* 12 (June): 293–303.

Janda, K. 1971. "Conceptual Equivalence and Multiple Indicators in the Cross-National Analysis of Political Parties." Prepared for the ISS/UNESCO/ECPR Workshop on Indicators of National Development. Typescript.

Johnson, S. C. 1967. "Hierarchical Clustering Schemes." *Psychometrika* 32:241–54.

Jones, D. 1988. "Third Party Actors in Symmetric and Asymmetric Disputes." Paper presented at the Annual Meeting of the International Studies Association, St. Louis.

Jones, R. 1966. "Construct Mapping." University of Missouri. Mimeo.

Kaplan, M. 1957. *System and Process in International Politics*. New York: John Wiley.

Kegley, C., N. Richardson, and G. Richter. 1978. "Conflict at Home and Abroad: An Empirical Extension." *Journal of Politics* 40:742–52.

Keohane, R. 1983. "Theory of World Politics: Structural Realism and Beyond." In *Political Science: The State of the Discipline*, ed. A. Finifter, Washington, DC: American Political Science Association.

Kerlinger, N. 1973. *The Foundations of Behavioral Research*. New York: Holt, Rinehart and Winston.

Klingemann, H. D. 1986. "Ranking the Graduate Departments in the 1980s: Toward Objective Qualitative Indicators." *Political Science* 19 (3): 651–60.

Klingemann, H. D., B. Grofman, and J. Campagna. 1989. "The Political Science 400." *Political Science* 21 (2): 258–69.

Knorr, K. 1956. *The War Potential of Nations*. Princeton: Princeton University Press.

Kravis, I. B. 1962. *The Structure of Income*. Philadelphia: University of Pennsylvania Press.

Kruskal, J., and M. Wish. 1978. *Multidimensional Scaling*. Beverly Hills: Sage University Papers.

Kugler, J. 1973. "The Consequences of War: Fluctuations in National Capability Following Major Wars, 1880–1970." Ph.D. diss. University of Michigan.

Labovitz, S., and J. P. Gibbs. 1964. "Urbanization, Technology and the Division of Labor: Further Evidence." *Pacific Sociological Review* 7 (Spring): 3–9.

Langer, W. L. 1972. *Encyclopedia of World History*. 5th ed. Boston: Houghton Mifflin.

Lankford, P. M. 1974. "Comparative Analysis of Clique Identification Methods." *Sociometry* 37:287–305.

Lebow, R., and J. Stein. 1989. "Deterrence: The Elusive Dependent Variable." Presented at the annual meeting of the International Studies Association, London.

Leng, R. 1979. "Event Data Validity: Comparing Coding Schemes." In *Measuring International Behavior: Public Sources, Events, Validity*, ed. D. Munton. Halifax, Nova Scotia: Dalhousie University Press.

Leng, R. 1980. "Strategies of Influence in Interstate Conflict: An Examination of the Realist Prescription." In *Correlates of War II*, ed. J. D. Singer. New York: Free Press.

Leng, R. 1983. "When Will They Ever Learn? Coercive Bargaining in Recurrent Crises." *Journal of Conflict Resolution* 27:379–420.

Leng, R. 1984. "Reagan and the Russians: Crisis Bargaining Beliefs and the Historical Record." *American Political Science Review* 78:338–55.

Leng, R. 1986a. *Behavioral Correlates of War: Coder's Manual*. 6th ed. Middlebury College. Mimeo.

Leng, R. 1986b. "Structure and Action in Crisis Bargaining." In *New Directions in the Comparative Study of Foreign Policy*, ed. C. Hermann, C. Kegley and J. Rosenau. Winchester, MA: Allen and Unwin.

Leng, R. 1987. *Behavioral Correlates of War Data: User's Manual*. Ann Arbor, MI: Interuniversity Consortium for Political and Social Research.

Leng, R., and R. Goodsell. 1974. "Behavioral Indicators of War Proneness in Bilateral Conflicts." In *International Yearbook of Foreign Policy*, ed. P. McGowan, vol. 2. Beverly Hills: Sage Publications.

Leng, R., and J. D. Singer. 1970. "A Multitheoretical Typology of International Behavior." In *Mathematical Approaches to International Relations*, ed. Bunge, Galtung, and Malitza. Bucharest: Romanian Academy of Social and Political Sciences.

Leng, R., and J. D. Singer. 1977. "Toward a Multi-Theoretical Typology of International Actions." In *Mathematical Approaches to International Politics*, ed. M. Bunge et al. Bucharest: Romanian Academy of Social and Political Sciences.

Leng, R., and J. D. Singer. 1988. "Militarized Interstate Crises: The BCOW Typology and its Applications." *International Studies Quarterly* 32(2): 155–73.

Leng, R., and S. Walker. 1982. "Comparing Two Studies of Crisis Bargaining: Confrontation, Coercion, and Reciprocity." *Journal of Conflict Resolution* 26:571–91.

Leng, R., and H. Wheeler. 1979. "Influence Strategies, Success, and War." *Journal of Conflict Resolution* 23:655–84.

Levy, J. 1983. *War in the Modern Great Power System, 1495–1975*. Lexington, KY: University of Kentucky Press.

Levy, J. 1984. "Size and Stability in the Modern Great Power System." *International Interactions* 10 (3–4): 341–58.

Levy, J. 1985. "The Polarity of the System and International Stability: An Empirical Analysis." In *Polarity and War: The Changing Structure of International Conflict*, ed. A. Sabrosky. Boulder, CO: Westview.

Levy, J. 1988. "Review Article: When Do Deterrent Threats Work?" *British Journal of Political Science* 18:485–512.

Li, R. 1978. "The Stochastic Process of Alliance Formation Behavior." *American Political Science Review* 72 (4): 1288–1303.

Li, R., and W. Thompson. 1977. "Interaction Opportunities and War Behavior: A Test of Two Theories." Mimeo.

Lieberson, S. 1964. "An Extension of Greenberg's Linguistic Diversity Measure." *Language* 40 (November): 526–31.

Lieberson, S. 1969. "Measuring Population Diversity." *American Sociological Review* 34 (December): 850–62.

Lingoes, J. C. 1965. "An IBM-7090 Program for Guttman-Lingoes Smallest Space Analysis." *Behavioral Science* 10:183–84.

Lingoes, J. C. 1966. "Recent Computational Advances in Nonmetric Methodology for the Behavioral Sciences." Presented at the International Symposium on Mathematical and Quantitative Methods in the Social Sciences, Rome.

Lingoes, J. C. 1972. "A General Survey of the Guttman-Lingoes Nonmetric Program Series." In *Multidimensional Scaling*, ed. R. N. Shepard, A. Romney, and S. B. Nerlove. New York: Seminar Press.

Lingoes, J. C. 1973. *The Guttman-Lingoes Nonmetric Program Series*. Ann Arbor, MI: Mathesis Press.

Liska, G. 1962. *Nations in Alliance*. Baltimore, MD: Johns Hopkins University Press.

Longabaugh, R. 1963. "A Category System for Coding Interpersonal Behavior as Social Exchange." *Sociometry* 26:319–44.

Lorenz, M. O. 1960. "Methods of Measuring the Concentration of Wealth." *American Statistical Association Journal* 9 (June): 209–19.

Lucier, C. 1974. "Power and the Balance." Ph.D. diss. University of Rochester.

MacRae, D., Jr. 1960. "Direct Factor Analysis of Sociometric Data." *Sociometry* 23:360–71.

Majeski, S., and D. Sylvan. 1984. "Simple Choices and Complex Calculations: A Critique of the War Trap." *Journal of Conflict Resolution* 28:316–40.

Manheim, J., and R. Rich. 1981. *Empirical Political Analysis*. Englewood Cliffs, NJ: Prentice-Hall.

Maoz, Z. 1982. *Paths to Conflict: International Dispute Initiation. 1816–1976.* Boulder, CO: Westview Press.

Masters, R. 1961. "A Multibloc Model of the International System." *American Political Science Review* 55 (December): 780–98.

McCleary, R., and R. Hay. 1980. *Applied Time-Series Analysis*. Beverly Hills: Sage.

McClelland, C. 1961. "The Acute International Crisis." *World Politics* 14:182–204.

McClelland, C. 1968. *International Interaction Analysis: Basic Research and Some Practical Applications*. Technical report no. 2, World Event/Interaction Survey. Los Angeles: University of Southern California.

McClelland, C. 1972. "Theoretical Problems." In *The Analysis of International Politics*, ed. J. N. Rosenau, V. Davis, and M. A. East. New York: Free Press.

McGinnis, M., and J. Williams. 1989. "Change and Stability in Superpower Rivalry." *American Political Science Review* 83 (4): 1101–25.

McGowan, P., H. Starr, G. Hower, R. Merritt, and D. Zinnes. 1988. "International Data as a National Resource." *International Interactions* 14 (2): 101–13.

McQuitty, L. 1957. "Elementary Linkage Analysis for Isolating Both Orthogonal Types and Typal Relevancies." *Educational and Psychological Measurement* 17 (Summer): 202–29.

Merritt, R. 1966. *Symbols of American Community, 1735–1775*. New Haven, CT: Yale University Press.

Michaely, M. 1962. *Concentration in International Trade*. Amsterdam: North Holland.

Midlarsky, M. 1988. "Rulers and Ruled: Patterned Inequality and the Onset of Mass Political Violence." *American Political Science Review* 82 (2): 491–510.

Mihalka, M. 1974. "Discovering the Diplomatic Structure of the European State System." Mimeo.

Mitchell, B. R. 1981. *European Historical Statistics, 1750–1975*. New York: Facts on File.

Moll, K. 1974. "International Conflict as a Decision System." *Journal of Conflict Resolution* 18 (4): 555–77.

Morgenstern, O. 1963. *On the Accuracy of Economic Observations*. Princeton, NJ: Princeton University Press.

Morgenthau, H. 1946. *Scientific Man vs. Power Politics*. Chicago: University of Chicago Press.

Morgenthau, H. 1948. *Politics among Nations*. New York: Alfred A. Knopf.

Morgenthau, H. 1961. *Politics among Nations*. 2d ed. New York: Alfred A. Knopf.

Morgenthau, H. 1967. *Politics among Nations.* 4th ed. New York: Alfred A. Knopf.

Morrison, D., et al. 1972. *Black Africa: A Comparative Handbook.* New York: Free Press.

Moul, W. 1973. "The Level of Analysis Problem Revisited." *Canadian Journal of Political Science* 6 (3): 494–513.

Moul, W. 1988. "Balances of Power and the Escalation of Serious Disputes among the European Great Powers, 1815–1939: Some Evidence." *American Journal of Political Science* 32 (2): 241–75.

Mueller, J. 1988. "The Essential Irrelevance of Nuclear Weapons: Stability in the Postwar World." *International Security* 13 (Fall): 55–79.

Mueller, J. H., K. F. Schuessler, and H. L. Costner. 1970. *Statistical Reasoning in Sociology.* Boston: Houghton Mifflin.

Muller, E., M. Seligson, H. Fu, and M. Midlarsky. 1989. "Controversy: Land Inequality and Civil Violence." *American Political Science Review* 83 (2): 577–602.

Mullins, A. F., Jr. 1975. "Manpower Data as a Measure of Arms Race Phenomena." University of Michigan. Mimeo.

Namenworth, J. Z., and H. Lasswell. 1970. *The Changing Language of American Value.* Beverly Hills: Sage.

Naroll, R. 1962. *Data Quality Control.* New York: Free Press.

Nelson, C. R. 1973. *Applied Time-Series Analysis.* San Francisco: Holden-Day.

Nelson, R. L. 1963. *Concentration in the Manufacturing Industries of the United States.* New Haven, CT: Yale University Press.

Newcombe, A. 1969. "Toward the Development of an Internation Tensiometer." *Peace Research Society International Papers* 13:11–27.

Newcombe, A., W. Eckhardt, and C. Young. N.d. "Voting Blocs in the U.N. General Assembly, 1946–1970: A Typal Analysis." Mimeo.

Newcombe, A., N. Newcombe, and G. Landrus. 1974. "The Development of an Internation Tensiometer." *International Interactions* 1 (1): 3–18.

Newcombe, A., and J. Wert. 1973. "The Use of an Internation Tensiometer for the Prediction of War." *Peace Science Society International Papers* 21:73–83.

Nicholson, H. 1946. *The Congress of Vienna.* London.

Nincic, M. 1983. "Fluctuations in Soviet Defense Spending: A Research Note." *Journal of Conflict Resolution* 27 (4): 648–60.

Noel-Baker, P. 1958. *The Arms Race: A Program for World Disarmament.* New York: Oceana.

North, R., et al. 1963. *Content Analysis: A Handbook with Applications for the Study of International Crisis.* Evanston, IL: Northwestern University Press.

Nutter, G. W. 1968. "Industrial Concentration." In *International Encyclopedia of the Social Sciences,* ed. D. Sills. New York: Free Press.

Organski, A. F. K. 1968. *World Politics.* New York: Alfred A. Knopf.

Organski, A. F. K., B. Bueno de Mesquita, and A. Lamborn. 1972. "The Effective Population in International Politics." In *Political Science in Population Studies,* ed. R. Clinton et al. Lexington, MA: Lexington Books.

Organski, A. F. K., and J. Kugler. 1980. *The War Ledger.* Chicago: University of Chicago Press.

Ostrom, C., and J. Aldrich. 1979. "The Relationship Between Size and Stability in the

Major Power International System." *American Journal of Political Science* 84 (3): 743–71.

Pearson, F. S. 1974. "Geographic Proximity and Foreign Military Intervention." *Journal of Conflict Resolution* 18(3): 432–60.

Pool, I. de S., ed. 1959. *Trends in Content Analysis*. Urbana, IL: University of Illinois Press.

Powell, R. 1987. "Crisis Bargaining, Escalation, and MAD." *American Political Science Review* 81:717–35.

Preston, L. E., and N. R. Collins. 1961. "The Size Structure of the Largest Industrial Firms." *American Economic Review* 51 (December): 986–1011.

Przezworski, A., and H. Teune. 1970. *The Logic of Comparative Social Inquiry*. New York: John Wiley.

Puchala, D. 1970. "International Transactions and Regional Integration." *International Organization* 24 (Autumn): 732–63.

Quandt, R. E. 1966a. "Old and New Methods of Estimation and the Pareto Distribution." *Metrika* 10:55–82.

Quandt, R. E. 1966b. "On the Size Distribution of Firms." *American Economic Review* 56 (June): 416–32.

Rae, D., and M. Taylor. 1970. *The Analysis of Political Cleavages*. New Haven, CT: Yale University Press.

Rapkin, D., W. Thompson, and J. Christopherson. 1979. "Bipolarity and Bipolarization in the Cold War Era." *Journal of Conflict Resolution* 23:261–95.

Ray, J. 1974a. "Inconsistency and War Involvement in Europe, 1816–1970," *Peace Science Society International Papers* 23:69–80.

Ray, J. 1974b. "Status Inconsistency and War Involvement among European States, 1916–1970." Ph.D. diss. University of Michigan.

Ray, J. 1990. "Friends as Foes: International Conflict and Wars Between Formal Allies." In *Prisoners of War? Nation-States in the Modern Era*, ed. C. Gochman and A. Sebrosky. Lexington, MA: Lexington Books.

Ray, J., and J. D. Singer. 1973. "Measuring the Concentration of Power in the International System." *Sociological Methods and Research* 1 (4): 403–37.

Reisinger, W. M. 1983. "East European Military Expenditures in the 1970s: Collective Good or Bargaining Offer?" *International Organization* 37 (1): 143–55.

Richardson, L. F. 1960. *Statistics of Deadly Quarrels*. Pittsburgh, Boxwood Press.

Riker, W. H. 1962. *The Theory of Political Coalitions*. New Haven, CT: Yale University Press.

Rohn, P. 1966. "Canada in the United Nations Treaty Series." *Canadian Yearbook of International Law*, 102–30.

Rohn, P. 1968. "The United Nations Treaty Series Project." *International Studies Quarterly* 12 (2): 174–95.

Rosecrance, R. 1966. "Bipolarity, Multipolarity, and the Future." *Journal of Conflict Resolution* 10 (September): 314–27.

Rosenau, J., and G. Hoggard. 1974. "Foreign Policy Behavior in Dyadic Relationships: Testing a Pre-Theoretical Extension." In *Comparing Foreign Policies*, ed. J. Rosenau. Beverly Hills: Sage.

Rosenbluth, G. 1955. "Measures of Concentration." In *Business Concentration and*

Price Policy, ed. National Bureau of Economic Research. Princeton: Princeton University Press.

Rothstein, R. L. 1968. *Alliance and Small Powers*. New York: Columbia University Press.

Rummel, R. 1970. *Applied Factor Analysis*. Evanston, IL: Northwestern University Press.

Rummel, R. 1972. *The Dimensions of Nations*. Beverly Hills: Sage.

Rummel, R. 1983. "Libertarianism and International Violence." *Journal of Conflict Resolution* 27:27–72.

Russett, B. 1964. "Measures of Military Effort." *American Behavioral Scientist* 7 (6): 26–29.

Russett, B. 1968a. "Components of an Operational Theory of International Alliance Formation." *Journal of Conflict Resolution* 12 (3): 285–301.

Russett, B. 1968b. "Delineating International Regions." In *Quantitative International Politics*, ed. J. D. Singer. New York: Free Press.

Russett, B. 1970. *What Price Vigilance? The Burdens of National Defense*. New Haven, CT: Yale University Press.

Russett, B. 1971. "An Empirical Typology of International Military Alliances." *Midwest Journal of Political Science* 15 (May): 262–89.

Russett, B. 1982. "Defense Expenditures and National Well-Being." *American Political Science Review* 76 (4): 767–77.

Russett, B., et al. 1964. *World Handbook of Social and Political Indicators*. New Haven, CT: Yale University Press.

Russett, B., J. D. Singer, and M. Small. 1968. "National Political Units in the Twentieth Century: A Standardized List." *American Political Science Review* 62:932–51.

Rusten, L., and P. Stern. 1987. *Crisis Management in the Nuclear Age*. Washington, DC: National Academy Press.

Sabrosky, A. 1980. "Interstate Alliances: Their Reliability and the Expansion of War." In *The Correlates of War II: Testing Some Realpolitik Models*, ed. J. D. Singer. New York: Free Press.

Savage, I. R., and K. Deutsch. 1960. "A Statistical Model of the Gross Analysis of Transaction Flows." *Econometrica* 28 (July): 551–72.

Schelling, T. C. 1960. *Strategy of Conflict*. Cambridge, MA: Harvard University Press.

Shepard, R. N. 1972. "Introduction." In *Multidimensional Scaling*, ed. R. N. Shepard, A. K. Romney, and S. B. Nerlove, vol. 1. New York: Seminar Press.

Sherman, F. L. N.d. "Recognizing and Responding to International Disputes." Ph.D. diss. University of Pennsylvania.

Siegel, S. 1956. *Nonparametric Statistics for the Social Sciences*. New York: McGraw-Hill.

Silberman, I. H. 1967. "On Lognormality as a Summary Measure of Concentration." *American Economic Review* 57:807–31.

Simon, H. 1954. "Spurious Correlation: A Causal Interpretation." *Journal of the American Statistical Association* 49 (September): 467–79.

Simon, H., and C. P. Bonini. 1958. "The Size Distribution of Business Firms." *American Economic Review* 48 (September): 607–17.

Simpson, E. H. 1949. "Measurement and Diversity." *Nature* 163 (April): 688.

Singer, E. M. 1968. *Antitrust Economics*. Englewood Cliffs, NJ: Prentice-Hall.

Singer, J. D. 1961. "The Level of Analysis Problem in International Relations." *World Politics* 14:77–92.

Singer, J. D. 1963a. "Inter-nation Influence: A Formal Model." *American Political Science Review* 57:420–30.

Singer, J. D. 1963b. "Media Analysis in Inspection for Disarmament." *Journal of Arms Control* 1 (July): 248–60.

Singer, J. D. 1965. "Data-Making in International Relations." *Behavioral Science* 10 (January): 68–80.

Singer, J. D. 1966a. "The Composition and Status Ordering of the International System, 1815–1940." *World Politics* 18 (January): 236–282.

Singer, J. D. 1966b. "Formal Alliances, 1815–1939: A Quantitative Description." *Journal of Peace Research* 3:1–32.

Singer, J. D. 1968a. "Alliance Aggregation and the Onset of War, 1815–1945." In *Quantitative International Politics,* ed. J. D. Singer. New York: Free Press.

Singer J. D. 1968b. "Man and World Politics: The Psycho-Cultural Interface." *Journal of Social Issues* 24 (July): 127–65.

Singer, J. D., ed. 1968c. *Quantitative International Politics: Insights and Evidence.* New York: Free Press.

Singer, J. D. 1970. "Modern International War: From Conjecture to Explanation." In *Essays in Honor of Quincy Wright,* ed. A. Leawsky, E. Buehrig and H. Lasswell. New York: Appleton-Century-Crofts.

Singer, J. D. 1971. *A General Systems Taxonomy for Political Science.* New York: General Learning Press.

Singer, J. D. 1972. The Correlates of War Project: Interim Report and Rationale. *World Politics* 24:243–70.

Singer, J. D. 1976. The Correlates of War Project: Continuity, Diversity, and Convergence." In *Quantitative International Politics: An Appraisal,* ed. F. Hoole and D. Zinnes, New York: Praeger.

Singer, J. D. 1977. "The Historical Experiment as a Research Strategy in World Politics." *Social Science History* 2 (Fall): 1–22.

Singer, J. D. 1981. "Accounting for International War: The State of the Discipline." *Journal of Peace Research* 18:1–18.

Singer, J. D. 1990. "Peace in the Global System: Displacement, Interregnum or Transformation?" In *The Long Postwar Peace,* ed. Charles Kegley. New York: HarperCollins.

Singer, J. D., S. Bremer, and J. Stuckey. 1972. "Capability Distribution, Uncertainty, and Major Power War, 1820–1965." In *Peace, War, and Numbers,* ed. B. Russett. Beverly Hills: Sage.

Singer, J. D., and B. Bueno de Mesquita. 1969. "The Minimum Winning Coalition in International Politics: A Test of the Hypothesis, 1816–1965." Ann Arbor, MI: MHRI Preprint.

Singer, J. D., D. Handley, and M. Small. 1969. "The Diplomatic Importance of States, 1816–1965: An Extension of the Basic Data." Ann Arbor, MI: MHRI Preprint.

Singer, J. D., and M. Small. 1966a. "The Composition and Status Ordering of the International System, 1815–1940." *World Politics* 18:236–82.

Singer, J. D., and M. Small. 1966b. "Formal Alliances, 1815–1939: A Quantitative Description." *Journal of Peace Research* 3(1): 1–32.

Singer, J. D., and M. Small. 1967. "National Alliance Commitments and War Involvement, 1815–1945." *Peace Research Society Papers* 6:110–40.

Singer, J. D., and M. Small. 1968. "Alliance Aggregation and the Onset of War." In *Quantitative International Politics*, ed. J. D. Singer. New York: Free Press.

Singer, J. D., and M. Small. 1972. *The Wages of War 1816–1965: A Statistical Handbook*. New York: John Wiley.

Singer, J. D., and R. Stoll. 1984. *Quantitative Indicators in World Politics*. New York: Praeger.

Singer, J. D., and M. Wallace. 1979. *To Augur Well: Early Warning Indicators in World Politics*. Beverly Hills: Sage.

Siverson, R., and M. Tennefoss. 1982. "Interstate Conflicts, 1815–1965." *International Interactions*. 9(2): 147–78.

Siverson, R., and M. Tennefoss. 1984. "Power, Alliance, and the Escalation of International Conflict, 1815–1965." *American Political Science Review* 78(4): 1057–69.

Small, M., and J. D. Singer. 1969. "Formal Alliances, 1816–1965: An Extension of the Basic Data." *Journal of Peace Research* 6:257–82.

Small, M., and J. D. Singer. 1973. "Diplomatic Importance of States, 1816–1970: An Extension and Refinement of the Indicator." *World Politics* 25 (July): 577–99.

Small, M., and J. D. Singer. 1979. "Conflict in the International System, 1816–1977: Historical Trends and Policy Futures." In *Challenges to America: United States Foreign Policy in the 1980s,* ed. C. Kegley and P. McGowan. Beverly Hills: Sage.

Small, M., and J. D. Singer. 1982. *Resort to Arms*. Beverly Hills: Sage.

Smoker, P. 1968. "Analysis of Conflict Behaviors in an International Processes Simulation and in International System, 1955–1960." Mimeo.

Snyder, G., and P. Diesing. 1977. *Conflict among Nations*. Princeton, NJ: Princeton University Press.

Sorokin, P. A. 1937. *Fluctuation of Social Relationships, War, and Revolution*. Vol. 3 of *Social and Cultural Dynamics*. New York: American Book Company.

Stoll, R. 1977. "An Attempt to Scale Major Power Disputes, 1816–1965: The Use of a Method to Detect Development Processes." Paper presented at the Annual Meeting of the International Studies Association, St. Louis.

Stoll, R. 1984a. "Bloc Concentration and the Balance of Power." *Journal of Conflict Resolution* 28 (March): 25–50.

Stoll, R. 1984b. "Power Capabilities: Indicators and Inferences." Presented at the annual meeting of the International Studies Association, Atlanta.

Stoll, R., and M. Champion. 1977. "Predicting the Escalation of Serious Disputes to War: Some Preliminary Findings." Presented at the North American Peace Science conference, Philadelphia.

Stoll, R. and M. Ward. 1989. *Power in World Politics*. Boulder: Lynne Rienner.

Stone, P., et al. 1966. *The General Inquirer*. Cambridge, MA: MIT Press.

Taylor, C. 1970. "Turmoil, Economic Development, and Organized Political Opposition as Predictors of Irregular Government Change." Presented at the Annual Meeting of the American Political Science Association, Los Angeles.

Taylor, C., and M. Hudson. 1972. *World Handbook of Political and Social Indicators.* New Haven, CT: Yale University Press.

Theil, H. 1967. *Economics and Information Theory.* Chicago: Rand McNally.

Theil, H. 1970. "On the Estimation of Relationships Involving Qualitative Variables." *American Journal of Sociology* 76 (July): 103–54.

Thompson, W., K. Rasler, and R. Li. 1980. "Systemic Interaction Opportunities and War Behavior." *International Interactions* 7 (1): 57–85.

Torgerson, W. S. 1958. *Theory and Methods of Scaling.* New York: Wiley.

Treaties and Alliances of the World. 1969. New York: Scribners.

U. S. Bureau of the Census. 1975. *Historical Statistics of the USA from Colonial Times to 1970.* Washington: U.S. Bureau of the Census.

Vasquez, J. 1987. "The Steps to War: Toward A Scientific Explanation of the Correlates of War Findings." *World Politics* 40:108–45.

Wagner, R. H. 1984. "War and Expected Utility Theory." *World Politics* 36 (3): 407–23.

Wall, R. 1972. *Bipolarization and the International System: 1946–1970.* Stockholm: Swedish Institute of International Affairs.

Wallace, M. 1973a. "Alliance Polarization, Cross-Cutting, and Major Power War, 1816–1965." *Journal of Conflict Resolution* 17 (4): 575–604.

Wallace, M. 1973b. *War and Rank Among Nations.* Lexington, MA: Lexington Books.

Wallace, M. 1979. "Arms Races and Escalation: Some New Evidence." *Journal of Conflict Resolution* 23 (1): 3–16.

Wallace, M. 1982. "Armaments and Escalation: Two Competing Hypotheses." *International Studies Quarterly* 26:37–56.

Wallace, M., and J. D. Singer. 1970. "Intergovernmental Organization in the Global System, 1815–1964: A Quantitative Description." *International Organization* 24 (Spring): 239–87.

Waltz, K. 1964. "The Stability of a Bipolar World." *Daedalus* 93 (Summer): 881–909.

Waltz, K. 1967. "International Structure, National Force, and the Balance of World Power." *Journal of International Affairs* 21:230–31.

Waltz, K. 1979. *Theory of International Politics.* Reading, MA: Addison-Wesley.

Ward, M. 1982. *Research Gaps in Alliance Dynamics.* Denver, CO: University of Denver Monograph Series in World Affairs.

Wayman, F. 1984. "Bipolarity and War: The Role of Capability Concentration and Alliance Patterns among Major Powers, 1816–1965." *Journal of Peace Research,* 21 (1): 25–42.

Wayman, F., recorder. 1988. "Minutes of the Rountable on the Next Twenty-five Years of the COW Project." Recorded at the annual meeting of the American Political Science Association, Washington, D.C.

Wayman, F. 1989. "Power Shifts and War." Presented at the annual meeting of the International Studies Association, London.

Wayman, F. 1990. "Alliances and War: A Time-Series Analysis." In *Prisoners of War? Nation-states in the Modern Era,* ed. C. Gochman and A. Sabrosky. Lexington, MA: Lexington Books.

Wayman, F., J. D. Singer, and G. Goertz. 1983. "Capabilities, Allocations, and Success in Militarized Disputes and Wars, 1816–1976." *International Studies Quarterly* 27 (4): 497–515.

Webb, E., et al. 1966. *Unobtrusive Measures: Nonreactive Research in the Social Sciences.* Chicago: Rand McNally.

Weede, E. 1976. "Overwhelming Preponderance as a Pacifying Condition between Contiguous Asian Dyads." *Journal of Conflict Resolution* 20:395–412.

Weede, E. 1977. "National Position in World Politics and Military Allocation Ratios in the 1950s and 1960s." *Jerusalem Journal of International Relations* 2(3): 63–80.

Weede, E. 1981. "Preventing War by Nuclear Deterrence or by Detente." *Conflict Management and Peace Science* 6 (1): 1–78.

Weiss, L. W. 1963. "Factors in Changing Concentration." *Review of Economics and Statistics* 44 (February): 70–77.

Wilkenfeld, Jonathan. 1968. "Domestic and Foreign Conflict Behavior of Nations." *Journal of Peace Research* 1:56–69.

Wilkenfeld, J., G. Hopple, P. Rossa, and S. Andriole. 1980. *Foreign Policy Behavior.* Beverly Hills: Sage.

Williamson, P., J. Warner, and S. Hopkins. 1988. "A Model of International Dispute Onsets with Preliminary Application to the Impact of Nuclear Weapons." Mimeo.

Woods, F., and A. Baltzly. 1915. *Is War Diminishing? A Study of the Prevalence of War in Europe from 1450 to the Present Day.* Boston, MA.

World Bank. 1983. *China: Socialist Economic Development, vol. 1: The Economy.* Washington, D.C.: World Bank.

Wright, B., and M. S. Evitts. 1961. "Direct Factor Analysis in Sociometry." *Sociometry* 24:82–98.

Wright, Q. 1942. *A Study of War.* Chicago: University of Chicago Press.

Yntema, D. 1933. "Measures of Inequality in Personal Distribution of Wealth or Income." *American Statistical Association Journal* 28 (December): 423–33.

Zinnes, D. 1967. "An Analytical Study of the Balance of Power Theories." *Journal of Peace Research* 3:270–88.

Zinnes, D. 1970. "Coalition Theories and the Balance of Power," In *The Study of Coalition Behavior,* ed. S. Groennings et al. New York: Holt, Rinehart and Winston.

Zinnes, D., J. Zinnes, and R. McClure. 1972. "Hostility in Diplomatic Communication: A Study of the 1914 Crisis." In *International Crises,* ed. C. Hermann. New York: Free Press.